Trade and Trade-offs

Trade and Trade-offs

Using Resources, Making Choices, and Taking Risks

M. Estellie Smith
Union College

WAVELAND PRESS, INC.
Prospect Heights, Illinois

For information about this book, write or call:
Waveland Press, Inc.
P.O. Box 400
Prospect Heights, Illinois 60070
(847) 634-0081
www.waveland.com

ISBN 1-57766-092-7

Printed in the United States of America

7 6 5 4 3 2 1

Contents

Preface

This book attempts to stitch together the increasingly raveled edges of areas of human concern that an institutionalized system of research and education compartmentalizes as "anthropology," "economics," "sociology," "finance," "business administration/management," "marketing," "psychology," "international studies," and more. Indeed, it seems that the more we talk about "crossing disciplinary boundaries," the more we create degree-granting programs, post-graduate institutes or schools, and special, concentrated seminars that create or focus on new niches—globalization, war and peace, entrepreneurialism, development, e-commerce, cognition, semiotics, ecopolitics . . . and on and on. Unquestionably, however, as those in the music trade would put it, this text is a "cross-over" publication.

The reason is simple: humans are complex and, as we move both up and down the scale on which they interact with each other—e.g., one-on-one; in small or large, informal or structured aggregates; or as representatives of institutionalized structures such as nongovernmental organizations, government agencies or the governments they represent, and multinational corporations—we increasingly realize how much there is we still need to discover about the dynamics of such interaction. We are continually discovering how various areas of activity, once treated casually or even ignored, have infinitely more twists and turns, greater depths, and many more ramifications than was realized even as recently as a few years ago. As each emerges, they attract a number of specialists who then begin to explore the various niches, while in the process developing their own special theories, methodologies, and language—and the barriers to cross-disciplinary communication begin to increase rather than decline.

At the same time, however, we all want "solutions," but the same sciences that bring the Good News also soon discover the Bad News. Thus, for example, if concerns about the health problems of automobile emissions emerge, a "clean air bill" is passed and chemists are told to invent a way to clean up the gasoline that causes such toxicity. They do—only to discover that the additive itself presents problems and is causing contamination to ground water supplies on such a scale that whole towns are being abandoned as their water supplies are declared unsafe to drink. Again, if we invent a vaccine to cope with a health problem, we discover that some people die from the vaccine. We then have to ask how many are we willing to put at risk to protect, say, 99 percent of the population. That is, we may never be able to produce a totally risk-free universe; if not, we have to debate and reach consensus as to what degree of risk is acceptable by managers, researchers, and, most important, those with the health problem.

Further, while it's true that many issues that involve various interests can be resolved equitably, many cannot—especially if the issue is to be addressed in a timely fashion. In the winter of 1999–2000, a large number of the North American population came down with the flu. Hospitals—in Canada, especially—were overwhelmed by the number of patients and, quite soon after the start of the problem, ambulances began being turned away because facilities were already stretched to the breaking point. Earlier, staffs had been trimmed, decisions to buy new and very costly equipment had been deferred, and even entire hospitals had closed down in order to fight "waste" and reduce costs that, under "normal" conditions were unnecessary. The dilemma was that no one wanted tax dollars wasted (there are critical areas of health care to which the money could be better applied), but no one wants to have a system that can't respond to periods of high demand (such as epidemics). Adding to the problem is that people are more quick to economize relative to "surplus" health care delivery when demand is "average," than in the midst of a catastrophe. Yet, the time to make decisions addressing the issue is before or after—not during—the crisis.

And that brings me to the main reason for writing this book. It is intended to speak to people whose life interests and lifestyles vary widely but whose lives are intermeshed by the exchanges that link us together at various aggregate scales. It intends to show how every decision, especially those about distribution/exchange, not only has benefits (the Good News) but costs (the Bad News), intended results but also unintended consequences.

Each of us increasingly is caught up in a world in which the demands of our personal lives, our work and our families, our roles as citizens—whether of our local community or the global society—are growing. We have two choices: we may live in blissful ignorance and make choices grounded in unenlightened self-interest, a self-interest that leads us to make decisions whose negative consequences for others—and to which we may give little if any heed—can boomerang on us; or we may grasp how important it is that we make thoughtful decisions. This isn't to say that, over the long haul, they will prove to be the "right" or the "best" decisions. But, at least, they will not be careless decisions. We'll have used the unique human potential for thinking in order to behave in ways that represent the best potential of this species, which impinges on all aspects of the world we inhabit.

The product I'm offering is a modest one and is designed to offer an overview of the wide range of issues involved. Since the only way that we can improve our decision-making sense is to make decisions about which we have thought in advance and which we review after the fact, one aim of the material is to show how frequently decisions are demanded of us. A second aim is to stress the difference between calculating costs and benefits in the short- and long-term. A third aim is to encourage readers to think about their own personally held values, beliefs, and norms as these are reflected in the ways they select and prioritize such nonmaterial Goods (and "Bads"). A fourth aim is to emphasize that, to the extent to which an individual's language skills—the tool with which we think, that organizes what we see (or fail to see)—are limited and inadequately utilized, to that extent the ability to think through and then review our decisions will be equally impoverished and poorly utilized. Finally, in order to stress how important it is that we improve our knowledge about how we use resources and make choices, the material aims to emphasize the degree of risk (some long-term and very remote indeed!) that accompanies *all* decisions.

The opening chapter poses a number of decisions, large and small, that introduce the reader to the costs and benefits involved in all decision making, even the most commonplace. Chapter 2 is a brief review of the anthropological—as opposed to, say, economic or psychological—tools that may be utilized to examine the way humans behave. The next chapter looks at how economists and anthropologists agree and differ on a few of the major concepts we utilize in common.

Chapters 4 through 8 explore economic behavior by utilizing a widely held framework that sees such behavior as a process consisting of (1) production, (2) distribution/exchange, and (3) consumption. Chapter 4 questions whether people produce in order to consume or, driven by the need to stay alive and sustain human societies, produce in order to meet the demands of consumption. It stresses that people produce both material goods and nonmaterial Goods. Chapter 5 looks at entrepreneurialism, a kind of behavior that is only now beginning to draw intense examination from researchers in a wide range of fields. It shows that entrepreneurs play a crucial role as agents of change, change that is necessary if sociocultural systems and the humans in them are to be capable of responding and adapting to context variability. Chapter 6 emphasizes distribution, especially as the allocation of resources is bound up in concepts of property—i.e., who has rights to whatever is identified as resources and their utilization. Indeed, property rights are the link between production and distribution/exchange. Chapter 7 is concerned with what happens after resources have been allocated to individuals and these individuals then make decisions as to how to exchange with others. While not a few see markets, and especially the capitalist market system, as the root of all that is wrong with modern society, the position taken here is that (as with most of life) there's always a trade-off between the Good News and the Bad News. Chapter 8 looks at the many curiosities of consumption—e.g., acquiring what we never consume (and never intended to), fads and fashions in consumption, how we identify what is good or bad to consume, and the problems raised because much of what the public sees as investment (or savings) economists describe as consumption.

Chapter 9 is rather unusual because it addresses problems that arise not just because of scarcity (cf. poverty) but also because of surpluses—not the least of which is a surplus of garbage. Chapter 10 provides an overview of the material presented, particularly as critical, moral, ethical, and geopolitical issues are involved.

Overall, some themes appear and reappear because there was a need to reassess them in different contexts. Unfortunately, other points had to be excluded because both the publisher and I were aware that few people will read a 1,200 page introductory handbook!

I'm deeply indebted to a number of people, first and foremost my husband, Charles A. Bishop, who patiently debated, tracked sources, and proofread numerous versions. My interest in all of this was stimulated by my parents (who became entrepreneurs during the 1930s' depression because they found no markets for their math and engineering degrees), who were and led me to be insatiably curious about everything. The people at Waveland Press have been enormously supportive and helpful. The referees of the original manuscript (Paul Bohannan, Bryan Byrne, Karen Curtis, and Susan Squires) gave detailed comments and raised a number of important questions. Not all were taken to heart, however, and I absolve them of any responsibilities for flaws in the material. Colleagues, students, and a host of other people provided insights, data, and provoking (as well as provocative) questions. Over the years during which this book was being formulated I became indebted to a long list of significant others. However, I owe too much to too many to list them—and in any case, not uncommonly, it was points of disagreement with them that forced me to hone my thinking. Thus, it's quite likely that several would not want to be acknowledged and thereby held as somehow responsible for any of the material.

M. Estellie Smith

Chapter One

It's All a Matter of Choice
Economic Anthropology and Today's World

—Hank and Debbie are making up a list of the people they'd like to invite to their New Year's Eve party. The list, however, includes (1) Joe and Mary—a rather dull couple who always end the evenings in a shouting match because Joe drinks too much and Mary doesn't want him to drive home; (2) Pete—who's trying to sell his house and, lately, can't seem to talk about anything but the real estate market and which way interest rates may go; and (3) Mike and Tamara—though Hank and Debbie met them only a few weeks ago and don't know them very well. It doesn't include two of their oldest and dearest friends, Jim and Allie, though they're still good friends and the four have always shared New Year's Eve. Why were these people included and excluded?

—Mr. Jones has been buying widgets from the ABC Company ever since he started his business. He recently received an offer from another company that said they could supply him the same widgets at a lower price because they were able to save on storage and shipping costs. Mr. Jones could add several thousand a year to his profit by changing suppliers, but he continues to patronize ABC Company. Why doesn't he purchase his widgets at the lower price?

—Money is tight this week and Jack is trying to watch his weight. Yet when the Scouts come around on their annual cookie sale he buys one of each of the six varieties, then gives them away to friends. Why did Jack buy them in the first place?

—The alarm goes off; Laura knows its time to get up and face a Monday-morning world. But she stayed up till 2:30 A.M. on the Internet, and an extra fifteen minutes of sleep seems to offer a return to paradise. After thinking for a minute, however, she pulls herself from her bed with a loud groan and starts the usual morning routine of getting ready for work. What helped her make one choice rather than the other?

—Student life can be a drag. Dave has an examination on Wednesday; his friends are urging him to go to the Tuesday-night beer blast at The Big-Frat-On-Campus house. However, one of his courses is proving tougher than he expected. Worse, it's important in his major. Finally, there have been so many of these parties lately that he has to admit he's not really especially turned on by the thought of this one. He decides to party and, despite good intentions, he doesn't get home early to do some studying before bed. On Wednesday, he cuts his first class to do some last-minute cramming, wishing that professors didn't seem to have a fiendish instinct for scheduling exams on the days after such events. Why didn't he just skip the party and decide to study?

—Leslie never liked brown; it's always seemed a depressing color, and Leslie has always thought that people who wear brown are the same kind who buy "sensible family cars"—secondhand. But the latest addition to Leslie's closet is a brown jacket. Can it be that Leslie's preferences have changed? Why?

All of the scenarios above involve making choices, deciding between alternatives. These are, say economists (and other social scientists, too), economic decisions because the outcome is arrived at by weighing costs versus benefits of each alternative relative to those of other possibilities—the Good News versus the Bad News that every alternative has.

It often surprises people to realize what very complicated mental bookkeeping they do many times a day. When you make a choice, you weigh the pros and cons of one possibility against another and usually end up calculating profits versus losses—in a Utopian world, greater versus fewer benefits (but in a dismal world, greater versus fewer losses). Are you skeptical because you can't see where that sort of thinking played a part in the above choices? Let me go back and show you a little more context for the above scenarios, the kind of context anthropologists look for in order to add depth to their search into the ways people organize their lives. And, let it be noted, it is one of the wonders of the human brain that humans can do many of these kinds of complicated processes so quickly that there is often little time between a choice being presented and a decision being made.

Hank and Debbie's guest list. Hank and Debbie know that inviting people to a party isn't just a case of picking your best friends, or the people who are "best" at a party. For openers, your best friends don't always mix well in a crowd (especially a New Year's Eve type of crowd), but those who are best at a party aren't always your favorite people. (1) Joe and Mary made the list because Debbie and Mary are core members of an office work team; it's important for the success of the team that, at the least, personal tension be kept minimal. If Mary weren't invited she'd be hurt, resentful, or both: life for Debbie might have some unpleasant surprises. (2) Pete invited them to his New Year's party last year; it's payback time. (3) Not only are Mike and Tamara a racially mixed couple (Hank and Debbie wouldn't want the couple to think they were prejudiced), but they live in the upstairs apartment—which means they'd know about the party and could complain about the noise. (4) Jim and Allie are going through a nasty divorce. You can't have both at the same party and you don't want to take sides.

Mr. Jones's buying pattern. X Company is run by his father-in-law.

Jack's Scout cookies. Jack was a Scout when he was young and doesn't like to feel he has let "his own" down. "You like to feel good about yourself—and," he adds, "what do you think my neighbors would say if I were too cheap to give the kids a couple of bucks? Everybody buys those things, even if they don't plan to eat them but plan just to give them away."

Laura's alarm. It took only a few seconds for Laura to work out the benefits of an extra fifteen minutes of sleep versus the costs those fifteen minutes would bring—of having to rush, cutting short morning coffee time and time spent at the mirror in the bathroom as well as deciding what to wear. "It just wasn't worth the extra hassle. I just had the feeling the whole day would go wrong if I slept in a little longer. Last night, it seemed like a good idea but today . . . no way, I decided."

Dave's examination. The situation that Dave was facing was one that required him to confront the fact that he had been mixing short- and long-term goals without any clear picture of which was what and when. He wanted to obtain the necessary credentials to gain entry into a job market when he graduated, and he wanted to create social networks that would be helpful at that time. He also wanted to enjoy college life ("before I have to go into the 'real world'") and have friends who were sources of valuable information about which courses/professors to search out/avoid, the "in/out" drinking places, and all the other things one has to know to "make it on campus." If Dave were an entrepreneur (and, in a way, he was), he would be confronting what in business is called "a cash flow" problem. Each expenditure increases or diminishes at least some of the costs/benefits that must be taken into account when making the next decision about yet another expenditure. Dave had not been "recosting" as events unfolded. Further, this particular decision also created a number of follow-up but immediate choices that had to be made: What time to quit the party? What were the short- and long-term costs/benefits of "one more beer"? Was it better to try to study after the party or just to go to bed and try to get up early to study? And, on the morning after, having done neither of the above, how should he weigh the profits versus losses of cutting the first class relative to the benefits/costs of gaining time for last-minute cramming?

The brown jacket. The favorite color of Leslie's current "significant other" (SO) is brown. Just last week SO pointed to someone who resembled Leslie and commented on how well the person looked in the brown outfit being worn, commenting that "People in that color always look in control, like, they don't have to run with the crowd but can do their own thing." Leslie decided that the way SO perceived people who wore brown mattered enough to buy the jacket and hope for the best.

Although the actors in all of the cases discussed did a social (versus a monetary) analysis, the process of calculating profits and losses, immediate or short- versus long-term benefits and costs, was not much different from the kind of monetary and social calculations done by all large organizations today.

- **Businesses.** Do we drop a poorly selling product or try to rebuild demand by adding to the advertising budget?
- **Government.** Should we cut out the school lunch program, delete funding for the arts—or make small cuts in both?
- **Charitable organizations.** A professional fund-raising firm says it will increase donations, but the charity wonders if the consulting firm's high fee will cancel out the increase in donations—and what if the campaign doesn't increase donations?
- **Hospitals.** A kidney for a transplant has become available, and two patients are eligible (one aged 20 and one aged 68)—the first is the skinhead leader of a neo-Nazi group, the second is a world-famous pianist. In any case, there are other issues: perhaps it's wrong to let age or personal lifestyle matter. Would it be fairer—and relieve physicians of the task of having to play God—to be guided by the simple rule of "first come first served?"
- **Religious institutions.** The Bishop must decide whether to continue to meet the rising costs of keeping open a church that has served a neighborhood for over a century but has been losing members for the last decade—or to close it and use the money for a youth program.
- **The military.** Told they have to close ten bases, the army has to decide whether to go ahead with plans to close low-priority Fort X. The elected political representative for the district in which Fort X is located also heads the committee that will decide next year's military budget—and has let it be known that the hardships the closing will cause for her constituents will lead her to take an equally tough line on the army's requested funding increase.

These examples are only a small sample of the kinds of choices available, factors to weigh, and decisions we make in everyday life. They also illustrate the difference between most economists and most economic anthropologists, as well as, say, sociologists, political scientists, or business managers—a difference that rests on what is taken into account (a neat phrase that reminds us that making decisions often involves a process rather like doing bookkeeping in one's head!) when trying to select, predict, or understand the decisions we and others make. Economists prefer to deal with things that can be counted and measured; they tend to discount (another neat phrase that we use in everyday speech to talk about reducing the value of something) the very things economic anthropologists see as critical. Here's an example:

> Jim and Lisa Marie, an inner-city couple with four children, won $10,000 in a lottery. After taxes (of course), they took $2,100 and used it to host a block party so friends and relatives could help celebrate their twenty-fifth wedding anniversary. They used the remainder as a down-payment on a six-year-old minivan.

An economist would say this was a poor use of the money; Jim and Lisa Marie should have invested in something that would bring them long-term benefits rather than wasting it on parties and a van that might soon require expensive repairs they couldn't afford. However, Jim and Lisa Marie calculated (note how often we use economic terms in everyday speech) that over the years they had been helped over tough times by those friends and neighbors; Jim and Lisa Marie knew they owed them. Said Jim,

> Hey, I can't tell you how many times those people came through for us. Now, we both know it's payback time. But you can't go to them and start counting up all the free meals, the help they gave when the apartment needed painting, all the times our friend Alice babysat for free; the money different people lent when the car broke down or when Jimmie needed Scout stuff—things like that. You could count them up, then try to pay them back. But you can't.
>
> We're not dumb enough to think life's going to change. What happens when this money's gone but there's another streak of bad luck? Do you think those people will come through another time after you forgot them when you had a little luck? Besides, that van will come in useful in lots of ways; Maybe we'll have problems with it—even a new car can be trouble—but my brother works in a gas station and can fix anything real cheap. And what if it's old? You think I'm dumb enough that I'm going to park a new car on the street in *my* neighborhood? Nobody's going to bother something like that. And you didn't think of how low my insurance will be on a car like that.

Jim and Lisa Marie were not being stupid or illogical in the way they spent their windfall. Nor—though some economists (and others) might claim it—are they using their unexpected resources[1] in ways that are not economically rational. Economically rational behavior consists of actions, activities, or choices selected by groups or individuals, using the means available to them that are appropriate to the ends desired. Given the context in which they currently exist, Lisa and Jim have, quite logically, worked out various ways to allocate the money; they considered the immediate and possible potential costs/benefits; and they allotted their windfall in ways that their "bookkeeping" showed made the most sense—that is, that promised them the optimum return, with the least risk, at the lowest cost.

In the pages that follow we'll explore the segment of human behavior that involves economizing behavior. We'll see how making many of our big and small decisions involves trade-offs that determine the quality of life—that yardstick we use to measure the degree of satisfaction we have with the gains and losses of day-to-day living as well as their long-range outcomes. Because we will be viewing economizing activities from an anthropological perspective, those activities will be selected from a wide range of societies—even some that no longer exist. Among the things we'll examine and questions we'll explore will be:

Where do we get the goods (and Good) and services that people distribute and exchange?

- **Production.** Is begging productive work? Is producing babies any different from producing fields of rice, automobiles, selling crack, delivering the mail or a sermon, interpreting dreams (for psychoanalysis or for help in picking the right numbers to bet)?
- **Distribution.** Who benefits from what I produce? Does someone buy from me simply to exchange my stuff with others, to help me by providing a market for my goods or services—or to exploit me by making an unfair profit on my labor?
- **Consumption.** How can some people argue that the less you have, the richer you are? Are the best things in life free? Can there be too much of a good thing?

What are the ways people can distribute and exchange?

- **Obligatory.** What do I have a right to receive? What are the "birthrights" to which every individual is entitled—which I have to neither earn nor be awarded, and of which, morally, I can't be deprived? What rights of others am I morally obligated to acknowledge? Can I voluntarily surrender a right? Do children have the right to be supported by their parents? Do parents have the right to be supported by their children? Does everyone have a right to expect that they will never lack for adequate food,

[1]If you should encounter a word that is unfamiliar on its own or in context, please turn to the Glossary, which contains definitions for many of the terms you will come across in the text.

housing, and medical care? Who determines what the adequate amount is? If you had to choose, which set of rights would you surrender—those just listed, or the rights to "life, liberty, and the pursuit of happiness"?

- **Equitably.** I give what you want, you give what I want, and each calls it an even transfer. Is there such a thing as fair exchange—all gain and lose to the same extent—my apples for your oranges, my labor for yours (I'll spend an hour tending your baby; you spend an hour fixing my teeth)?
- **Variably.** One or both parties perceive that the exchange was unequal—and, possibly, unfairly so. Though, as with the previous two exchanges, coercion may be the basis for the exchange, threat or actual use of force is more likely to occur in this type of transaction. Is "your money or your life" an unequal exchange—and, indeed, how can you "gain" what you already possess?

What are some of the tools that aid in the distribution and exchange process?

- **Money and barter.** It's often claimed that "money is the measure of all things." Is it? Why is the original handwritten score of Beethoven's Fifth Symphony worth more ($100,000) than the outstanding recording of that music by the world's leading orchestra ($15)? Are food stamps money? What can plastic poker chips buy in Las Vegas? What can't they buy? How can a business pay you in money that it prints itself and that can be spent only in company stores? If money has replaced barter, why does France sell military planes to Iraq in exchange for barrels of oil?
- **Marketplaces.** How do the Saturday flea market and the global commodity market for oil resemble and differ from each other? How has the cybermarket changed the world? Is the Global Economy completely changing the world's economies and, if so, how? What may and may not be priced, bought, and sold in the marketplace? What property rights do you need to have (and perhaps don't) to sell things? How do goods and services differ in terms of their production, distribution, and consumption?
- **Accounting.** There are various ways of keeping track of costs and benefits, profit and loss, and appreciation and depreciation. How does the government measure things that don't get counted and for which the records (if they exist at all) are hidden? What does theft cost? What does wasted time cost? How much money is circulated in the drug trade? Should kids pay taxes on money earned for babysitting or collect a sales tax on worms they sell to fishermen? Should charitable volunteers calculate the hourly worth of their labor and receive tax rebates—and, if they do, can we really count it as charitable work? If 80 percent of the people

in a certain poor locale work off the books, and 40 percent of these "unemployed" people make an average of $20,000 a year, how does the government calculate the taxes needed to support the official number of unemployed? How do we calculate the costs of the decline in nonrenewable resources such as oil, water, or clean air? What's the difference between price and value? (For example, what's the price of a college education, what's its worth, and why do people pay different prices for the same B.A. degree earned from different universities? How is it that, at the same university, people get different value for their money?)

- **Budgets and budgeting.** Think about how you allocate your resources. How do you really spend your time (yet another of those interesting everyday, economic phrases) as well as your money (how often have you heard the phrase "Time is money")? How do you budget work and play—and what do you define as work versus play? Are professional sports people playing or working? Is sleep a waste of time? When was the last time you just sat and did nothing? Is thinking work? When you buy a gift for someone, are you spending, investing, or wasting money?

There are other issues that will be examined in order to understand the themes in the material presented here: the impact on our lives of the High-Tech (HT), Information Technology (IT), Biotechnology, and the Internet revolutions; the growing importance of commodities and, more important, the process of commoditization in the lives of the world's peoples; problems of growing waste and declining natural resources; and the way sentiment, emotion, and other noneconomic considerations affect economic processes.

Our modern world is increasingly centered around commodities—their production, distribution and consumption. But just what is a commodity? A common definition is "any good or service produced for its exchange rather than use value." Until a few thousand years ago, most people, most of the time, produced for their own use and within a small circle of kin and group members. If they had an occasional surplus, it was unplanned and shared with others, given to the gods in thanks, or simply left to rot. Nowadays, the majority of the earth's people are engaged in producing, distributing, and consuming commodities: They aim to provide goods and services to others so that, usually, they will receive, through a salary or share of the profits, some monetary reward (workers rarely anticipate going unpaid and company personnel or shareholders rarely expect the company will go bankrupt though, in point of fact, companies do collapse and, during the late 1990s, many workers in Russia and other parts of eastern Europe hadn't been paid for a half year or more).

However, it's not uncommon that goods originally produced for self-use ultimately enter the market and are exchanged—think of native crafts produced for self-use and personal adornment, or another possibility, antiques that were once items that people made for their own use. Thus, the definition of "commodity" used here is "any good or service that can be exchanged in an institutionalized marketplace or system of trade."

Now, there is a great deal of concern being expressed by people in all segments of society about the ways in which modern humans are allowing the chase after commodities (goods or services) to dominate—indeed, to become the only thing that matters—in our lives. A growing number of people, or so it's claimed, center their lives around chasing wealth, on getting money in order to buy a constantly expanding array of "things." We allow the possession (or lack of possession, as the case may be!) of things to color our opinions of others, and we are deeply concerned about the way in which things color their opinion of us. People all over the globe are, increasingly, driven either to catch up or keep up with the Joneses: the citizens of emerging economies must play catch-up with those of developed economies; the economically depressed regions of the European Union must be given subsidies to catch up with the prosperous regions; and you and I need to worry about debt (or find more income) in order to keep up. Concerns about "overconsumption" are valid as we see its effects in a depletion of resources, a creation of waste, a despoiling of the environment, and mounting levels of personal stress. Despite all the gains, many feel a disquieting sense of loss.

That said, those who are concerned can't just wish away the phenomenon. Indeed, it's difficult if not impossible to address the concerns we have about the process, if we ignore the legitimate aims that underlie it and the complex conditions that sustain it—as well as make it difficult to alter. Gathering statistics may be informative of the costs and even supportive of our concerns, but they don't always enable us to work together to redirect or modify the chase after commodities in realistic ways—ways that take into account the very real need for some to catch up, or the equally real aim of others to use the market system and patterns of consumption to express their public persona. However we make judgments on the process, it is unrealistic to deny it exists. The way people are ranked by others is often used to measure their eligibility for a promotion, for invitations to events where valuable social networks are built, for their children to be invited to parties—and how such friendships may affect their future quality of life.

This emphasis on the way in which the possession of or access to certain goods and services are judged to be important for how others evaluate our social position isn't new; archeologists find evidence for it in both small-scale societies and early empires. For example, we find emblems of valor or special spirituality once worn by warriors, priests, or rulers, or a set of pots used for ordinary cooking and eating but other finer, thinner, more elaborately painted pottery used to serve high-ranked elite, important visitors, or supernatural beings. Differential access to Good, goods, and services appears in ancient societies when only some few, high-ranked individuals were allowed certain foods, the wearing of clothes made with costly dyes or the furs and feathers of particular animals and birds, or special funeral arrangements. Differential access is also evident when leaders of different societies exchanged rare gifts with each other while entertaining at magnificent banquets to impress visiting leaders and their followers with the abundance of resources the hosts had at their disposal. Control of resources is a form of power, and a commonly recognized belief is that whoever negotiates from a position of inferior power is likely to come out a loser in the distribution of available resources. The ostentatious display of expensive, rare foods and wines; fine porcelain; crystal, silver, and gold tableware; linens; and exotic flora are a standard part of international gatherings. Even when the host nation is applying for a loan, a display of wealth indicates that their need is (a) only temporary and (b) the loan is likely to be repaid because the country does not lack resources but (like many individuals from time to time) is currently experiencing a temporary cash flow problem. Lenders can be reassured that both the debt and its servicing (i.e., making interest payments) will be honored.

People may, of course, limit the distribution of their resources and, instead, live modestly, displaying their thrift and frugality by neither accumulating nor distributing. But how much and to what extent may thrifty individuals ignore the rules of production, distribution, and consumption followed by most of the people most of the time? How long will it be before they begin to incur the social costs of a frugality that causes others to question their work ethic or creditworthiness (in terms of reciprocity), before others would feel uncomfortable around them because they can't just relax and enjoy life—because they have forgotten that "All work and no play makes Jack a dull boy"? At what point are people identified as lacking in ambition, as hoarding, stingy, or cheap? Are such persons using up the resources of others while conserving their own—and, if so, to what end? How much frugality and saving (or investing) can you practice and still meet those social obligations that are necessary if you wish to have a safety net?

Resources are redistributed, reallocated, and shifted around whenever humans change location in real as well as sociocultural time and space. As you go through the average Euroamerican life cycle—living at home, living in a dorm while attending college, sharing an apartment, getting married and raising a family, watching your residential unit shrink as children grow up and leave home (and possibly come back alone or with child(ren) and/or spouse), living alone when your spouse dies—all require a shift in the distribution of resources, goods, and services.

There are more ways than ever to distribute and exchange goods and services within the global population. There are still the traditional marketplaces (e.g., the farmers' markets, flea markets) as well as the door-to-door salesperson and the telephone solicitor; there are monster malls, cybermarts, shopping by mail from a thousand different catalogues, and TV home shopping. You can shop while at 13,000 feet above the earth, in the middle of the ocean, and, possibly, those in submarines may order online as well!

It's hard in today's world to realize that only five hundred years ago, most of the world's people engaged in market exchange only at periodic fairs held annually or at most weekly. Now, people can shop around the clock, around the calendar, and around the world. People in Nepal, Nigeria, New York, or Moose Jaw are able to purchase a book from Amazon.com whenever they decide to buy. This has changed our personal lives in ways only beginning to be understood. When we moved goods by, say, camel caravans, the caravan stopped at night and everyone bedded down for a night's sleep. Today, a trucker moving goods from Rotterdam to Moscow is monitored by a computer in the main office, a thousand or more miles away, where a computer screen shows a dispatcher precisely where the truck is, how fast it is traveling (or not), and estimated time of arrival within a time frame of fifteen minutes. And truckers have to eat, sleep, and take rest breaks according to a schedule as laid out by the computer.

Because people work around the clock, they must have the ability to get goods and services around the clock. This explains some of the popularity of cybershopping; for many people, the only available time to buy goods and services is outside the traditional marketplace hours (witness twenty-four-hour, seven-day-a-week supermarkets, drug stores, restaurants, ATMs, TV, and movie houses. One may even have dental work done, order eyeglasses or hearing aids, and even have certain types of plastic surgery done at any hour of the day or night. There are problems, of course: those who live near such twenty-four-hour markets object to the traffic, the noise, the lights, and so on. Despite the fact that mall developers are anxious for tenants, mall operators may not be able to afford to have one large twenty-four-hour tenant if none of the other shops find it profitable to be open at all hours. The expense of heat, lighting, and security would offset the rent received.

Despite all this emphasis on marketplaces, it must be remembered that there is an important area of exchange that takes place outside marketplaces and, only recently, has begun to be taken into account in the market system. It's the exchange between humans and the ecosystem. We may trade in commodities, especially minerals (oil, gold, and silver) and food (wheat, corn, coffee, etc.), but little attention has been paid to the benefits of natural ecological systems, benefits that are disrupted by the extraction/production of such goods. Yet soil, water, and air are critical components of the human life-support system. When they are negatively affected, human society is also negatively affected. And, very importantly, the poor of the world bear a greater share of such costs than the affluent. As one moves down the ladder of wealth, one finds an ever larger segment of the population at risk relative to the quantity and quality of potable water, clean air, and uncontaminated living/leisure places.

Although we have begun to make attempts to calculate the value of the global ecosystem (generally estimated as being worth several trillion dollars), we have no true mechanism with which to price the earth. Furthermore, decisions about ecosystem resources are often made in an arena where the choice seems to be a necessary trade-off between economic development and environmental degradation. The real choice, of course, is whether we want to have sustainable (i.e., long-term) development or instant gratification. And here we have a poignant dilemma. Much of the so-called First World developed its wealth at a time when we had little knowledge of and little interest in the impact of various types of development. Having begun to see the results of a shortsighted building of wealth, First World nations now urge the emerging economies to learn from our mistakes: "It's all one global system, and we must work together," we say at what often seems to be an unending chain of international conferences on the issue.

But those who speak for the poorer countries of the world respond:

> We're suffering for your mistakes; why shouldn't you suffer for ours—especially since we're the people who have no running water, medical facilities, adequate housing, and the like. We need to improve our lives now. How many wars need we fight—and how many people must live out their lives blinded or crippled as a result—because we must compete with our neighbors for a few acres of land or access to water? How many old people die because they lack adequate caretaking or facilities to make do themselves? How many babies die from diseases that could be eliminated for a few cents per person—if we had the money? How many people will work in the fields or the mines (if they work at all) because they lack the education to do anything else? We need the wealth that comes from economic development now, not a generation or two down the road.

Indeed, this is not just a complaint from emerging economies. There are many pockets of poverty in developed countries that look to economic development to improve their lives. In North America, for example, there are segments of Amerindians, rural dirt farmers, and an urban underclass who lack the skills to move from towns and cities that have lost as much as 75 percent or more of the businesses that would offer them employment and who live "lives of quiet desperation." And the poor of the Euroamerican world are much more likely to live in those portions of rural and urban areas where their quality of life suffers relative to those whose higher incomes allow them to live in more affluent neighborhoods. It is in the locales where the less affluent live that the waste disposal landfills are located, the sewer system is faulty, the yards and playgrounds are contaminated by factory waste and agricultural fertilizer runoff deposited in years past and in some cases still going on. Again, it is those at the bottom of the ladder who bear a disproportionate amount of the costs of ecosystem spoilage. The affluent are able to move away from unattractive locales, buy water filtration systems for their homes, and have more access to legal and political avenues to correct problems when they are affected by them.

Every society has rules about the distribution, allocation and exchange of goods and services. In our society, for example, one is not supposed to sell babies; the trade in sex—especially if it involves the sexual services of children (those under the age, say, of twelve)—brings up issues not of price but of morality. There is a growing concern around the world about the issue of child labor (especially in hazardous and unsafe conditions or where the children have been sold and are, literally, enslaved—although one might assume that such labor conditions would be unacceptable for adults as well!). There is an increasingly heated debate as to whether blood or human organs should be available on the open market, to be bought/sold rather than given free by altruistic donors. All of these cases reflect our concern with a broader issue: market prices don't always reflect true costs.

Another question: What should be exchanged in the market, and what should be distributed by the government? Many North Americans are in favor of universal health care (the system that already exists in Canada, though not all services—e.g., a test for prostate cancer—are covered without a small copayment). However, rising medical costs are leading to a deterioration of the Canadian health care system (e.g., people waiting fifteen hours or more for emergency health care, critical surgery postponed as long as two or three months). To provide a minimum standard level of care for all, should the program be adjusted so that those with higher annual incomes must augment the system through a private, supplementary insurance program, freeing up more resources for the truly needy? Or should all citizens have an equal claim to equal coverage? (It should be noted that a growing number of more affluent Canadians supplement the program by purchasing private insurance; those who want to be in a private or semiprivate room rather than in a ward must pay for it themselves or with private coverage. They are, as well, bypassing the system and using private providers, usually located in the United States.)

One aspect of the issue brings us back to the broad claim by economists that, behind most of the decisions people make, there is a weighing of the balance between costs and benefits. If this is the case, we must assume that people in government—whether elected, selected (e.g., through civil service examinations), or appointed (as with positions in the cabinets of our leaders to serve as secretary of defense or minister of education)—are guided by the same model. But is it in line with that model to find that an individual seeking public office—a position held for, say, four or six years and paid, say, a salary of less than $100,000 a year—may spend as much as several million dollars to get elected? The people who give campaign funds may have special interests in having a particular representative of those interests voting on government laws, regulations, policy decisions, trade tariffs, subsidies, budgets, and various social programs, to mention only a few of the issues. It's rare, however, that a campaign ends with money to spare; usually the candidate is in debt and more attempts to raise funds must be made to pay past campaign debts—often at the same time that fund-raising attempts are being made to finance the next campaign.

Are these individuals altruistically compelled to employ resources for the mere potential to do public good (after all, many candidates lose) and sacrifice not just their own but their family's resources? Many politicians are trained in law; their government salaries are far less than most could make in private practice. They actually incur debt to earn less money. Why? As for civil servants, they often seek raises on the grounds that they receive far less than comparable jobs would pay in the private sector. When they applied for and accepted their posts, were they unaware of this? Does ignorance account for their initial choice to enter public service? Or, in both cases, are individuals selecting a choice that offers added value beyond the monetary costs of the campaign or the lower salaries? If so, what might that extra value be?

We're going to be examining these questions in a world that stands at the beginning of a technological revolution. One of the things we'll address is how and when innovations occur—and when they are rejected to retain existing patterns. We'll also look at the role of the entrepreneur—the risk taker and niche-creator, individuals who, in today's world, seem to be everywhere.

More and more, each of us is facing a world in which innovations appear at an increasingly rapid rate, each building on all the others to create a whole next level of even more rapid and more complex innovative changes. We're going to try to see how we can make sense out of a system spewing forth never-ending (and cumulative!) "newness," innovations, along with a growing accumulation of bits of data that are woven together in an increasingly intricate network of cause and effect, costs and benefits, trade and trade-offs.

No one wants to be a puppet, manipulated by people as well as events or processes not understood. When you come to realize that you, like everyone, spend a large part of daily life making decisions, engaging in actions that you hope make sense, economizing and wasting, you should be awed—and concerned. But if you realize that you already have an impressive inventory of tools and already know how to calculate at least some of the social and monetary costs/benefits of everyday life that play an important role in the choices made, you'll know that you're not incapable of understanding how you and, importantly, others, make decisions affecting your life. This should go a long way toward your taking a more active role in making better decisions. No matter how you define and, through life, continue to redefine your goals, this new self-awareness cannot help but increase benefits and decrease costs.

Chapter Two

It's a Great Place to Visit, but I Wouldn't Want to Live There

Get ready for a hard sell. Before going into the way trade and trade-offs are part of many of the everyday things most people do, I'm going to try to persuade you to buy the claim that the findings of anthropology in general, and of economic anthropologists in particular, are very useful in dealing with the kinds of issues and concerns that bedevil us in everyday life, especially when we have to make decisions.

Let me begin by emphasizing that the major utility of the anthropological eye lies not in our ability to provide "answers" or "solutions" but to learn ways to identify problems more accurately and be more creative in suggesting ways to address them. Indeed, the sooner we rid ourselves of the idea that we or anyone can come up with "the answers," the sooner we'll be partway out of the woods. The world we live in is too complex, too full of information, too full of innovations that bring unexpected consequences instead of anticipated results, for some sort of magic formula that works for everyone all the time—or even the majority of the people much of the time. But anthropologists are able to use the insights and information we've gained from looking at sociocultural systems that are the products of thousands of years of attempts to decide "what do we do now"—and how, when, where to do it.

Despite this, our work is not well understood. Anthropologists are used to people saying to them—after class, at parties, or in job interviews (yes, anthropologists hunt for jobs, too!), "But what can you *do* with anthropology?" The sense behind such questions tends to stem from the popular conception that, while interesting, there's little practical use for what many identify as the research concerns of anthropology. In economic terms, people question its utility. This gives rise to various attitudes that lead people to question the time and money spent to research such typical anthropological topics as "exotic" languages and communication in general (Dismissive: "Isn't English the global language these days?"); early human fossils (Petulant: "Hey! I've got enough problems finding the right computer links without worrying about Missing Links."); the archeological remains of early societies (Conscientious: "Those Egyptian pyramids are fascinating, but wouldn't those millions of dollars serve a better use in medical research?"); or "primitive" people (Belligerent: "Thousands are dying in the Balkans, and you people are studying puberty ceremonies among some group of fifty or sixty Indians in the Amazon jungle!"). In short, what has any of this to do with our lives—our jobs, our personal difficulties and goals, the much-discussed global economy, the computer-based IT system, and our concerns about social issues both locally and internationally?

First, and most important, many anthropologists do address today's problems. A significant amount of our research has been done in modern industrial societies—but frequently such studies are assumed to be "sociology" (and, despite similarities, there are major differences between the two fields).

There are two keys to anthropological research. One is the belief that human behavior must be studied in its entirety, that is, holistically. It is assumed that our biology plays an important role in affecting individual and group behavior; that such behavior is deeply affected by and, in turn, affects the environment; that aggregate sociocultural patterns unfold in a historical time frame of hundreds, thousands, and even millions of years because the consequences of decisions may take many generations to emerge; and, finally, that as people try to understand and communicate with each other, they create structures and processes intended to facilitate the day-to-day problems of living together and the long-term concerns of survival.

The second key to anthropological research is the imperative that we look at issues cross-culturally and cross-temporally. We not only study particular aggregates or societies (e.g., single parents, the teenage consumer market; the Navajo, Korean society; a comparison of legal systems in modern state systems) in fairly limited segments of time (e.g., a given period of, say, 12 months, a decade, during the Renaissance), but we also compare and contrast diverse sociocultural units over extended periods of time. For example, we may study the geopolitics of north Ireland over the last 3,000 years; compare the governing councils of Australian aborigines, the Mayflower settlement, and the European Union; or study the ways in which gambling has emerged as a way to redistribute wealth. Our aim is to explore how very different historical, demographic, technological, ideational, and environmental factors affect various aspects of sociocultural behavior.

Hunting and gathering groups are an especially interesting example of how something that appears to be of little relevance to those of us who live in the world of computers and high tech presents us with evidence of problems and ways to address them that are not so different from ours. Few human groups still practice this way of life (and certainly not as they did in ancient times—for their sociocultures have changed and adapted as much as any other). Yet, for most of humanity's history, humans survived by hunting and gathering. The ability to control the growth of food through the planting of small gardens, stock raising, or farming has only been developed in the last ten thousand years—a very small proportion of the four million or so years in which hominids have been around. One of the reasons hunting and gathering became impractical was the growth of population; much more land is needed for hunting and gathering than for agriculture. Hunting and gathering (as many modern people will agree) is actually quite a pleasant way of life, not the least because a mobile lifestyle discourages the accumulation of "things." For many, being unencumbered, being able to just pick up and go when the notion strikes—or conditions require—can be just as attractive as building a cozy little nest and settling down. When you're mobile, it's important to travel light: it's not only less tiring, you are also able to defend yourself more easily. People who own their homes accumulate more stuff than those who rent—for one thing because the latter often don't have attics, basements, spare rooms, or garage space to store things, and for another reason, renting is the expectation of mobility. Conversely, "opportunistic foragers," people who rely on what they hope to find in each day's quest for food, don't carry surplus baggage. They are, as Marshall Sahlins suggested, "the original affluent society"; given that they wish to accumulate little and desire only to fulfill their daily needs and minimal wants (often nonmaterial—e.g., time to think, to talk with friends, to engage in games), their immediate desires are easily satisfied. In short, they have the level of resources that leaves them satisfied with what they have. This is what most people identify as being "affluent." They still, however, have the same long-term concerns and try to plan ways to insure against scarcity. Kinship ties and marriage obligations, rituals, and rules of sharing are some of the ways they do it. But they, too, make economic decisions, that is, they weigh the costs and benefits of certain decisions that must be made in, say, the quest for food.

A modern and urban kind of hunting and gathering is still practiced. Let me give two examples from my own fieldwork.

I once lived in Tallahassee, Florida, and hired a cleaning woman to come in one afternoon a week to clean my apartment. After a few weeks, however, Ella made it known that I wasn't living up to some sort of unspoken contract that, apparently, she and I had made. Initially, new to the rules of southern living, and unaccustomed to having a cleaning person, I didn't realize that the employer is supposed to indicate that there are certain "leftovers" for the cleaner to take home at the end of the day.

One day I discovered that a steak I had planned for dinner on the weekend had mysteriously vanished. I mentioned this to Ella, indicating that I thought I was losing my mind because "I know I put it in the fridge." She replied, "Oh, I took that; I thought it was leftovers." I wasn't happy with Ella: How could she think an unwrapped steak was a "leftover"? But when I told the story to a friend, expecting sympathy or outrage to match mine, she scolded me for not asking some local how things were done in Tallahassee. She explained that such foodstuffs were a standard part of the deal. Ella was just letting me know I hadn't been following the rules—and one important rule was that the various day-employers indicated, on Ella's arrival, the "leftovers" that we would appreciate her "cleaning out" (and the linguistic rules for how to offer such things are as important as the things themselves!). After that, I always made sure to buy an extra pork chop, a slightly larger pot roast than I needed to meet my needs, a six-pack of soft drinks (even though I never drink them), and so on.

I realized that, with her various clients, Ella practiced a new variant of the age-old technique of hunting and gathering. Ella was "opportunistically foraging," going out each day with a specific resource target (food and wages) in mind and collecting whatever edibles turned up in the day's activities. Indeed, as I eventually found out, a large part of the family food came from these kinds of activities, helped out by Ella's daughter, who baby-sat several times weekly. Additionally, Ella's husband and sons went hunting and fishing at least one or two days a week, storing excess amounts in rented freezer space as well as trading it with restaurants or friends for other kinds of foods. It may also be noted that, among hunting and gathering groups, sharing is a basic component of their social organization. In typical hunting-gathering tradition, Ella was expecting me to share with her.

I encountered another kind of hunting and gathering group in Buffalo, New York. It was a motorcycle club whose group organization and many of the internal rules were surprisingly similar to those of "standard" hunters and gatherers. Granted, the kinds of stuff male gang members were "hunting and gathering" came from stores or from parked cars—radios, tape decks, and other items left unsecured in the cars (as well as, occasionally, the cars themselves!). Females, considered as attached to but not an integral part of the gang, used a rather sophisticated shoplifting scheme. Still, their way of viewing such stuff as "free resources" from their environment, the extent to which their subsistence base rested on such foraging, and their attachment to this way of life (as compared to those who "settled down and had regular jobs") was much the same as that of aboriginal groups following the same lifestyle. Their social organization was male-dominated; women were useful but subservient. The club had elaborate networks with other autonomous (motorcycle) groups—even to the extent that a large number of such small bands gathered together periodically, much in the style of the Australian gatherings called *corroborees*. Australian native peoples who still follow the traditional ways have supernatural objects (*churingas* or "bullroarers") that make a heavy roaring noise when whirled over one's head in rituals. Motorcycle males have a similarly mystical relationship with their powerful Harley-Davidson motorcycles whose engines are revved to increase the noise whenever the bikers want to express their identity or intimidate their prey. The main difference is that the motorcycle gang persists in time by recruiting new members from outside (pregnant females are either expelled or told to abort), while aboriginal groups value children and maintain continuity primarily through internal reproduction.

There is other, less "exotic" research. For example, in one developmental project in eastern India, people in the region resisted being relocated to a proposed new town, a coastal site that urban planners selected as ideal for creating an industrial port. The locals, however, claimed the locale was cursed; evil spirits, they said, punished people who invaded the area. Ridiculing such "primitive superstitions," urban planners went ahead with the development.

Eight years after completion, a massive typhoon (hurricane) hit the area and over twenty thousand people died. It later emerged that not only did such typhoons hit the area every thirty or forty years—and time spent talking to the older people might have informed the planners of such a risk—but, in recovering the bodies and clearing the debris, the remains of an urban area dating some five hundred years earlier turned up, destroyed by the same kind of catastrophe. Records of the events (if there were any) had been lost in time, or no one had bothered to check on such things. Any concerns about the probability of typhoons were dismissed with claims that provisions had been made for such events and that possible risks had been adequately addressed in the development plan. Nevertheless, the local people had accumulated the knowledge that over the long haul this could be a very hazardous place to live, and their memory aids for warning future generations of the occasional monster storm were phrased, as they often are, in the language of the mythic and supernatural.

Anthropologists are not so quick to dismiss such folklore and superstitions as "prescientific thinking," or as groundless, foolish, and ignorant. Had anthropologists been involved, such statements would have led them to do more research for clues as to real-world factors to account for such "superstitions." They might look into the region's history (e.g., was it a place vulnerable to coastal slave raiders?), geology (was it an earthquake zone?), climatic conditions (how intense could storms be in the monsoon season?), or even—by analyzing human bones recovered from long-vanished villages—indications of repetitive food shortages and malnutrition or starvation. Any or all of these might have provided clues that could have helped bridge the lack of cooperation between locals and experts, between the explanations given by the locals for resistance to settlement and the scientifically trained outside personnel whose focus was the economic potential and structural design needs of the projected port.

Another example from my own research: An urban renewal program was designed to help a once prosperous New England mill town attract new industries by making the town less dreary looking because of the large number of slums. I attempted to convince the city managers that their plan to tear down a large area of multifamily dwellings in a designated slum area was misguided. To be sure, the exteriors showed peeling paint and other signs of dilapidation, but the interiors were in excellent condition. I explained that people left the house exteriors in poor condition (while spending considerable sums to remodel interiors) because homeowners knew tax assessors simply drove around the neighborhoods and assessed homes on the basis of their street appearance. Assessors rarely, if ever, left their cars, some from fear of such "bad neighborhoods," others because a quick eyeballing through their car windows required less time and effort. Homeowners (rightly) believed that taking care of the exteriors would result in increased taxes on the property.

A large majority of the houses had been built in the late nineteenth century and were very sound structurally. Rather than tearing them down, I recommended a freeze on property taxes for ten years and a tax rebate for those who remodeled the exterior. Such changes would have cost, roughly, one-tenth that of razing the homes and building new structures—and, importantly, would have maintained a neighborhood stability and sense of community that went a long way toward keeping such areas relatively crime free. The city managers, however, argued that, in addition to providing employment (albeit short-term), the renewal program would "modernize the city" and attract new businesses. Urban renewal went ahead.

When they were considering various plans for the new buildings, I then recommended that they should not construct high-rise apartment buildings. The majority of the residents were immigrants from the Portuguese-owned Azores, a group of islands located in the mid-Atlantic. They had come to North America because it offered these mostly rural peasants, skilled at farming but little else, jobs and the opportunity to learn new skills. Just as important, living frugally and earning cash income, they could save and buy their own homes, places with a bit of green space where they could plant kitchen gardens. They would fulfill a dream; they would become landowners, "rich people." High-rise apartments, I said, would not attract these people as tenants. But, for those new arrivals who would be the likely tenants, space for kitchen gardens would be an important inducement to rent such flats.

Despite such arguments, the decision was made to erect high-rise apartments. Ten years later, however, the apartments had less than a 40 percent occupancy rate and vandalism was a constant problem. Those forced to sell their homes for "slum clearance" were angry that they received much less than they believed (accurately) their homes were worth, and most agreed they wouldn't go back to being renters and, above all, be unable to have gardens. Non-Portuguese townsfolk, planners, and politicians were baffled and angry that what they categorized as an impoverished minority group should reject the low-rent, "well-planned" apartments. Typical of their complaints were the comments of one person: "When you try to give that kind decent housing they turn it down. They like to live in dumps; that's what they're used to."

What did the former residents of the area have to say? First, drug dealers moved into the area, and those long-time residents of neighborhoods adjacent to the rebuilt area began to have discipline problems with their children. There was also an increase in robberies and vandalism. Next, both former area residents and new arrivals were reluctant to move into the new apartments because they would be tenants in public housing where they faced a number of restrictions, such as an inability to make any changes in what, for them, was a cramped and colorless environment. They couldn't paint walls or hammer nails to hang things; they couldn't invite visitors or friends down on their luck to stay for a few weeks. One woman moved out after a few months because, she explained, "Imagine! They told me my nephew and his family couldn't stay with us till he found another job." They were told to expel their newly arrived kin because "It's not sanitary for that many people to live there." Another said, "But you have to help family. So I moved." And another case: "I put a crucifix on the wall and the manager came and told me to take it down; I couldn't put nails in the wall. I wouldn't want to live where you can't put Christ on the wall."

The city finally sold the buildings to a private developer for twenty cents on the dollar. He, in turn, did some relatively low-cost remodeling that transformed the apartments into middle-income condominiums—and made a nice profit on buildings originally constructed with (scarce) taxpayers' dollars.

There were also telling social consequences: Along with an increase in drug sales and other street crime, ethnic factionalism intensified, resulting in more fights in neighborhood bars and at the high school. Because the original inhabitants began buying the least expensive housing in other areas of the city, local talk programs on both the English- and Portuguese-language radio stations were filled with ethnically explicit attacks on the immigrants—"They're coming in and turning our neighborhood into a slum, too!"—while the Portuguese retaliated with equal heat and ethnic slurs.

When I asked council members why they hadn't accepted my analysis, one answer was that none of the four expert urban planners hired had raised such issues, and "We figured that some anthropologist who was studying folklore [I wasn't] didn't really understand the situation."

One final example: In the Province of Quebec, schooling in the French language is required of all immigrants whose native language is not English. In Quebec, unless one's parents have attended English-language schools, children are required to attend schools with instruction in French. Acquiring English is difficult for many, especially the parents. Many immigrants from Italy, Portugal, Spain, and French-speaking countries (e.g., Haiti) opt to go to Quebec when they decide to immigrate. Already speaking a Romance language leads them to believe that settling in a French-language context will make for an easier transition than moving elsewhere in Canada where English is the dominant language.

When I interviewed thirty-eight families, about three-quarters of them residents for more than three years, over one-third of family adults said they were sorry they had chosen Quebec. Now that they understood Canada better, the majority (twenty-one males and twenty-three female adults) said they would like to leave the province and were encouraging their children to do so should it become possible. They claimed that, as new arrivals lacking job skills and sometimes low in literacy and math ability, "the only employment opportunities are in low-paying, dirty jobs that Canadians don't want." As one put it to me, "The problem is the French make it hard for immigrants to learn English. And if we can't learn English, that makes it hard to move and get better jobs in other parts of the country. But, as long as we stay here, people don't hire us for better jobs because they like to keep those for people born in Quebec."

Statistics show that this claim is somewhat overstated: it is possible (though not easy) for these immigrants to French-speaking Canada to learn English and other skills while earning a livelihood and adjusting to their new lives. But the reality of the situation is not the issue here. From the perspective of many such immigrants, they're paying too high a price for their decision to move to Quebec. There is a sense of isolation from Quebeçois society, an isolation that makes it difficult for the immigrants to begin to feel at home or that discourages them from moving outside their own ethnic enclave and adopting the language and culture of their Quebec hosts. Children are growing up listening to their parents' view of the situation and to what the adults perceive as its inequities—and not uncommonly they either disagree, which leads to family conflict, or they acquire the same view, preferring to stay with "their own kind" rather than cross the boundaries. "And, besides," said one seventeen-year-old boy, "even if I really wanted to, you should listen to what happens if I try to bring anybody home who's not Portuguese!" It's a situation that gives rise to various urban problems that, in turn, create still more problems—as when one Quebeçois politician blamed such "outsiders" for the failure of a recent referendum as to whether Quebec should withdraw from the rest of Canada.

How could an anthropologist help address the issues? Again, we often work in the countries from which the immigrants come as well as with them in the new setting. We also work with members of the host community along with newcomers; we rely on establishing long-term relations of trust with those with whom we work (frequently taking up residence in the area over a period of months, a year, or even longer). These relations as well as wide social networks allow us to verify by repetition various pieces of information and allow us to test the extent to which reports from individuals are biased or relatively factual reporting (only relatively, because, after all, we all employ different perspectives). Importantly, we arrive prepared to listen to what people want to talk about, the aspects of their life with which *they're* concerned, rather than carrying a clipboard with a prepared list of questions in which *we're* interested—some of which would have preconceptions, biases, and assumptions built into them that would skew the research findings in advance. And we listen to people from all quarters (not just the "problem" population), discovering new angles that might not have been considered in designing the study in preresearch ignorance. We allow those interviewed to engage in thoughtful, open-ended discussions, to change their minds after they review our conversations and mull over what was said. Once assured that we won't make judgmental responses, they'll even voice "politically incorrect" answers rather than giving the type of responses they know it's "good to say"—especially to a stranger whose announced motives they suspect. Again, the anthropologist doesn't come in prepared to provide answers or solutions; rather, we work to clarify the issues and identify techniques that assist those with whom we're working to select ways to address them.

Why do people persist in thinking of anthropology as having little more than entertainment value in their own lives ("I really enjoy watching all those archeology programs on TV"; "*National Geographic* has been favorite reading of mine since I was a little girl")? Certainly, one reason is that anthropologists tend not to translate their work into presentations that address the everyday concerns of people living in a twenty-first-century world. Because we describe people and places to which many other social scientists pay little heed, such studies can be interesting, entertaining, occasionally even thought provoking—but, as John Hunt, professor of organizational behavior at the London Business School recently charged in the analysis of cross-cultural issues (*Financial Times*, London, May 5, 1999), "Most of the academic literature on culture is very complicated and often boring." For many people, however, our work is interesting *because* it looks at places, people, and activities that are disengaged from their everyday world, from the people next door, the company where they work, the places in which they worship and play. Our lives are filled with concerns about college costs, pension plans, the activities of our children, the need to put a new roof on the house, the cost of groceries, and the taxes we pay. The TV programs, coffee-table books, and magazines present us with sketches of people and places that are interesting to visit, although most never expect (nor perhaps ever want) to live there.

Such worlds often hold a special attraction. People in these exotic worlds seem to spend a great deal of time relaxing, dancing, having festivals. In our world, yours and mine, there never seems to be enough time for what *needs* to be done—let alone what we would *like* to do. Even if we thought we had all the leisure time we think we really need, the mental calculations of how best to spend our time rarely lead us to think it worthwhile to explore in greater depth the kinds of questions raised by some TV special on, say, a South Sea island community whose fishing has been destroyed by nuclear bomb testing. We believe we already know enough on these kinds of subjects to toy with any of the ideas, questions, and thoughts to which, briefly, they might give rise.

It seems to be a case of what one scholar has labeled "rational ignorance." When we weigh the costs (i.e., time spent) of acquiring more in-depth information about, say, the economic crisis in Africa, the effects of overfishing in the North Atlantic, the chaotic deterioration of Russia, or politics in the national capital—events over which we perceive ourselves as having little control or which seem to have little impact on our daily lives, we judge that time and effort will be better spent on problems nearer to hand—the information we need on our new job, how to deal with a problem at the plant, the way to budget our money, the colleges to choose, and the small stuff that makes up the quality of everyday life—whether to go out to dinner or stay home, or what to wear to Saturday night's party. We might want to spend the time becoming better informed about important issues, but can we really afford to?

At bottom, when we work out decisions on such matters, we are addressing one of the fundamental questions of both life in general and economics in particular: how, given limited resources, do you best budget the use of your available resources to get "the biggest bang for your buck"? If you have only so much time and energy (and resources such as money), why spend it studying things that may be neat to know but seem to have no special relevance to today's problems?

Following a lecture some years ago, a member of the audience commented that she didn't understand spending all that money to study the high suicide rate on the Navajo reservation: "On any given weekend here in L.A. more people probably OD [overdose on drugs] than commit suicide for a whole year on the reservation. L.A. is a problem I have to live with. Study *that* and fix it." Still, it seems probable that most people will rarely spend time seeking more information so as to make a better informed decision as to the amount of funding that should be allocated to study Amerindian problems, despite that such funding represents your tax dollars at work. As with so many topics, the costs of ignorance appear to be far less than the cost of acquiring information that "doesn't really matter," because either it appears to have little or no impact on one's personal life or "I probably won't have much to say about what happens."

What such queries really address is the problem of scarcity. There's never enough of what you need to go around. All humans always have and always will face scarcity of one thing or another; even the earliest humans faced food and water scarcities, energetic insufficiencies to fight off an attacking beast or, from time to time, inadequate supplies of persons with whom to mate. What is scarce might be time, information, money, friends (or, sometimes more important, friends in the right places), food, clothes, space, quiet, good looks, job skills—the possibilities are endless. What's important to understand is how often and in how many ways we need to make choices dealing with alternatives that relate to the scarcities.

Basic needs come first: most living creatures spend much of their time looking for food and water, a safe place to play or rest, and sexual partners. Once the basic needs of immediate, day-to-day survival are taken care of, people begin addressing more general issues. One of the most important is acquiring what we call a risk fund—resources for that "rainy day." If you're healthy, you worry about what might happen if you become ill. Your income may be adequate now, but what will happen if you lose your job, if the stock market crashes, if you are robbed, or if your house is destroyed by some natural catastrophe? How will you cope if your car breaks down or the rent on your apartment jumps up 20 percent? And, sooner or later, you begin worrying about old age when you start facing a scarcity of hair, sexual prowess, memory, or physical agility, when you either can't or don't want to keep working. Do you have enough "set by" to cope? This risk fund even includes a fund of goodwill among friends on whom you can depend to help out when you need it.

Although the problem of dealing with various kinds of scarcity seems to differ when one compares the lives of those in industrial versus nonindustrial societies (we'll return to this issue in chapter 10), the differences may be more apparent than real. An underlying issue that is rarely addressed in this context is a disagreement as to the nature of human nature.

On the one hand, we have those who believe that the earliest human sociocultures were marked by a sharing and cooperative mode of interaction. Various social forms and cultural rules were institutionalized through, say, the unfolding of structured kinship, religion, and associational groups—that is, those who collaborate in the performance of work, play, or ritual performances. Such unfolding structures and processes, it is said, worked to insure that obligatory distributions and reciprocal exchanges were satisfied in ways that bonded all members together in a seamless whole. It is further held that people in these types of groups did not make economic decisions because (a) there was no distinct, institutionalized system of market exchange, and therefore (b) there were no choices to make that would involve concerns about costs or benefits to any individual or group. Any flow of goods and services was determined by relatively fixed and stable rules, for example, of kinship or religious obligations. Any change was the result of slow, consensual adaptation, not conscious choices made between the costs/benefits of various options.

This position seems to assume that it is human nature to be sharing and cooperative. Indeed, those who posit early groups as behaving in this way—let's call them the "seamless society" (SS) proponents—argue that it wasn't until market exchange became a major if not the dominant mode for the transfer of goods and services that human sociocultures were contaminated by such economic concepts as personal costs and benefits, that humans began to exploit others in order to serve their own best interests. The cooperative and egalitarian characteristics of nonmarket sociocultures that existed for most of human history became corrupted by the economic perspective that weighed the price for rather than the value of goods and services. Resources that at one time were freely shared became commoditized and obtainable only through the market mechanism. Once this occurred, the members of sharing sociocultures became divided into aggressive, competitive, and exploitive social segments.

On the other hand, there are those who take their lead from economists who, in turn, take their lead from such pioneers as Ricardo, Jevons, and especially the father of modern economics, Adam Smith. Smith assumed that humans are acquisitive by nature and, as he put it, "have a propensity [an instinct] to truck [trade] and barter." This group—let's call them the "acquisitive society" (AS) proponents—maintain that economists have provided us with a model that explains much of human productive, distributive, and consumptive behavior. A major point of disputation with the SS crowd is that, unlike the economists who limited their analysis to the study of market societies, AS analysts apply the market-based utilitarian model to groups that lack concepts such as "price," "cost," "profits," "debits," or "credits"; who rarely if ever produce "commodities"; and who, lacking markets, are devoid of the "market mentality" that surely must provide the basis for such concepts.

Now, the positions of both the SS and AS proponents have a certain appeal. The SS people (those who hold to something akin to the idea of the original Garden of Eden) offer a welcome corrective to the depressing claims that people are basically selfish, that it's human nature to "get what you can while the getting is good," and the gloomy outlook that ultimately we humans will destroy the world. On the other hand, the view of the AS crowd is attractive for its simplicity. Here's a model that explains a wide range of human behavior: just apply the cost/benefit model to people's actions, and why people do what they do becomes clear. They select whatever allows maxing out at the least cost.

So which is it? Are we naturally cooperative and sharing or instinctively acquisitive and maximizing? Put that way, the answer must be,

"*Naturally*, we are neither." Behaviorally, and especially in groups, humans are so complex and have such a long history of sociocultural experimentation and adaptation—often with no record of which were failures and which successes—that it would be an act of hubris to claim that anyone is able to peer into the depths of time and say, "This is what our species was like at the earliest stages of the invention of human society and culture."

Sometimes, our individual cognitive processes and adherence to group values and norms lead us to behave selfishly; sometimes we behave generously. Furthermore, much of the assessment of behavior results from the cognitive processes and evaluations of those around us. It's their option to decide whether what I consider adequate and appropriate—even generous—behavior is that of a spendthrift or a penny pincher (think of the variations in tipping and children's allowances). What *our* socioculture might see as managed and prudent care of limited resources over which we exercise stewardship, other groups may see as selfish hoarding that denies *their* need for and right of access to those same resources.

Why does this debate matter to the world at large? Well, how many times have you heard people say, "Well, that's just human nature"? Often, certain kinds of behavior are expected ("Oh, boys are just naturally more aggressive than girls") or denied any real generality ("There are no atheists in foxholes") because "everyone" assumes that the presence or absence of certain behavior is universally present. It is, it seems, in the biological nature of hominids as a species. Even when anthropologists and others point to groups that do or don't fulfill such "natural" expectations, opponents counter that what they assume to be "natural" has been disguised, buried, eroded, or has emerged due to the introduction of some new phenomenon. Thus it has been argued, for example, that the feminist movement is to blame for the perversion of women's natural role as loving (and subordinate) caregivers, or that the growing acquisitiveness of modern humans that has required women to work outside the home has led such women to behave as aggressively as their mates in order to compete in the marketplace. When it's pointed out that people do go through life-threatening crises without "rediscovering their need for God," the reply is that this is because science or secular humanism has corrupted the instinctive need of humans to deal with the world by looking to and believing in supernatural forces.

The bottom line? What is important is not the nature of human nature but an awareness that, whether selfish or sharing, cooperative or competitive, there's no blaming most kinds of behavior on nature. *We* make the choice, and *we* may take credit or must bear responsibility for it.

The point is that humans are and have long been a species with exceptional cognitive abilities, and that's what really makes us interesting. We think a great deal about what we do. And, I would argue, we think about the majority of actions we take, have taken, or might take, weighing our actions relative to things we realize we might or should have done: Surely, early hunters thought, "If I had stopped and taken the rabbit, I would have lost the deer. I went after the deer but it got away, and by the time I got back to the injured rabbit, some animal had eaten it. And now I'm back in camp empty-handed. What should I do next time? What shall I teach my son is the smart thing to do?"

Anthropologist Robert Carneiro ("The Evolution of Horticultural Systems in Native South America," 1961) gives an example from the Peruvian Montaña. The residents of a number of small villages (with an average size of about thirty people) live by hunting, gathering, and gardening. The settlements consist of easily constructed houses, and villages are relocated every few years. Yet, points out Carneiro, in nearby regions there are other villages, some of them five times larger, known to have been on the same site for almost a century. Why do some people keep shifting villages and building new residences? Carneiro notes that, over time, gardens are moved ever further from the existing settlement; the villagers have two options and both involve weighing alternative energy costs. The villagers, he says, make an "economic" choice between the energy costs of (a) building new houses nearer gardens, or (b) remaining in the present village but spending time and effort walking ever further as the distance between house and gardens increases. Further, at times of local warfare, the longer the distance, the higher the risk costs. He concludes that ". . . the abandonment of a plot after a brief period can best be understood . . . as the most economical way of carrying on subsistence farming under the prevailing conditions of technology and environment" (p. 57). This would seem to indicate that we have "economic" decisions being made in what is clearly a nonmarket and therefore seamless society.

But wait a minute. What about the way in which kinship and religion play a role in a world dominated by the market system par excellence, global capitalism? Muslim, Jewish, and Christian businesspeople choose to forego profits rather than violate their religious temporal rules, or rules governing charging interest. People everywhere allow kin, friendship, and associational ties to determine certain economic decisions—decisions that, again, result in lower economic profits or even a collapse of their venture. Finally, people often make decisions that result in higher costs and lower rewards rather than violate their ethical guidelines. They make less (or even nothing) in transactions with kin and friends because they feel obliged to do so. They donate free labor to various community organizations because, they feel, it's expected. Doesn't it seem that many of the economic decisions of those in market societies are fairly well embedded in the sociocultural matrix of such segments as kinship, religion, and the like?

Well, now the waters have really been muddied! First, I dispose of explanations based on human nature. Then I point out that, whether seamless or acquisitive, members in both types of sociocultures both make cost/benefit-based choices and, as well, satisfy rules of obligatory sharing and reciprocity. Where do we go from here?

Try this: What do we look at when we address "economic" activities? The kinds of behavior we've been including or excluding (depending on whether you're an SS or AS adherent) is what economists over the last two hundred years or so have defined as the domain of the "economic." Perhaps we should challenge their view of what constitutes this realm.

The position taken in this analysis is that the difficulties we (including economists) have encountered in understanding many important aspects of human interaction stem from our acceptance that certain kinds of behavior and certain tools of economic analysis are indeed economic—uniquely and specifically invented to address market issues. This, let me suggest, is simply wrong-headed.

Let me propose, instead, that cost/benefit analysis is and has long been one of the ordinary ways that humans have employed when trying to weigh options and decide between alternatives. Granted, such decisions may indeed be economic and, granted, outside that economic sphere, the weighing of alternatives, especially when dealing with issues of scarcity, may not utilize the terms "cost" and "benefit." *But the process is the same.* We have actions to take; we see possible alternatives, we weigh the Good News and the Bad News of taking other actions, and we accept or reject them on the basis of possible outcomes.

The point is, these need not be economic decisions just because we use what we now accept are terms specific to the economic domain. The words cost and benefit are mere labels, shorthand terms we use to evaluate the ordinary tasks of weighing the pros and cons of various alternatives for action.

What seems to have happened is that early in the development of modern economics, economists seized upon this quite familiar conceptual model, and they redefined and reworked the well-known and broadly utilized approach to adapt it for their use. Most damaging of all for those who would try to apply the reconstructed model outside the narrow field to which economists then confined it, they proceeded to surround it with what over time became an impenetrable thicket of other specialized analytical tools. The ordinary process of employing a cost/benefit analysis became monopolized by those in the process of constructing the new science of economics.

Since the idea of weighing cost versus benefits of various alternatives had long been an important tool in everyday decision making, it was easy to understand and noneconomists were quick to accept the now-enhanced "economic" model. But noneconomists were expected to buy the whole package. They seemed to have only two options and both required accepting a very Eurocentric definition of cost/benefit analysis.

The option selected by the AS adherents sometimes requires a kind of mental gymnastics. Frequently, it either dismisses relevant data from market societies or distorts another socioculture's ways of behaving and thinking. The studies end up being rejected both by colleagues and those who were studied.

The other alternative, chosen by the SS proponents, throws the baby out with the bath water and argues that, in nonmarket sociocultures, individuals and groups have no options; they never seek alternatives, weigh options, and make choices. Actions are determined according to tradition and by obeying the rules of obligatory sharing and reciprocity.

Both camps need to readjust their sights. The AS people need to break free of the restrictions imposed by modern economics and reclaim the cost/benefit model—call it the Optional model or the G/BN (Good/Bad News) model, whatever you choose. We need to return the concept to its original general utility in the broader sociocultural sphere. We might even consider being innovators and inventing some new tools of our own. The SS people need to accept that traditions are invented (and reinvented), that people everywhere need to make some choices and have some options to weigh. They need to discard myth-based assumptions about the characteristics of sociocultural systems before sin (in the form of the market) was invented.

One note to both: It's not uncommon for the kinds of cost/benefit criteria developed for one segment of the sociocultural system to be applied to another segment. Thus, for example, I may apply the bargaining rules or barter techniques of the marketplace to work out parenting relations with my children; I may use religious cost/benefit standards to evaluate the costs/benefits of the performance of those in the governing system; I might use standards of kin-based costs/benefits to make productive decisions centered on the utilization of natural resources. This sort of shifting can be useful or it can cause disarray. It would be useful for those who must make decisions to be shown that such shifts have been or could be made. Introducing such shifts is capable of opening new avenues of negotiations to explore. Making them explicit can assist in ridding some negotiating "noise" when participants are unaware that such imports have been made.

Anthropologists have always been concerned that the kinds of studies we do will not only be ethnographic accounts but will also provide insights for addressing issues in the lives of First World people. It's a generally held notion among anthropologists that the kinds of sociocultures that emerged as people grappled with these concerns illustrate the strategies people developed in the hope (but only the hope) that these strategies would address their problems. Often, the problems of others were and are not so very different from ours. For example, all people have worked out ways to store up food for hard times. It might be by preserving it or—if "nomadic" and unwilling to burden themselves by carrying preserved food—by sharing it with others, building up the potential for future returns by "storing surplus food in someone else's belly," and expecting these others, when the tables are turned, to reciprocate.

In today's world, we deal with the same concerns in similar ways. Thus, for example, numerous studies have shown how rural people in Newfoundland, the urban poor in New York, and North African immigrants in Paris have cooperative sharing networks to build up goodwill for times of scarcity—just as do hunting and gathering bands in the Australian Outback.

In short, anthropologists study all sorts of sociocultural ways to deal with life's problems, seeking to address the variety of ways that people in varying situations have developed to try to deal with such common human concerns as scarcity. They study the ways in which people come up with new ideas when things change (becoming better or worse, or just different) and ways to try to build in a margin for error, ways to have a safety net in case their ideas don't work out. Interestingly, we find that it makes little difference whether someone is a hunter-gatherer in the Kalahari Desert, a farmer on the North American Great Plains, the head of small business firm, a software programmer in Silicon Valley, a displaced bureaucrat in eastern Europe or China, or a college student. Certain concerns and general techniques for addressing problems that arise have much in common.

The main focus of this book is on alternatives and the making of choices. We'll look at the ways that people deal with scarce resources and the need to allocate our limited supply of resources among competing wants and needs. Part of this problem stems from the difficulty of weighing the differences between short- versus long-term wants and needs.

Sometimes, as we've noted, people don't have a choice—or at least perceive that they don't. You have a choice only where there are two or more perceived possibilities that offer various costs and benefits. When told, "Your money or your life," for most people there is no real choice. Despite Patrick Henry's statement of preference—"Give me liberty or give me death!"—how many slaves see these as balanced alternatives? Still, even a slave has the choice of staying captive or risking escape. And, just as free laborers do, they have a choice between expending little effort (and facing the consequences imposed for "laziness") or working diligently—though the only benefits of the latter might be the absence of punishment.

Interestingly, though most of us wouldn't want to live in a world where there is no choice, it's not uncommon to complain that making decisions is very stressful. Now, there's a problem for cost/benefit analysis: Weighed against the stress of making decisions or taking the lead role, do you find it more pleasurable to let others make your decisions and benefit from rational ignorance, or do you find the costs of time and energy expended are outweighed by the pleasure of being free to make your own choices?

There is another issue with which this book is concerned. It's a muted, secondary theme but is just as important as the emphasis on making choices about how to use resources. In the midst of increased innovations and decreased time to understand how to incorporate them into our fast-changing life, there is a growing need to try to make sense of all this complexity. Hardly a day goes by that we don't find ourselves facing some situation that frustrates or confuses us either because we feel overwhelmed by the magnitude of it all or because there's some seemingly trivial glitch. While this shouldn't seem to matter, it obviously does. Indeed, it's not uncommon for us to be so baffled by some situation or tool that we don't even know where to start asking questions about it. At such times, I suggest, it's the difference between making sense and having meaning that presents us with problems.

Now, anthropologists have long recognized the difference between information, sense, and meaning. Having an abundance of information (i.e., many bits of "stuff") is not enough. First, unless information has some structure or organization, it is just noise. It's stuff that makes no sense and, not uncommonly, strikes us as nothing more than a confused and confusing jumble. Thus, after obtaining or being presented with information, our next step usually is to try to make sense of it. But, again, in the real world, usually that's not enough. Something can make sense but lack meaning. A simple example: The statement, "I studied the table," both provides information and makes perfectly good sense to any speaker of English. But that single statement may be meaningless if the person I addressed and I are standing in the middle of a grain field somewhere in the Great Plains ("What table? There's no table anywhere for miles!"). On the other hand, if the person addressed was a farmer, an agronomist or hydrologist, it would probably be assumed that I meant I'd studied the regional water table. But if I were talking to my hydrologist friend in a furniture store (where we stopped after lunch because I'm looking for a new dining-room table), she might assume I was talking about the water table while a nearby salesclerk hearing my comment would come over and ask if I'd also looked at the chairs that accompanied the table. If my comment was repeated later in my company's conference room, the director of sales would wait to hear how I'd analyzed the table showing differential widget sales in various countries around the world. Thus, something can make perfectly good sense but fail to communicate to another the meaning the sender of information intended.

Most of us are aware that we may have an abundance of information and still find that making sense of it all eludes us. We're even more aware of how difficult it is to go beyond superficial sense and grasp underlying meaning—for example, we know music, art, and poetry when we see it and we recognize a friendly versus a threatening gesture, but why something is considered timeless music, art, or poetry while something else is trashed in a few years is not so easy to understand; nor can we understand why total strangers should chose to go out of their way to be friendly or, on first sight, make threats. We grow up knowing that people who say the same thing can mean different things; that the same thing can mean different things in different contexts or at different times; that, for example, mother's "No" really meant "No," but father's "No" usually meant, "—unless your mother says it's okay"; and that "Wake up and smell the coffee" can be an invitation to get out of bed and smell the fresh coffee—or an insult to your ability to understand the subtleties of a hostile gesture.

Now, it's one thing not to understand how combustion engines work; most people lack such knowledge and still are able to drive a car. It's another thing to be so bewildered by something that we can't even begin to ask the right questions or be reasonably confident that we have enough of the general idea that we can take a chance on doing the right thing or making an appropriate response. It happens to all of us because, in these times of increasing information (that requires increasing specialization), much of the world must be taken on faith. The most brilliant mathematician can be so baffled by the arcane income tax laws that he simply carries a shoebox full of bills, receipts, and other bits of paper to the tax preparer; the company's top expert on programming can become enraged with frustration when she can't get her key out of the car ignition (unaware that there's an automatic control that locks the key in the ignition until the car's lights are turned off). For many today there is that endless source of aggravation, the source of mysterious glitches, the computer. Nothing is simple anymore: Looking in the computer manual to get help, a beginner comes across "Warning! Be sure not to hit the RFP button twice; it will cause the DKJ to LPM." This leads to real panic because several hours of searching fails to inform us as to where or what the RFP button is—let alone the identity of DKJ or LPM. Eighty percent of North Americans don't know how to use their VCRs for anything except to play rented videotapes. But, then, how many practicing Christians understand such theological concepts as transubstantiation or the difference between the Immaculate Conception and the Virgin Birth? How many investors understand the bond market or the vagaries of the stock market? Even traffic engineers are baffled by certain types of traffic jams (which are quite different from fruit jams!). And how can I really explain rather than simply guess at the causes of why my friends/competitors, women/men, parents/teenagers, serial killers/store clerks, whatever, behave as they do?

Not being able to make sense of this or that is, in many ways, more confidence shattering than not grasping the deeper issue of what something means. After all, not being able to understand the meaning of really important things is fairly common; it takes time and concentrated effort and, with time so scarce, we often claim we have none to spare for such mentally demanding labor. Meaning is deep, meaning is knowledge; sense, on the other hand, is getting enough of a handle on something to be able to take some action or make some response that seems to work—sometimes for the wrong reasons but adequately for the moment.

I may not understand the theological meaning of the religious rituals I practice, but their performance satisfies my sense of being a participant in a significant and special life activity. Many members of my staff don't want to understand the grand organization of the company; they're just concerned with grasping the arrangement, the functioning and the function of the specific material that flows over their desks everyday. Students often come up and say, "Will this be on the exam?" They're not concerned with understanding the complex theoretical issues that underpin the points being made but are concerned only with how to get the information they'll need to pass the course.

So, for example, I recently read an ad in a leading financial publication that set up what the ad labeled "The Problem," namely, "So many great business books. So little time." It offered "The Solution": subscribe to their new publication, the staff of which reviews "all the new books" and selects "the year's best," then condenses each into eight pages "of only the essential information." The ad assures you that your access to the publication means you'll "never be caught off guard in a tight spot." Now, I wonder why, if the essential information can be distilled into eight pages, the authors of these "best books" didn't do it themselves. (Were the authors just trying to make bigger royalties on more expensive books? And if two hundred fifty pages could be boiled down to eight pages, why not make it five or just two pages and make it even faster and easier for me?) Can I be sure the staff will be able to read all the year's books in all different languages? How does one select the best book when all such publications are hot off the press and before the contents have been assessed in the marketplace or been tested by being applied? Clearly, the need being addressed here is the barrage of information (and occasionally some knowledge) with which we're being bombarded. We have a situation in which even making sense (forget about meaning) is discarded for the trade-off of getting out of a tight spot with a nod of recognition at the author's name, a few buzzwords, and what Oscar Levant once called "a smattering of ignorance." With time so scarce, we often adopt the strategy that buzz phrases and a nodding acquaintance will have to do for the moment.

However, in today's world, we cannot simply ignore or sneer at the desperation that drives the desire for "instant knowledge." In a global socioculture of increasing linkages among and interdependence on other people, this kind of flimsy control over the activities we perform will increasingly result in important outcomes being caused by initial, seemingly "trivial" occurrences somewhere in the chain of events. We don't know why something is happening, has happened, or seems to be about to happen—and, sometimes, even that it has happened (until it's too late to do more than make an ad hoc response). Rarely a day passes that we're not thrown into new situations, get new information, and realize we have to do something—but what? The situation is ambiguous; the information is complex as well as suspect as to its reliability. It may not even be relevant in terms of our needs. Now what?

What follows won't give you the answers, but it will provide you with some tools to help address the problems. As long as you come away with an understanding that the world really is difficult and full of complexities, that it's not just you, and that "dumbing the problems down" or "smarting the answers up" in the hope that these strategies will be enough *isn't* enough. The more we think it is, the worse the problems will become. All of us are struggling with the situation because, for one thing, we're in a transition phase; we may even be undergoing a revolution, one of those rare quantum leaps in human history. Indeed, that's the very reason behind that growing mountain of self-help, how-to books written by people, some of whom are doing the really hard thinking for us, putting in a great deal of their time to help us make sense of what's going on—occasionally even digging down more deeply and providing genuine and creative insights.

How does an overview of the turmoil and confusion help? Well, for one thing, it may offer encouragement to admit that you don't have perfect information and knowledge; no one does or can. It may encourage you to admit to a lack of understanding—even to ask questions without the feeling that such queries indicate stupidity. The important thing is to try not to fake your ability to grasp the sense or understand the meaning of people and things and processes that surround you. Keep asking questions and really listen to responses. It may provide enough confidence that you'll accept that you don't always need to try for "the quick fix" and the fast way out of tight spots. It may teach you to avoid putting a constant emphasis on being "a better communicator" (translation: "Listen to me talk") and instead embolden you to seek ways to ask better questions. More important, it may encourage you to be a better listener—hearing what people say, seeing what people do, and waiting to see longer-term results rather than jumping to conclusions. In sum, you may be able to learn better ways to address the universal human need to make sense when confronted with uncertainty, to make decisions when confronted with choices. You may even find yourself with a greater understanding, not of just your life, but the life of others and the world we all inhabit in common.

Chapter Three

Economic Laws and Sociocultural Truths

It's an interesting thing about economics: Most people say they really don't understand it. Yet, in a nationwide poll conducted in 1998, over 95 percent said they knew as much as they needed to know about finances—which is surely a subset of economics. However, only 34 percent of that group could define what buying on credit meant, and only 40 percent were able to describe what it meant to budget. Add to this our lack of knowledge about the regional, national, or global economies, plus the unpredictable buying patterns resulting from millions of self-interested decisions about how to manage distribution, what to exchange or when to make certain exchanges, and you must ask how something called the market system emerges. If, on the one hand, a system is defined as an orderly, integrated entity of interdependent parts, and if, on the other hand, most people (including economists) admit to a degree of ignorance about how economic systems operate, how can such a complex system develop and be maintained? If there's a system, why is it so hard to understand and predict? Are we fooling ourselves that there's a system there at all? And how, given the gaps in our understanding, are we able to surmount what we don't know and use what we think we know to make predictions that shape personal, national, and international decisions with an important impact on people's lives?

There is, to be sure, a core of basic economic laws or axioms, but a review of them reminds one of the story of a famous physicist who for years baffled his classes by always looking up when something fell from his desk. One day a student summoned up the nerve to ask why. "Because of the law of gravity," was the response. "But," said the confused student, "that says you should look down, not up." "No," said his professor, "since any 'law' is only a probability statement, I want to be sure I'm looking in the right direction when what is only a probability fails."

Events in today's world seem to be defying so many economic laws that some who study the latest technological revolution are arguing that we should throw out the traditional rule book. The new world of instant global networking has changed so many patterns (e.g., the movement of capital and information around the world in milliseconds) that it needs to be announced that we're playing a whole new game in a whole new ballpark.

For example, the Law of Diminishing Returns states that, sooner or later, the return on an additional unit of input designed to increase output will decline (relative to the return for previous inputs) rather than increase. You may double the amount of productivity in your office by hiring a second person, and it will probably go up again when you hire a third, and so on. Eventually, however, hiring extra workers doesn't keep increasing productivity by as much as the extra employee costs; you may even get to the point where hiring another worker causes productivity to decline. Imagine, for example, if you just kept adding employees, extra desks, and more equipment but didn't change the size of your work space; people would start getting in each other's way and slowing each other down; crowding would produce stress; workers would complain about their unpleasant work conditions and productivity would decline still more. Further, if you invent a new work practice (such as piecework on an assembly line) or a new piece of equipment (e.g., the cotton gin), eventually others will copy these ideas and machines and your market share will decline as your competition increases.

Once upon a time, if you wanted to produce oil, you had to find it first (exploration costs), then bring in a well (production costs), then find ways to move it to markets (distribution costs). However, despite these initial costs, oil would gush forth and you'd earn windfall profits. That's the good news. The bad news is that over the long haul it all would be downhill. Annual profits would decline as the well started to run dry and extraction costs increased to the point where they outweighed the price the oil brought on the market. Similarly, a farmer plants wheat and fertilizes the crop, thus increasing bushels per acre. But again, ultimately, the farmer reaches the point where no additional amount of fertilizer will increase production sufficiently to pay for the cost of the fertilizer and the labor of adding it. Indeed, too many farmers producing too much grain will probably cause the world market price to decline because supply will exceed demand. This is one illustration of the Law of Diminishing Returns.

It's rather interesting to know how many people understand this concept despite knowing nothing of economic laws. In my early research on fisheries, many fishermen told me that government management of the commercial fishing industry was unnecessary because, to quote one typical remark, "Long before we can wipe out a species, our catch per trip will drop to the point where we're catching too few to pay for the trip.

Then we'll switch to some other species and, with nobody going after it, the first species will have a chance to recover." Unfortunately, other factors were at work, and while the economic theory might be correct, whole segments of the fishing industry are now facing the same extinction as some of the stocks that industry members once claimed were economically impossible to overfish. Interestingly, the so-called "Fish-crats" (i.e., federally-employed fishery managers) in the government can't understand why so many people still want to keep on fishing, even though their economic returns keep diminishing as the costs of fishing go up and catches go down. "The fishermen don't have a clue about basic economics," said one government economist to me. In the social accounting of many fishermen, however, other benefits of life as a fisherman far exceed the costs of declining income.

This law is supported by another: the Law of Diminishing Utility, which states that the more you obtain of something, the less valuable each additional unit becomes. On a hot summer day, you might be willing to pay $5 for a cold beer, even for a second, a third and so on. But eventually, you won't be willing to pay another $5 for another beer. You might be willing to pay $1 but, sooner or later, even the willingness to do that will end. You've had enough. You've maxed out your desire for beer, reached the edge, that is, you're at the margin of its desirability to you at that point of time.

When it comes to consumption in general, it's assumed that you may have a big enough house, enough leisure, and sufficient money to do whatever you want, but there's always something else to which you can shift your list of wants and needs. Perhaps it's a perfect body, perpetual youth (or as close to it as they can get), a new style of house furnishings, a new spouse, more education, whatever. Your desire for one set of goods may have reached its limits, and your desire for more of the same has begun to decline or even ceased to the point where you donate or sell whatever you've accumulated. But your preferences shift. This may be a shift forced by circumstances other than how much something costs. In addition to the ceaseless creation of new goods and services, we are also discovering new risks in certain existing goods and services—as when people start worrying about certain foods and health risks or when war or natural catastrophes lead tourists to revise travel plans. People change preferences when certain places become dull or too popular or when, to attract clients, prices are dropped and attract the more price conscious. We'll pick up again later on the problem of preferences.

Returning to the Law of Diminishing Returns brings us face to face with the new developments in today's world because of the emergence of the computer and, more important, the Internet. In today's world, as in previous eras, millions may be spent on development costs. In this, there may be little difference between developing a new type of car, a new oil field, or a software program. However, in what some are calling the new economic environment, the cost of putting the first copy of the software program on a store shelf may be, say, $13 million, but, unlike the costs of producing the car or the oil, once in production, the cost for successive copies of the software program keeps dropping. Ultimately, it costs only a few cents to produce the software; we can even afford to give the program away (indeed, we're now giving computers away!) in order to create potential customers for peripheral services or the next upgrade. In short, return does not eventually level off but has a seemingly infinite capacity to keep going up—though some say this defies the law of economic gravity. In the new economic world this may be called the Law of Expanding Returns. The logic behind the claim that we've now entered an era where we have an infinite capacity to grow rests on the fact that the basic resources of the HT industry are not raw materials or land or capital; they are information and knowledge. These differ from traditional resources because human creativity and imagination are unlimited and, unlike other resources, the more widely such resources are used, the more creativity is generated and the more the market expands. In other words, the more such resources are utilized, the greater the future supply. This is the main reason why, through the course of human history, the rate at which innovation occurs has increased exponentially.

To be sure, as in the old economic world, some firms keep growing because they have the capacity to buy out or inhibit the market entry of new but smaller competitors. This lack of competition can produce what is in fact, or effectively amounts to, a monopoly (think Microsoft). Whereas land can produce only so much wheat or provide enough food for so many cattle to graze, and while there is a finite supply of water and mineral resources, what are the limits to Internet creativity? What are the limits to how many times Microsoft or any other of the new companies of the new economy can reinvent themselves?

In the world in which humans have lived for some four million years, there have always been limits: limits to how many animals could be hunted before we hunted them to extinction; limits to how much corn, or rice, or wheat could be grown year after year on an acre of land; limits to the growth in production of or demand for cars, refrigerators, typewriters; limits even to leisure activities or beer consumption. Growth is a characteristic of living things, but in nature there are inherent limits to growth; trees, no matter how old, don't just keep growing taller; humans do not keep increasing in height throughout their lifetime (actually, many shrink as they age and their bone mass compresses). Thus, in nature there are limits to growth.

An increasing number of scientists and businesspeople alike say that in the world of HT or IT, the only limit in a world that will soon be upon us is the capacity of humans to invent new ways to think about the world. If there are limits to that, we've yet to discover them. It's rather like trying to imagine limits to the kinds of games we can invent to play, or the novels and music that can be written—even the words that can be added to the language. If we can keep inventing new goods and services to meet (as well as create) consumer demand, there seems to be no limit to the number of more useful, more practical, more necessary (as well as more silly and more dangerous) goods and services we may create.

Since new inventions spark other new inventions, it's easy to understand why 95 percent of human technology (and knowledge) has appeared in the last one hundred years. The IT revolution is causing us to invent new things faster than ever; we're accelerating the processes of change. A mere two decades ago, who would have imagined cybershopping, chat rooms, archeologists' Web sites that let you walk through an ongoing site excavation via your computer; the entire *Encyclopedia Britannica* on one slim CD—and for less than U.S.$70.00 instead of four feet of bookshelves at a cost of some U.S.$700; and worldwide networks of scientists sharing their latest findings (e.g., this morning's research) in real time rather than waiting months, even years, to get an article published?

Further, new ideas create spin-offs. People discover a gap, lack, or opening and create a good or service to fill it—and a new business is formed. Adobe Postscript—initially, only a language for printers—became the impetus for the whole new occupational niche and leisure activity we now call desktop publishing.

It's important to keep in mind, however, that although the tempo of the change is new, the capacity of an innovation to spread as well as to spin off an array of other new inventions and ideas isn't. Even in the ancient world, people might go to one locale because it had spiritual significance or offered some resource such as gold or furs—and they would return home having discovered some totally new way of, say, honoring their gods, fashioning gold, or preserving fish. Thus, for example, gunpowder was invented in China and used for fireworks displays that entertained, but when early European travelers brought the invention home, it became the basis for a revolutionary new concept of warfare. New ideas produce new avenues of performance for whole new occupational categories—priests, architects, and embalmers; goldsmiths, merchants, and counterfeiters; net and boat makers, shore-side fish buyers, and fast-food vendors (yes, they had them in ancient Pompeii!). These new goods and services created new preferences.

Ah yes, preferences. What about that point made earlier, that human consumers seem to have an infinite capacity to want things but that, over time, their preferences as to what they must or would like to have change and shift? I've previously indicated that this is more than a small problem for many economists whose modeling of economic behavior tends to assume that preferences are fixed and unchanging. They're not interested in why you want what you want (leave questions of motivation and taste up to the psychologists, they say), they're interested in *what* people do, not *why* they do it. For an economist, preferences simply are.

The issue of preferences is an important question for most social scientists, however. Take, for example, the role of preferences in social welfare programs. Why do people refuse some kinds of housing or reject some kinds of jobs, even, occasionally, jobs that pay more than the one currently held? What causes us to change preferences? For example: "I don't feel like having a steak dinner today; let's have seafood"; "I can't imagine why I used to wear that jacket every chance I could—now I can't stand it." Under what conditions do we prefer chicken to lobster today, and under what conditions do we prefer lobster to chicken tomorrow? Why do buyers prefer open-plan houses this year but next year demand defined-activity rooms?

The importance of the rule of thumb used by economists—that people have fixed taste—leads to the theory that, all things being equal, if I prefer fish to steak, I'll buy fish. However, if the price of fish goes up (and it has!), the usual cause being scarcity, or the price of steak relative to fish declines, I'll buy steak. The change in my buying pattern is a response to the price change. Producers and merchants are equally responsive to price fluctuations, and the expanding or contracting supply or consumption of such goods and services leads to the demand/supply being labeled "elastic." On the other hand, a stable demand for or supply of some goods and services, for example milk or bread, regardless of price fluctuations, leads to the demand being labeled "inelastic."

Be cautious, however. Economists tend to qualify hypotheses with a caveat. They hypothesize or state that research shows that "if X then Y, all things being equal." In the real world, however, all things are rarely (some would say never) equal, and even when they are, they rarely remain so. For the economist, only scarcity (supply and demand) and price distinguish fish from steak or BMWs from Chevrolets. If prices remain constant and supply meets demand, there should be no change in consumption over time.

Now, if economists want other social scientists to grapple with such questions as to how—holding price constant—preferences change or how they are formulated in the first place, and if they want to let others explore the interesting issues of what happens when all things aren't equal, I'll accept that. It helps justify my existence as an economic anthropologist who studies the activities that economists don't.

Let's explore the problem. (Note: I have avoided saying "answer the question" because, as noted earlier, to think you have "answered" a question is always dangerous. For one thing, many so-called answers are at best ill-founded rationales and, at worst, knee-jerk solutions.) Take the argument that people buy things they want but don't really need because humans seek novelty. Yes, some do. But, then, some don't. How, for example, do we gain a better insight into the behavior of that segment of the population (say, 30 percent) that consists of people who consistently are the last to put in electricity or cable TV, to have a phone, or to buy a TV, a computer, a food processor, or a cellular phone; the 5 to 10 percent who will never buy them; and the 5 to 10 percent who seek a good or service before it's even available (who, for example, stood in line for several hours to buy a ticket for the opening, at midnight, of the latest *Star Wars* film)? Why do some people have as a motto, "Out with the old and in with the new," while others avoid the latest gimmicks because they subscribe to the theory of "better the devil you know than the devil you don't know"?

First let me suggest that we accept that preferences change as our personal store of experiences and information changes and as the world around us changes. I have friends who are now vegetarians, not because meat and fish are expensive (so are vegetables these days!) but because they are deeply troubled by the information they're receiving about the slaughtering of animals. New information caused their preferences to change. However, this suggestion doesn't help very much, since we're left with the question of why some people respond to the information about animal cruelty and change their preferences while other people just keep eating their chicken or veal and shrug off publicity about inhumane methods of raising and killing chickens and young calves.

Second, we also know that people tend to imitate people; as more people express a preference, the more likely it is that others will also shift to that preference. Sometimes it's because no one has raised the issue before and, once in the public eye, people begin to consider their activities in the light of the approval or disapproval of others toward such activities. Further, the reluctance to go against the crowd or SO may be based on the fact that, in many cases, some individuals have no strong preference for one thing over another. It's not only easier to go with the flow, but playing follow the leader relieves such people of any necessity to explain or justify their preference change—that everybody is doing it is enough of an explanation for those who observe the behavior. How many times do people justify their desire for something on the grounds that, "Gee, Mom, everyone is wearing them," or "Well, everybody else does it, so it must be OK." Conversely, it may be that some individuals did have a particular preference but were reluctant to express it for various reasons ("I always hated the smell of cigarettes, but everybody smoked so I kept quiet"). The preference was always there; they simply substituted one kind of preference (a smoke-free environment) for another (the desire not to seem to be some sort of oddball). Again, however, this doesn't really get us far because we still don't know why some people follow the leaders or why leaders usually change preferences as soon as they discover a large number of people are imitating their preferences.

Years ago, when the Big Three of North American car manufacturing still accounted for 95 percent of autos purchased in the North American markets, and long before anyone worried about emission pollution or the price of gas, each year the buying preference of most North Americans was for a bigger car than their current vehicle. Yet, a small number of people started buying Volkswagens, nicknamed "Bugs," initially a term of derision but adopted and used with pride and affection by VW owners. How come? And what caused the shift to Japanese cars? Why not an increase to Italian, French, or British cars? The rationales are many (better made, better styling, cheaper, etc.) but don't always hold up in the face of empirical data. And how is it that some people who could easily afford a new car always buy secondhand vehicles while other people, even those deeply in debt, never buy a used car? Why don't people defer purchase, bank the money they'll need to buy a car, then pay cash rather than spend several thousands of dollars extra in interest payments on their car loan? How do you account for the shift in consumer preference from buying to leasing cars? And why do more women prefer to buy while more men prefer to lease? Marketing experts can explain some of these patterns, but for other questions the response is likely to be, "Go figure."

Third, preferences rarely stand alone; that is, in any given situation they become bundled with other preferences—some trivial and some very important, that for whatever reason(s) appear to be part of the way we think about and sum up our position on an issue, problem, decision, or goal. It may cause a dilemma for an individual who belongs to a rod and gun club to oppose killing animals for their fur. On the other hand, a fellow club member will see no problem because she is against animal suffering and sees controlled killing of excess wild animals as a humane act (it reduces the number of animals who face death from slow starvation because humans have invaded their natural habitat and reduced their food base). Regardless of whether you agree with one or the other position, it is simply the way an individual will bundle preferences so they make sense.

Next, we may compartmentalize our preferences in ways that allow us to justify isolating preferences on one issue from preferences on another. For example, over the years I've asked students to pick any combination of seven numbers and letters to be used by them whenever I ask them to write their opinion on an issue on a slip of paper that will be passed to me. Two issues, separated in time by a few weeks, are presented. The first: What is your position on the right to choice/right to life issue re abortion? The second: What is your position on whether we should abolish the death penalty? Over the last fourteen years, approximately 70 percent of the students have opposed the death penalty, but about 60 percent approved of abortion. One might suppose that some would see some contradiction in the two positions, but when this is pointed out, students marshal very different arguments to support their stances. The bundle of preferences that support/refute each position tends to be very different.

Finally, people adapt their preferences to what they believe are reasonable expectations for them as individuals. These include ease or difficulty of actually attaining their preferred choice and the windows of opportunity or barriers to success that they are likely to encounter at any given time. They may believe that the "best" choice is not realistic and that they'd be better off opting for a "good enough" choice. Thus, unsure as to whether I'm capable of being accepted by or competing at the "best" school, I pick a lower-ranked school where my chances are better relative to other applicants or to the performance of other students. I may turn down a promotion (despite a welcome pay increase) because I'm afraid I can't handle the demands of the new position; or I don't attempt to strike up a friendship with a beautiful, talented, and popular female because I'm sure she'll reject any overtures I make.

Another illustration: My fiancé and I are at a jeweler, picking out my engagement ring. Joe says, "It's up to you." Now, my real preference is a five-carat diamond, but I pass it up and select three rings, each with a one-carat stone, from which Joe and I make our choice. My three preferences were based on what I knew Joe could afford at the moment, and I didn't want to embarrass him.

A final example: Studies have shown that women tend to aim lower on the corporate ladder than males. This, in turn, is sometimes used to justify omitting women from consideration for top-ranking positions on the grounds that it's difficult to attract women to apply for the posts. Many women indicate that they decline such opportunities to apply because they believe they would have less opportunity to be successful in the job, anticipating difficulties they would encounter due to a negative bias on the part of male colleagues ("We have to be twice as good to be considered half as competent as a man").

When economists try to create models that will help guide policy choices, design social programs, and determine budget allocations, they look at the statistics of actual choices people have made or that they indicate they would make. In some cases such models may be helpful at predicting what people will do in the future, but circularity of reasoning can create serious social problems. Planning based on such models creates future opportunities of choice on the basis of past choices made, ignoring the processes used by the people who made the choices. Thus, for example, when children in inner-city high schools choose classes in office skills or auto mechanics rather than in physics or biology, it may be because they assume that they have few opportunities for the advanced training required for such skills; they may have little knowledge as to employment opportunities. Thus, they adapt their choices of instruction to the opportunities already available and the life expectations they have. However, because they select auto mechanics and bypass physics, the school limits (or even eliminates on budgetary grounds) opportunities for training in courses that would lead to such employment on the grounds that there is too low a demand for such courses. Low expectations result in low-end choices, and low-end choices result in low-end instructional opportunities—and so the vicious circle goes.

Finally, preferences are ranked relative to other preferences but the rankings often change, depending on time, place, and SO(s). I may have an equal liking for both fish and meat but prefer turkey at Thanksgiving and fish when I'm on vacation at the seashore. My pickup may be my vehicle of choice—but I wouldn't choose it to drive my daughter to her wedding. On the other hand, if I could really pick the car I want, it would be that $65,000 sports car.

Okay. So preferences shift, and my cost/benefit analysis doesn't always lead to selecting the choice that would bring me the greatest pleasure at the least cost (never mind that sports car). But we have another problem linked to these same two aspects. It's one thing to say that I may pick a good enough rather than best choice, but how do we explain bad choices—selecting an option with high costs and a low, even negative pay-off?

1. I've been told I'll lose my job if I don't stop drinking. I don't stop. One day, I come back to the office and, no question about it, I'm drunk. I get fired. Why did I choose to get drunk? Why didn't I at least wait until after work?
2. I'm embezzling funds from the company in which I'm employed, even though I know there's a high probability that any careful audit of the company books is likely to uncover my theft. It does—and I go to prison. Why didn't I live within my means or save up to buy the things I wanted?
3. I gamble and keep gambling even though I rarely win, and when I do the winnings are small. Most of the time I lose. My car has been repossessed, and I'm up to the limit on credit card debt. Why do I keep gambling?
4. A group of us decide to go skiing, even though there have been several avalanches in the area in the last week and people are being warned to stay away. The avalanche in which we're caught kills four of our group. Why, given the risks of which we were aware, didn't we avoid the activity?

Let me give one more example, perhaps the most inexplicable of all: Is suicide a rational choice? Do its benefits outweigh its costs—and, if so, how?

In all of the above cases, decisions were made that logically and in terms of economic rationality seem likely to bring more costs than benefits.

These cases bring us to the role played by perception and emotions. No economist denies that they are factors. However, by definition, in their dollar-and-"sense" world, perception, cognition, and emotions are excluded. For one thing, how do you quantify the monetary costs and benefits of emotions such as anger, love, timidity, or happiness? They certainly have a qualitative dimension, but how do you measure them, count them, and especially take into account that there are degrees of such emotions (I'm happier today than I was yesterday, but how much more happy today and how much less than yesterday? And am I happier today than I was angry last week)?

Curiously, over two hundred years ago, Adam Smith, the father of modern economics, didn't exclude such considerations. He pointed out that hunger and thirst were less influenced by social learning than fear or desire. It seems reasonable to argue that many bad preferences—and, in North American socioculture, suicide would seem to be a prime example—are based on how we perceive what is happening in the world around us and how we emotionally respond to that perception. The anthropologist recognizes that, for most individuals, the world of perception is not created out of nothing. Events (real, known, or perceived as real or known) and people encountered in specific sociocultural contexts shape our perceptions. People living in tropical rain forests don't experience and therefore don't fear drought. But a recent study showed that a majority of highly successful (i.e., seven-figure income) female CEOs (Chief Executive Officers) in New York City have a major fear that a series of economic disasters will lead to the loss of all they possess and result in a future as a homeless street person, a bag lady. How reasonable is this concern? Such a fate is not impossible, but how probable is it? Does it affect their economic behavior? We don't know; there are few studies of female CEOs and none that focus on their insecurities and fears regarding their futures.

The things, people, and events that create perceptions as well as the emotions that accompany them are based on the things, people, and events that exist around us, not just in our specific socioculture but in the world as we know it. Some people don't pay much attention to geopolitical events in other parts of the world (e.g., the collapse of the Russian economy; the wars in the Balkans). Yet, for others, these events are so deeply felt that I know of one well-known scholar who recently committed suicide because of the despair he experienced when thinking about the future in the light of events in eastern Europe.

People who live in different places don't face the same experiences: A farmer along the banks of the Mississippi fears the spring floods because they destroy crops; people along the Nile look forward to floods because they deposit new soil with rich nutrients for crops. I once heard a doctor phoning a colleague to tell him he was referring a patient to him because, as he gleefully noted, "You have to see this! It's the only classic textbook example of the disease I've ever seen." One doubts the patient felt the same exhilaration.

Yet people in the same place don't experience the same reaction to the same event. A few years ago, at the height of the violence in Northern Ireland, I was walking down a street in Belfast. A car backfired several times, and I watched dumbfounded as people around me ducked into doorways and even flattened themselves on the sidewalk. I stood thinking to myself, "These people are really nervous!" A brief moment later, however, more such sounds and from a nearby doorway a call of "Hey, you loony, get down!" made me realize, "Hey! People really are shooting!" The man in the doorway and I experienced the same events, but our perception of them and the emotional response they elicited differed. (A final note on this last example: Even as I dropped to the ground, my response was not fear but a rather silly, "Damn, I just bought this dress and now it'll be ruined.")

The actual events are the same; what differs is our perception of them and what emotional response they elicit. And those perceptions and emotional responses are shaped by our sociocultural experiences.

There are still other aspects to weighing trade-offs and making choices, as well as trying to make sense of the world. All societies and the individuals in them have a history. The little world we know and experience as individuals and the larger world beyond our immediate experience (including natural phenomena, some of which are not even known to us, as when we are unaware that we are residing in a polluted environment that is causing deadly health problems), together with the sociocultural institutions people have constructed over the years, work out common ways to address common needs—ways of teaching the young; addressing concerns about the forces of nature, life and death, defense, sustenance, and caretaking; and ways of arriving at decisions that affect the group as a whole.

All of these and more are designed to capture the individual in a net of others. On the one hand, sociocultures are the organized networks that groups of humans have consciously as well as out-of-awareness created over time to offer alternatives to and balance with individual self-interest. On the other hand, sociocultures are self-organizing systems. Further, the whole is greater than the sum of its parts and is marked by synergy—the collective energy and activities that exceeds the additive energy of the parts. Synergy is capable of creating structures and processes that were not in the original design of the system as a whole. Such synergistic dynamics create certain aspects of a system that are, at best, unintended consequences of human planning; and nothing that the individuals consciously or unconsciously do accounts for some of this aggregate activity. Take a simple example: Watch the behavior of an individual bird (any species). No matter how thoroughly and how long you study that bird, you can't predict how it will behave when it becomes part of a flock flying through the sky. Where will it be in the flock—at the lead, at the end, on the edge, or in the center? More interestingly, how is it that the whole flock, composed of individual birds, manages to wheel in a coordinated fashion? How do the inner birds "know" at any given moment that they should make a tighter turn than those on the outer edge of the flock (who must also know to make a wider turn)? Is it simply a nearest neighbor response? What does the flock do when predators attack—and could you predict that response by knowing how an individual bird behaves when attacked by the same predator?

Now, take a large corporation: Would knowing the individual life history of every single member of the corporation allow you to predict how the company, a corporate entity but involving specific individuals as well as groups of individuals (such as the board of directors or the stockholders), would respond to a hostile takeover? Or how the members of a department or division would respond to an unexpected loss of their section head?

Take another example: For all the similarities in Canadian and American life, the rules, institutions, and many other sociocultural characteristics of each nation can be strikingly different. (Remember, of course, that the comments below are generalized and that people move from one country to another because personal preferences may lead individuals to find one or the other system more responsive to their individual wants and needs.) One difference between the two sociocultures is the way that the young are taught the rules of behavior. A parent from the United States trying to teach a young child—say, less than five years old—how to behave is likely to focus on what the child shouldn't do. A large part of the interaction consists of the adult (even the most permissive) saying no to the child: "No, that's bad to do," "No, that wasn't nice," "Don't hit your brother," "No, that doesn't make daddy feel good," etc. This kind of instruction may account for why it is that most Americans assume that unless something is explicitly forbidden, anything else is permissible. Unless there's a sign that says "Keep off the grass" (and even when there is), it's hard to predict whether an individual will take a shortcut or go the long way around by using a sidewalk. This, in turn, leads to more individualized decision making—and less emphasis on the possible effects of that decision on other people.

In Canadian socioculture, on the other hand, parents are more likely to train their children by emphasizing positive rules, for example, "Be nice to your friend," "Respect other people," "Let's all get along, eh?" "Be kind to your brother," "Play fair." The "eh?" that is so much a part of Canadian speech, something that is tagged on to a declarative statement and almost (but not quite) turns it into a question, seems to open up an opportunity for other people to have their say, as in remarks like, "Gretzky's the greatest, eh?" or "She's a good doctor, eh?" Similarly, if there's no sign telling you to "Keep off the grass," Canadians are likely to respond by erring on the side of caution—and keep to the sidewalk anyway, perhaps even remarking that "There really should be a sign to stop people from destroying the greenery, eh?"

Look at those preferences again. We may change some of the specifics as we mature and age, and our preferences may seem to change. Sometimes, however, the change is more apparent than real; we alter the form but the substance remains the same. For example, take those who reject what they see as the excess consumerism of their parents, friends, and society in general. They opt, instead, to adopt the so-called "minimal lifestyle" (now being labeled the Voluntary Simplicity Movement [VSM])—spending less, consuming less, wasting less, practicing thrift and frugality, and living on less. Yet, such individuals spend just as much (perhaps more) of their lives focusing on deciding how to consume less as others spend wondering how to consume more. In a mirror image of their former lifestyle, consumption as such is still their central concern and critical to their perception as to the quality of life. The only difference is that their energies are directed to consuming down rather than consuming up.

One of the dilemmas in economic thinking (plaguing economists and anthropologists alike) is: If the concept of rationality/utility in decision making is true—that is, people will choose whatever offers the greatest return (pleasure) for the least cost (pain)—(a) how do you test it, and (b) how do you explain why people incur higher costs than necessary to accomplish something? Why, for example, do they spend more to acquire a good or service when a cheaper and equally adequate version is available? Take an extreme example: If I am able to worship God by standing in what some call God's Cathedral (some awe-inspiring natural setting), why build a large and costly cathedral? Why not use all of those resources to care for the ill, orphaned, elderly, and so forth? If I can tell time with a $9.95 Timex, why buy a $15,000 Rolex? If it's the thought that counts, why spend $5 to have a birthday present gift wrapped when I can simply present the gift in the box or plastic bag in which the purchase came? Why does the North American public spend over $60 billion a year on diet pills, weight-loss programs, and exercise equipment to lose weight? Couldn't that same weight be lost (and resources of time, money, and food saved) simply by eating less?

One response to such questions is to note that, in most of the examples just given, there is value added in the more costly choice. I show the depth of my engagement with God by making an extra effort to enhance a particular shrine to my God; I impress my friends (and reaffirm my own sense of accomplishment) by wearing the notably expensive Rolex; the wrapping tells the recipient that he or she is worth the extra effort and expense; and two raw carrots from a brown bag at my desk will never satisfy my craving to have a very large piece of chocolate truffle cake in an elegant dining room.

Let's take the case of how various individuals select a watch from a universe in which the commodity ranges in price from $9.95 to $12,500 (this seems to be the top price for a watch that does not have added value by including precious jewels on the case or watchband). We know that if you ask *N*-number of individuals the purpose of a watch, a near-universal response is "to tell time." Why, then, do individuals pay thousands of dollars for a timepiece when another watch may be had for a few dollars?

Indeed, more fundamentally, what determines their sense of style, their choice of one particular watch when they have thousands from which to select?

The range of answers includes: the design of the face and the numbers (if there are any and whether they are Roman or Arabic), the kind of watchband (curious because, even though significant at time of purchase, many people change the band later), and so on. Of equal—perhaps greater—importance, however, is that when you ask why someone didn't buy a less expensive model, the most frequent answer is that the more expensive watches are much more accurate. Frequent answers also include: "People judge your taste by your watch," "People can tell how successful you are by the watch you wear," "I wanted something feminine/masculine-looking," "I think wearing a cheap watch says something negative about a person," and "Cheap watch bands turn my skin green" (why not just change the band?).

The claim that the more expensive watch was purchased because of its extraordinary accuracy may be one of those cultural truths mentioned above. Accuracy is prized in our technologically oriented society but, in the case of expensive watches, (a) they are often no more accurate than less expensive timepieces, and (b) most people who buy expensive watches do not need hairline accuracy fine-tuned to an atomic clock on a mountain top in the Alps. When asked the time, a majority of people round it off and, instead of saying "Twelve minutes and thirty-two seconds past two" will say something like "Ten after two—unless you need the precise time, in which case it's twelve after two."

In short, in deciding which watch to select, not only is monetary price only one measure of value, it is not the determining factor in an individual's socioculturally grounded cost/benefit analysis.

But we still have the problem of testing the claim that people make choices on the basis of an economically rational cost/benefit analysis. Again, as noted earlier, the model has been criticized because it's a tautology, a circular definition. No matter what choice you make, it will be claimed to be a choice that you perceive as bringing the greatest benefits for the least cost—perfect maximizing; otherwise you wouldn't have made that choice. Only a fool would select something that costs more and returns less. Thus, any choice you make is a rational choice: That Rolex watch, if it leads people to treat me more courteously and more deferentially and gives me better service, is likely to incur lower social costs and give greater value than my cheap (note: not "inexpensive" but cheap, cheap, cheap!) watch if friends and business acquaintances, seeing it on my wrist, treat me like an oaf with no taste. Viewing me as a cheapskate, a nerd, and assuming I'm a nobody, the maître d' seats my client and me next to the kitchen. It seems impossible to predict under what kind of conditions an individual is likely to make what the rational model would label an irrational choice. You seem to end up with a model that, because it "explains" everything, doesn't explain anything.

The problem, however, is not insolvable. First, one never tests (i.e., examines the truth or falsity of) a theory. For one thing, theories are general statements that serve as the basis for creating testable questions. The utility of a theory is its ability to generate interesting questions about the world, questions that may be framed in the form of testable hypotheses. The value of the utilitarian model is that it leads us to formulate testable statements, as for example the following: In expensive restaurants, people who wear Rolex watches will receive better tables and more deferential treatment from waiters than people wearing Timex watches. A second hypothesis: In making choices, individuals are, along with economic considerations, as likely to include and give equal weight to sociocultural costs/benefits. Another hypothesis: If individuals select a more costly option over a less costly option, they will be able to clarify their choice by describing (a) value added in the more costly option, or (b) value lost in the choice rejected.

Much of this chapter has focused on a few of the concepts or issues that economists contribute to or neglect in the study of human behavior. Let me return briefly to two concerns regarding the rational choice model: first, the issue of "rationality" in the decision-making process and, second, the kinds of contributions anthropology can make to understanding more about how the world operates.

On the first point: Over the past several decades there has been a debate among, for the most part, economists, philosophers, psychologists, and political scientists about the extent to which rational choice theory—with its emphasis on the way individuals seek the greatest benefits at the least costs—interferes with or even negates the possibility of individuals compromising their own benefits (or increasing their own costs) in order to cooperate with others; such choices would be, it's claimed, nonrational. If people cooperate, the model must be flawed; if people follow the dictates of the model, cooperation is doomed. While certain components in various debates rest on a misreading or willful exaggeration of the economists' model (even by other economists), problems also stem from the use of situations that fail to take into account the human ability to use new information to alter behavior.

First, the scenarios are often unrealistic. For example, a group of one-armed people are seated around a table and, while they all have spoons, the utensils are so long, no one is capable of putting the spoon into their mouths. What do they do? Answer: They feed each other; cooperation brings rewards. However, goes the argument, perfect maximization would lead one "perfect maximizer" to save time and energy by letting others feed him—or, if all at the table were attempting to conserve energy and waited for others to feed them (i.e., they were being totally rational—in the economic sense—and attempting to be "perfect maximizers"), totally rational, they would all sit and starve. Now, in addition to being a silly example (heaven knows there are plenty of real-world examples to which the scholars' time and energy could be directed!), the outcome of all perfect maximizers starving to death is hardly a choice of action that could be classified as "perfect rationalization." In the real world, if one diner didn't make a contribution to the cooperative feeding effort when it was his turn, he simply would be excluded from future rounds. Others would eat a full bowl of porridge; the perfectly rational (and now we're using that term in its other sense, i.e., not crazy) individual would receive only one spoonful and then starve to death. The perfectly rational individual knows this would be his fate, and at this point his cost/benefit analysis accepts that cooperation and playing by the rules is required if he is to survive. The Old Wise Woman used to say, "Cheat me once, shame on you; cheat me twice, shame on me."

Second, many of the widely used examples claim to show how people are prevented from engaging in "perfect maximizing." Yet "perfect" is a problematic term (would we label as "perfect" situations in which scam artists use their own resources to pay their "marks" high returns on a nonexistent fund or what are in fact losing poker hands, in order finally to cheat their target out of all their resources?). Third, cases are presented in which people have no ability to anticipate and formulate alternate scenarios for various outcomes. The classic Prisoner's Dilemma is one example since it would seem that the "prisoners" would have discussed the eventuality of being caught and induced by their captors to betray each other.

The rational choice model does not require some mythic component called "perfect rationality." Further, it recognizes that short- and long-term maximization involve different interim strategies and, unless one knows the ultimate aim, different strategies may, at different times, seem to be less than maximizing. Additionally, given other factors at work, optimizing or satisficing strategies may prove to be the least costly. I could, for example, max out on fame and fortune if I rowed solo across the Atlantic—as one woman in fall 1999 did—but, compared to traveling with one or more companions, my risks of not surviving would expand exponentially. Finally, the everyday world usually presents us with situations in which cooperation is the only way anyone gets anything; members of team A must work together and, further, some other team(s) must agree to cooperate both as to the rules of play and in a willingness to compete. Without cooperation there is no game and, in more ways than one, no one wins. Thus, not only does competition require cooperation, rationality often drives us to cooperate.

As to the second concern—how anthropology contributes to our understanding of human behavior—anthropologists (not alone in this) understand that the test of falsifiability does not lie only in comparing what people say with what they do, selecting the latter as the real measure of behavior. Talking is also behavior, and what people say to themselves or to others is just as much actualized sociocultural behavior as planting seeds, buying a TV, or selecting a dentist. In asking people how they make choices and what they take into account, what they tell us is true—in the sense that it is true that this is what they said. What they say may be false and they may be aware it is false, but if you examine why they told a falsehood, you will usually discover a cultural truth. The truth would shame, embarrass, or otherwise threaten them relative to the world of which I'm a representative.

Now, when anthropologists find that the information we received from those who work with us does not coincide with their behavior or when statements they make seem to contradict each other, or when other people present contrary evidence, we have a problem. We may have been told something that was true as far as the speaker was concerned, but perhaps the speaker had been told a lie and, unaware of this, repeated the lie as a truth; or the speaker received only partial information and what we heard was a half-truth (or was it a half-lie?). Further, people may not really know all the reasons for doing what they do, or their memory plays tricks on them and they rewrite history, remembering one thing though other evidence indicates they did something else; or, as said above, for their own secret reasons they just plain deceive us.

An example: The U.S. Government accused Bill Gates and Microsoft of engaging in illegal restraint of trade. During the trial, Bill Gates was on camera and, looking the government (and us) earnestly in the eyes, vowed that the accusation was not only untrue but, in point of fact, Microsoft had done much to encourage competition. Who is deceiving us, Bill Gates or the government? How can both be telling the truth? For the anthropologist, at one level of analysis, an objective measure as to the truth or falsity of specific statements doesn't matter; our concerns may focus variously on obtaining sociocultural data about, say, the law, the government's relation to trade, entrepreneurialism, competition/cooperation/collusion in business, the new HT economy, or whatever we are interested in exploring.

Thus, the anthropologist treats what people say as well as what they do as equally valuable information. Their deceptions—of us or of themselves, the rewrite of history in their memory banks, their attempt to keep certain things secret, their decisions on what to say and how to say it—are all critical sociocultural information. Deceptions or, if you will, lies are especially interesting because, for one thing, they often provide information about an area difficult to research. People are not always able to articulate their values, beliefs, norms, and the like. Saying to someone, "Give me a list of your values" usually elicits a puzzled frown, a laugh, a shifting of the body to indicate discomfort with the question, and a response something like, "Well, uh, . . . uh . . . what do you mean?"

But when people deceive us, tell half-truths, or hide certain aspects of their behavior, they often are revealing the important rules and norms whose violation they can't always articulate or don't want to reveal, especially to an outsider. Thus, it's a basic tenet in anthropological research that not telling the truth (deliberately or unknowingly) occurs because there are sociocultural rules, norms, laws, and the like that both Ego and others use to evaluate behavior, awarding benefits or imposing costs as seems appropriate. If, for example, I claim that I never waste money, this makes me feel good and—because while spending money is one thing, wasting it is another—I assume that making such a claim will restrain you or others from ridiculing me or thinking when they see me that "a fool and her money are soon parted." Similarly, though gossip is commonplace in all societies, many (as in much of North American society) frown on it. So most people will tell you they never gossip—even though those who gossip the most are often most vehement in their disclaimers as to the value of gossip.

In short, lies and other deceptions are grounded in sociocultural truths (for example, the small white lie of telling someone he looks good in an outfit when you think he looks terrible, or the upstanding pillar of the community, involved in numerous good works, who hires her household help from among the undocumented [i.e., illegal] immigrant population because "they work harder and get paid less"). In what follows, we'll spend a great deal of time trying to get at some of the sociocultural truths about economizing behavior in all of its various guises.

Chapter Four

Production
Is It the Chicken or the Egg?

Common sense tells us that just as reproduction is the basis of all human societies (since without new members, families and even whole communities die out), so the basic building block of human interaction—exchange—is based on the production of various goods or services that people want from each other. I am able or have the potential to produce something someone else wants; they, in turn, have something I need or want, now or in the future. The needs or wants may range all the way from such basic human necessities as sex, food, caretaking, or security/defense to someone with whom I can share a joke or play a game, or who can be a sympathetic listener when I'm melancholy or distressed at the unfairness of life.

Even very young children are aware of the role of production in their lives. They learn at a very early age that certain behavior that they produce for adults (a smile, a hug, sounds made) will be rewarded—or not, as the case may be. As we get older, we add to the list of goods and services we have to produce: academic performance, homework assignments, and good grades in schools; certain athletic activities (not uncommonly done as much if not more to please one's parents than for self-use); chores around the house; after-school jobs; doing things that win favor with our crowd; caretaking younger siblings or older relatives. The list of goods and services keeps growing as we mature.

When we reach adulthood, production becomes really central in our lives. In remote pockets where villages survive by hunting, gathering and gardening, it is the male capacity to hunt, clear lands for planting, or impregnate women, and the female capacity to gather foods, tend gardens, care for elders and children, and produce offspring that are the foci of production. In the HT global society, we are expected to produce ideas, new products and markets, and solutions to social, economic, education, or health problems; we're also supposed to volunteer labor; maintain our homes, patios, or gardens; participate in civil society; take care of our children and elders; entertain; or even just play the role of consumer. And take note: shoppers work very hard to find "just the right thing" for their homes, for a gift, or for self-enhancement and self-presentation (how we want the world to think of us). Further, in all societies, we spend much of our time learning new skills as well as unlearning old ones that have little use or may even have become counterproductive.

When studying the relationship between production and consumption, it's a question of which comes first, the chicken or the egg. Production certainly stimulates consumption, since people will consume that which is in front of them—but consumer needs and wants also stimulate production. Despite concerns that too much consumption continues to deplete nonrenewable or slowly renewable natural resources as well as spoil the environment, the global economic crisis of the late 1990s led to the paradox of governments telling their citizens, on the one hand, to save more, stop acquiring debt, and, especially, stop being wasteful of the world's resources. On the other hand, the same governments took to giving incentives to these same citizens in order to encourage them to buy more and increase consumption. When spending drops, production drops; when production drops, payrolls are cut back. People who are employed pay taxes and fund the work of government; people who are unemployed pay fewer taxes and consume a higher proportion of government revenues. In most of the world's countries, a high percentage of the unemployed are under twenty and over sixty—precisely the segments of the population who are the heaviest consumers of health, education, and welfare funds. Therefore, many governments (not to mention those people seeking jobs) see high unemployment as a national issue of major concern. For example, in 1997, the French government gave a U.S.$1,000 rebate to every citizen who bought a new car within a given period. In November 1998, the Japanese government established a U.S.$5 billion economic stimulus program, one component of which gave every family on public assistance with adults over sixty-five or children under fifteen years of age U.S.$165 worth of "Hometown coupons," valid for six months and to be used only to purchase goods. The point is that, beginning with the reproductive process, production is a key activity for whole sociocultures as well as for individual survival.

Production, in all of its complex forms and whether for self-consumption or trade, requires the expenditure of human energy, broadly (but not always) labeled "labor." In some sense, and more often than we recognize, we are all laborers, spending much of our waking hours working to produce or seek information, perform services, and make things.

But for many, backbreaking and tedious labor many hours a day, every day of the week, and every week of the year is required simply to produce the most minimal requirements of food and water, never mind shelter or medical care. And, indeed, in many locales in the world there are those who count themselves among the lucky ones if they have such labor to perform. Put a farmer on a piece of land with poor soil and lacking sufficient water, and even the most intense labor may not be able to produce an adequate supply of food. Farmers and hunters need land and water, as well as plants and animals, which themselves require access to the resources they need to exist. Yet for some urban poor the only productive activity is begging or stealing because, as the Wise Old Woman used to say, "You can't make something out of nothing." So we're back to the need for resources.

Resources are of two kinds: natural and sociocultural. We all know that we need the renewable and nonrenewable resources such as water, minerals, air, plant and animal life, land with the capacity to sustain life, and so on. But most of the activities of many humans around the world today require other resources, the kind that they must have to earn wages. Some of the most obvious resources of humans are other humans ("It's not what you know but who you know—and who they know"), reasonably good health, information, and, in today's world, money. Without money many find it impossible to get an education, start a business, have the collateral to get a loan, buy the clothes to make the kind of appearance required for being hired, afford transportation to their place of employment—or even to leave a poor community, migrate to where there are income possibilities, and survive until an income starts coming in.

Most important, people need a space to stand on—land. We need land to live on and land to build the structures in which we perform most of the actions of daily life. So, for example, those who work with the urban poor know that one of the most pressing problems for the homeless is the lack of a stable place in which to live, having a place to store possessions, a place where a potential employer can contact them, a place where they have a certain degree of assurance they are safe from harm. Even one of the latest fads produced by the growing role of cyberspace, flexible offices—"rent office space for a day, the way you rent a car"—plays on the fact that from time to time, we all need a physical space to operate our business.

There are other resources needed. Single parents need some way to have affordable care for children; life and work experience is a resource (e.g., most of us don't like to hire a physician or a lawyer fresh out of school, or a waitress or house cleaner who has never done such work before); entrepreneurs need business contacts and ideas as well as capital and customers. People need a reasonable level of mental and physical well-being in order to be a reliable worker (how long would it take you to switch a service provider if your doctor or babysitter kept canceling appointments?) just as much as house builders need construction materials. But more, social workers, doctors, and lawyers need clients; politicians need supporters and campaign funds; bankers need depositors and borrowers; large agribusinesses in the North American Great Plains need ways to ship their wheat and livestock to markets.

It is especially important to remember that no two societies or individuals have the same access to resources. Sometimes this differential is the result of a natural unevenness in distribution. Some locales have plenty of water and open space, while others have very little; some individuals spend much of their lives surrounded by a supportive and widespread kin group, but others are left orphaned and alone when quite young. Sometimes the differential is due to the way sociocultures value certain personal skills, talents, or attributes. For example, given three males, all relatively similar in skills and background, in over 75 percent of the cases the tallest of the three is the one selected for the job; similarly, in our society, manual dexterity is less valued than mathematical skills. Thus, personal and social resources are as critical as natural resources for a satisfactory quality of life. People seek resources for one reason or another and are willing to make trades and trade-offs in order to obtain them. These two facts of life, unevenness in access to resources and the need as well as willingness to exchange, are the basic motivation for the creation of microsocieties such as families and neighborhoods, as well as macrosocieties such as nation-states, the United Nations, NATO, the European Union, or the World Trade Organization—and the global exchange network.

For much of human history, productive units were the household and closely linked communities (mobile hunter-gatherers and pastoralists as well as fishing and agricultural settlements). In such units, labor was viewed as free despite various costs such as providing for the young until they were old enough to make a contribution to production. Also viewed as free resources were those foods whose only costs were the energy expended to produce them, for example, housing, clothing, the manufacture and maintenance of the tools used, and the energy used in their preparation.

Despite several million years of human existence, it is only in this century that we have become sensitive to the costs of such free resources. The costs of many of the goods that we take for granted—for example, water, clean air, fuel, even space for leisure activities and the deposit of the dead or waste—are becoming so expensive that, in much of the world, growing numbers can no longer afford them. In some parts of India, for example, people spend as much as one-third of their meager annual cash income to purchase the firewood they need to cook their food. Increasingly, the ethically and morally challenging triage model is being employed in situations where limited resources require that, according to urgency, we prioritize the variety of needs demanding allocation of scarce resources.

Our present awareness about the costs of exploiting nature began with making a distinction between renewable resources (such as trees or fish) and nonrenewable resources such as oil, minerals, and fresh water.

There is growing pressure to price goods and services for which we've never before been charged. When a couple divorces, what is the value of a woman's services as a helpmate who enhanced her husband's career development? Even scenic views now have "a market value," and numerous lawsuits have been filed because, say, Hotel X is blocking the view from the windows of rooms in Hotel T, or a new structure of Mr. A has deprived Mr. and Mrs. B of a view they enjoyed for years from their front porch.

It's in this area of production that some of the most difficult trade-offs have to be made. One of the poorest countries in Africa, Mauritania, has to sell licenses to the European Union so that fleets of highly industrialized, capture-efficient fishing vessels from countries such as France and the Netherlands may fish in their waters. Indeed, so much fish is being taken that Mauritania has prohibited its own citizens from going fishing. But despite recognizing that such fishing can devastate the stocks, Mauritania needs the money from such licensing agreements to import food, run schools, pay its police and schoolteachers, build roads, and buy medicines. The difficult question: Do the decision makers opt for meeting the immediate needs of the citizens or looking ten years down the road, when they will probably still need to meet at least some of the same needs but when there are no more fish, thus no more licenses to sell? Currently, the several hundred fishermen who bring in a few hundred pounds of fish each day in a country with a poor distribution system cannot provide the food that hundreds of thousands need. So Mauritania sells the licenses and buys the flour that is sold at a subsidized price in an attempt to meet the food needs of those who are hungry today.

Another trade-off in resources is that faced by Israel. Its growing population has a different kind of hunger, the need for housing. High-rise concrete apartment houses are the solution. But concrete requires sand, and builders are disturbing the coastal shelf to obtain it, causing problems for both the fishing fleets and the coastal fisheries. What's more important, the preservation of fishing habitats or the production of housing?

The next thing that is essential to production is capital—but not capital in the narrow sense employed by most modern economic theorists. A useful way for an anthropologist to identify capital—given the wide range of societies and the different ways people have of surviving—is "resource-producing resources," that is, any resource, material or nonmaterial, that may be put to use producing more resources. Capital focuses on the role of resources not consumed but invested, that is, used to create ways to produce more resources. If hunters kill so many beavers that the remaining amount lacks a sufficiently large reproductive pool (and the remnants of the beavers move elsewhere to join a larger population), there will be no beaver next year; if a farmer turns all of his seeds into flour for current consumption, there will be no seeds to plant for the next harvest. Resources must be used in a way that allows for future production. Humans have understood this for thousands of years and have made rules limiting either the number of people who can exploit the resources or the amount of resources utilized. Many villages in the emerging economies had strict rules regulating the amount of water to be used, the wood taken from the forests, or the time of year that certain game, fish, and birds may be hunted. These rules have been ignored by the outsiders who come into these locales to exploit the natural resources.

It should be noted that sociocultural knowledge is what humans use to identify resources, things, or ways of behaving that can be utilized by people. We don't always identify all potential resources and may ignore or waste some material and nonmaterial stuff until we acquire knowledge of how they may be put to some practical use. That is, we must first learn how to extract some utility from that material, activity, or idea before we label it "a resource." Many land areas are identified as wasteland until humans discover that they have a use value (say, a scenic tourist locale, or a place to extract valued minerals or to race off-track buggies): Strangers can die of hunger or thirst in locales where the native population can find adequate supplies of food and liquids to survive; for centuries, humans have drained ecologically valuable marshlands ("swamps"), unaware of how necessary these ecozones are as breeding grounds; and oil was nothing but a nuisance until the emergence of the fossil fuel revolution that accompanied the Industrial Revolution.

In some societies, at some times, elderly men and women, living alone in forests because they were unable or unwilling to be part of the tightly knit villages of medieval Europe, learned how to use wild herbs and roots, at first simply to supply their own needs. Most of the time people recognized the utility of the medicinal services provided by such mysterious figures ("mysterious" only because it's always difficult for people to fathom why anyone doesn't want to be an integral part of a community: "What secret reasons—to do what mischief or evil—does she have for living apart?"). While these solitary people were utilized as a resource, they were viewed with a certain wariness: they were "strange." Thus, when some misfortune struck, it was often blamed on these vulnerable loners. A productive resource for the village (a healer with knowledge of herbal medicines) would suddenly become a dangerous, polluting threat to the community's well-being (a witch practicing satanic arts). Villagers could make sense of and "explain" what was otherwise inexplicable catastrophes; a cow dies, a house burns, people sicken from a plague, floods wipe out the fall harvest. Blame a malevolent agent—the witch in the woods. Similarly, asbestos—once viewed as a resource for its use in controlling fires—is now viewed as a dangerous pollutant; and the military (or the police) may be variously viewed as an evil force in civil society or a collection of heroes willing to lay down their lives to protect us.

A final note: Styles change, and knowledge of how to use a resource is lost. Many plants once eaten as food or used as medicines are now treated as weeds and chemically targeted for destruction (today few people use the lowly dandelion to make wine or to eat as a vegetable). Similarly, where small, rural communities once had a place for those mentally capable of learning only a limited number of simple but very useful tasks, the complexity of the modern world now leaves many such people with few options—and the larger community frequently opts for institutionalizing these people. The elderly, once treated as a valuable resource for what was believed to be their storehouse of information and wisdom (though there's no reason to assume that age is an automatic marker of ability or skills), today face a world in which, at best, they frequently are treated with tolerant condescension and, at worst, abandoned or institutionalized and forgotten.

It was really the invention of agriculture—first in the Near East some ten thousand years ago, then in China, and, finally, in the New World—that changed people's thinking about resources. Before this technological revolution, people relied on the largesse of nature, believing food availability rested with super-natural (or supernatural) forces. If one was respectful of the rules for social and religious behavior that Elders over the centuries had worked out, and if one asked in the right way for the bounty of the land to appear, the resources would appear—unless someone had violated the rules. As an Old Religion priest in an Amerindian village in the American Southwest explained it to me:

> It's not that some action can "make the gods angry" the way the movies say. We believe when people do wrong things, it's not a sin, it's just dumb. When you tell your kid not to put his finger in the light socket, you don't say not to do it because it's a sin. There's electricity there. Electricity works good—if you respect it. You learn the rules—the right way to live with the energy of nature—and bad things don't happen. Don't follow the rules and you can expect things to go wrong.

Along with the resource of expanded technological knowledge as to how to control the production of food resources came the usual spin-offs of expanded knowledge; humans began to develop various technologies to preserve the resources, whether for another year or simply from one harvest or run of salmon to another. They learned, for example, how to preserve foods by salting, dehydrating, and freezing them; how to redirect water into irrigation channels, thereby expanding the land available for planting; how to construct granaries in which to store grains.

Once humans began to understand that they could invent ways of managing nature—domesticating animals and controlling their location and reproduction patterns; planting seeds in particular locales, tending them, and harvesting them—they began to shift from supplicating nature to be generous to performing religious and magical formulas—rituals, prayers, dances, songs, and spells—which, when done properly, would bring the desired result. When the expected result didn't occur, it was assumed to be due to human error; someone did something incorrectly or in the wrong frame of mind.

With all of this came the necessary technology of governing, the making of rules and the management of people to control their production and use of resources. Rules were invented to make sure that people didn't cheat on the amount of water they took and that all did their fair share of the work in building the dams, irrigation ditches, and storage buildings; that all were willing to negotiate disputes that could upset the necessary cooperation among community members; that all shared the fruits of their labor with the sick, elderly, or orphaned; and, very importantly, that all worked to produce a surplus for future consumption—or, when food production slipped, deferred consumption to protect future productivity.

I said earlier that, in the relation between production and consumption, it's difficult to determine which drives which. One of the most interesting problems about production, however, is the extent to which humans often spend time producing things that no one needs (or sometimes even really wants), producing things that are never "consumed." The most obvious example is what is often labeled "busywork," people laboring to produce things and services that neither they nor anyone else will utilize. The aim of the labor is to occupy the laborer—period. Children, the elderly, and institutional inmates are examples. Think of the difference between those who live in coastal villages and fish for food versus those who go recreational fishing and throw the fish back after landing them. The labor and productive routine is the same, but in one case it is to obtain food for consumption; in the other case, it is—what? What is being produced if the fish are thrown back? Leisure time; a temporary capturing of Nature; the good feeling that one has not ruined it for the next in line; the photo quickly snapped before the fish is returned to the sea? Perhaps there should be a distinction between "activities of production" and "productive labor." But then what of the various religious people, such as Buddhist monks, who pray? They consider this productive labor, but would those who don't believe in Buddhism or prayer agree?

Governments and businesses often put people to work simply to put them to work, that is, to pay them wages for work whose only utility is to provide an income to citizens and keep them busy in a controlled workplace setting (in a classroom, say, "learning work skills" rather than on the streets causing civil unrest). Even if business is slack, a company may keep people on the payroll for a variety of reasons: it may not want to lose skilled workers or government incentives, or disincentives make it worthwhile to keep the workers or too costly to dismiss them.

Cultural norms act as powerful constraints against idleness. In today's world, it's not uncommon that people find themselves doing a task, then undoing it, then redoing it. They may change the filing system, paint machinery, or (as an example from the economically depressed area of southern Italy) build a road that stops in the middle of nowhere—but provided months of employment for the roughly 40 percent unemployed of the region. In Japan, about 20 percent of voters are dependent on construction-related industry and so, as the London *Financial Times* quotes Eisuke Sakakibara, an official in the Japanese Ministry of Finance, "Even if you just get people to dig holes in the ground, you still get an economic boost."

I know several people whose aging parents continue trying to perform the jobs they've done all of their adult lives, unable or unwilling to imagine an alternative—and often viewed by others as simply getting in the way or forcing others to follow after, undoing and then redoing the jobs properly.

Sometimes what seems to be productive labor is, in reality, a ritual. The performance—the act of production in and of itself—is the real product rather than the ritual goal claimed for the performance. It has, for example, been suggested that colleges be allowed to hire football players and, in effect, sponsor professional teams rather than continue the farce that their teams consist of students who attend classes and must meet academic standards to continue to play. Too often, it's claimed, the productive labor of the faculty is not intended to teach such students but instead to provide products for football teams that keep alumni financially supportive of the institution. Another and more commonplace example is the Thanksgiving dinner. Though a major ritual event in the North American calendar, few people actually gather to give thanks for God's bounty (less than 35 percent offer a prayer of thanks at the beginning of the meal). However, note the productive labor the feast requires in the home, the marketplaces, the travel industry, the TV and sports industry, and so forth. But at least in these two examples there is some product—though not the one claimed as the intent of the productive process. When, however, the National Anthem is played at the beginning of, say, a baseball or hockey game, the performance seems to achieve little or nothing. Many ignore it, some use the time to check their programs or to go to the stands for a snack. Yet, though we might question the utility of the bands playing and the singers singing, and though many fans indicate their impatience with this segment by starting to cheer and talk during the final few bars, the production of the anthem seems to be an important part of the game. Why?

The final component of production is innovation. If people didn't invent new things and new ways of doing things—that is, if we simply learned what things to use, how to use them, what to do when, what to think or not think—we would still be living as hunters and gatherers. Sociocultural systems are open—that is, no group lives in an unchanging environment, isolated from the world around it and from other groups. New demands are constantly made of us as, for example, when populations grow or shrink, when the natural world alters (especially the supply of whatever it is we label "resources"), or when some catastrophe takes place that the group is not equipped to handle.

And so, of course, sociocultural changes are constantly occurring. People forget instructions and introduce change without intending to. People also are prone to tinker, to try something different just to see what happens (people who cook do this all the time). Some changes become widely accepted by simply passing along a grapevine without any effort made to sell the innovation as such. This happened with Skin So Soft, an after-bath skin softener made by Avon Products. Someone discovered that it made a grand mosquito repellent. Within a few months, word of mouth (especially among people who like to go fishing) led people all over North America to use it for that purpose (it took Avon several years to become aware of why sales had jumped for the product). Another example: When I was a child there was no such thing as a babysitter; if one could afford it, children had a full-time nanny; otherwise families took the children with them when they worked in the fields or in a shop or asked kin, neighbors, or older siblings to care for children. And you never paid a fee to those who acted as caretakers; neighbors exchanged favors or kin obliged when asked, because that's what neighbors and kin did. But during World War II, the idea of hiring babysitters was introduced, and soon even older children expected to be paid for taking care of their own younger brothers and sisters. Such innovations and changes slip quietly and unnoticed into the pattern of things, though sometimes people will remark, "Funny, I don't know when that first appeared, but we didn't use to do (or have) things like that," or "I thought that had been around forever" (e.g., it was only in 1928 that broccoli was introduced into North America from Italy).

Of course, goods and services also disappear, slipping quietly out of the pattern of things. People used to have their milk delivered and their weekly laundry picked up; doctors used to make house calls (and most doctors were general practitioners); insurance agents came to the house once a month to collect your premium payment. Similarly, numerous children's games and various toys have vanished. And people say, "You know, it's been years since I thought about (whatever), but you just don't see/do/think about it any more."

Change is everywhere, and it's inevitable because no two people do everything exactly alike. When we learn something; there is always some slippage in the transmission, something that we do just a bit differently from the way our instructor (a parent, a friend, the crowd, whoever) did it. Some things we don't consciously learn, we just "pick them up," and because people have different interests and skills (or lack of them), ways of doing and saying vary. But an important question is: When we decide to follow the way someone else does it, do we always know if their way is just a personal quirk or habit or if it's the way "everybody" does it? Most people at some time or other find themselves in a situation where they quietly glance around to see how others are behaving. We don't want to be conspicuous, appear ignorant, or look like a dweeb, nerd, fool, or, worst of all, behind the times, out of date, unfashionable. So we learn without explicit instruction—and, sometimes, we miss something that may be crucial in the performance.

And here's a trade-off: Is it better to be an innovator, a trend-setter, someone who is self-confident enough to set the style, create the new—but risk being ridiculed or ignored, or is it better to be safe and follow the crowd? Was Frank Sinatra right when he said he always did things "My way"? How do innovators know they can carry it off and get others to accept or at least tolerate it? Why do most people try to do or say "the right thing," even when it's awkward, uncomfortable, and even distasteful? Sometimes we do or say something, fully aware that we really don't like doing it that way; occasionally, we are even resentful that we feel pushed to do it. For example, a number of college men and women, talking about certain aspects of campus life, complain about this pressure to follow the crowd. After a course I taught was over (and the grades turned in), a born-again Christian told me he never really believed "all that stuff about evolution" he had to write on the final exam. And, every year, there are a few students who confide to me that, rather than pleasure, their main emotional response to the sexual activities in which they felt pressured to engage was concern about possible consequences—sometimes mixed with boredom.

All of this has to do with productive activities—old ones carried over and transmitted from older to younger, passed through the network—as well as innovative activities. We're all concerned with the result of those activities and how we decide whether to produce the traditional things in the traditional ways or risk a loss of time, money, respect, friendship, social standing with friends or work mates, and so forth, and try something new. The interesting thing is that numerous studies have shown that most people, most of the time, don't consciously seek to be innovators. Rather, they try to avoid taking risks and tend to prefer to be safe rather than sorry.

All of this makes the entrepreneur a most curious person. For here are individuals who thrive on innovation and deliberately search out the new. They are people who take risks, work to organize and manage new markets, and introduce changes, all with the conviction that, in their scheme, the benefits will outweigh the costs and that their ideas and innovations will succeed. They look for openings, for gaps, for needs that can be met. Those people we label entrepreneurs are famous for creating needs and wants that never before existed. Something frustrates them and before you know it, they've gone out and done something to solve the problem. They hear someone say, "Why isn't there a way to do this more easily/quickly/cheaply," or "I wish someone would . . .," or "Why can't there be something that does . . .?" and they're off trying to fulfill the need—inventing the paper clip, frozen TV dinners, the zipper, traffic lights and road maps, much of the new computer software, some new service, and on and on.

Since these individuals play a crucial role in production—and never more than in this global society in which we are all producers and traders and consumers—let's take a closer look at them.

Chapter Five

Innovation, Entrepreneurs, and Risk

I've already touched on the claim by some anthropologists that members of nonmarket societies do not make rational choices as the term is used to apply to the weighing of costs and benefits before deciding on whatever actions seem likely to bring the best outcome at the least cost. As the argument goes, people in nonmarket societies are too embedded in a web of traditional social relations with production, distribution, and consumption organized around relations that are fixed by morally grounded obligatory rules and norms. In such societies, it's claimed, labor is more than an economic necessity, especially when performed for others; it is part of one's social persona, and all labor, most particularly when performed for others, is social labor. Such an analysis must rest on the assumption that change is minimal (if it exists at all). Otherwise, these "webs of traditional social relations with fixed exchange relations" would be subject to change—and change requires decisions to be made.

But no socioculture exists through time without changing in response to internal and external variations. Populations grow and decline, resources expand or contract, natural catastrophes occur, and new people appear next door. All these and more require a response, and responses require weighing the costs/benefits of continuing to do things the old ways versus the costs/benefits of trying something new.

In the approach presented here, it's assumed that the claim that many societies are locked into traditional ways results from the gaps in our knowledge about such societies. Though the groups may have no written records—and even these always are suspect—we do have their oral histories as well as information provided by archeological research. Still, we miss much of their history and, in the complexity of everyday life, we cannot recover material that informs us as to the amount of innovation that does go on and does have a cumulative effect, one generation to the next. Change in the makeup of human groups and the context in which they must make a living is so much an everyday fact of life that human sociocultural systems cannot persist without many minor and some major changes being made.

Now, admittedly, some societies do "die"; that is, the societies lose members and eventually cease to exist, even in memory. What really happens, of course, is that either people start moving away and the population dwindles till the last survivors die, or, gradually, as with Imperial Rome or the Aztec empire, the socioculture changes so much over time that at some point people start identifying not, say, as Romans but as Venetians, French, or Spanish. Rome and the Latin language, for example, didn't just disappear overnight, nor did people one day say something like, "Last month, we were Romans and spoke Latin, and this month we're Italian and speak Italian." In every part of the world, humans migrate, separate, and gradually become very different from those groups with whom they have common historical roots.

Thus, humans have to respond to change. It is difficult to imagine that, being human, they have not done this with the tools that humans employ whenever they must make choices. True, even when change is perceived, groups sometimes choose to do nothing or, worse, refuse to recognize a crisis until a genuine catastrophe envelops them and they have no options but to appeal to supernatural forces to intervene, or they make a decision by doing something like flipping a coin or reading the entrails of a chicken. Real (and rational) decision making, however, requires that we: (a) recognize there is a crisis—that is, a turning point, a fork in the road, where one must either stop dead—sometimes literally!—or take a different path today from that taken yesterday (note that though a catastrophe may create a crisis, the two terms are quite different); (b) believe that a response to the crisis is capable of being worked out by humans; (c) identify the components of the problem or issue; (d) list options; (e) work out which options offer realistically attainable results and which seem impractical and unworkable; and (f) attempt to calculate unintended consequences (risks and uncertainties of each option) and how we might respond to these new problems. This process is the same, whether the question is what to wear or what to eat for dinner, what investment decisions to make, or how to deal with ecological issues.

Humans look at the risks and uncertainties of continuing to do what "everyone" (i.e., various aggregates to which they belong or with which they're familiar such as the family, neighborhood, work or religious group, women/men/age group, town, region) has "always" done, or, as individuals, thinking it out as well as checking around and talking it up in groups. The old and familiar will be contrasted with the risks and uncertainties of trying something new and unknown in its consequences.

Sometimes—rarely, I think—even when they know there's a problem, people simply will opt to keep on doing what they know—recall the old folk saying, "Better the devil you know than the devil you don't know." The people of Easter Island may have responded in this way as their overloaded ecosystem became less and less capable of supporting the population. Though there is no evidence to support the possibility that some wanted to change and were hindered in their attempts, it seems reasonable to assume that at least a few might have decided to leave. But, even so, what of those who stayed? Are we to argue that they didn't go through a decision-making process, weighing the costs and benefits of remaining and, if the latter, trying to decide what would be the best way to meet the obvious catastrophe that was threatening? Certainly, deciding not to change is no less of a decision than choosing to innovate. Such a choice may have been forced on the group by circumstances other than the obligatory and embedded social relations—as when, for example, on the southern rim of the Sahara, the desert started to invade the green areas, and most inhabitants had no choice but to move where there was adequate water.

Whether in premarket societies or in the global village, all people have been and continue to be embedded in obligatory exchange relations, performing labor that contributes to the social identity of an individual as well as contributing social services beyond the immediate economic needs of the laborer. When individuals lose their jobs, even jobs about which they grumbled, and even when provided with generous "golden handshakes" or a State-provided safety net, they often bemoan the loss—especially if months or even years pass and no other employment is forthcoming.

In the developed world, especially in cities, it's the young people (aged sixteen to twenty-five) who have the highest rate of unemployment and who have not been able to gain entry into the job market. Currently, in France and Germany, for example, despite an adequate safety net that provides for their basic *needs*, the long-term unemployed of all ages are angry because it is their *wants* that are going unsatisfied; they have "nothing to do," "nothing to look forward to," and, most of all, they see no opportunities in the future. Their desire to work—as witness the way they flock to apply even for "mind-numbingly dull" factory work—is grounded in the same desire to be part of a sociocultural web as is held by those in nonmarket societies.

It may also be noted that Karl Marx charged that in capitalist societies, the working class is entrapped in the web of a society built around the drive for profit. By the logic of his argument, it would seem that those who live under capitalism are at least as embedded (if not more so) in a sociocultural system organized and dominated by "the ruling class," whose members' major (even sole) concern is their own increase of wealth and power. Given Marx's views on the powerful position of capitalists and the "enslaved" position of the workers, it seems odd that any Marxian scholar would argue that it is only in nonmarket societies that economic means tend to be translated into social ends, or that relationships depend on the social status and relations of the person concerned. For example, in nonmarket societies it's usually the male elders who determine what rules and social relations should prevail (often to their own benefit and at the expense of women and young, junior males). It's also agreed by the same scholars that in market societies it's the owners of the means of production who determine what rules and social relations will prevail. These simultaneously held positions seem, however, to force us to the conclusion that in *all* societies, the majority of people will live out much of their everyday lives fulfilling their major sociocultural obligations and only rarely challenge the rules that sustain those relations.

However, since change is just as much a part of all human life as is whatever we label "tradition," we must understand how change (and nonchange) occurs. What follows is based on the assumption that change is ubiquitous, and many minor innovations are made every day. Most are perceived as simply trivial adjustments in the business of having to make do. We've all improvised when faced with the need to perform some household chore that is lacking the right tool, improvised by using something else; we've all made what we perceive as some minor adjustment to have things function more efficiently. We don't identify such adjustments and variations as Important Innovations nor as offering entrepreneurial opportunities. They are ad hoc changes; many may be forgotten once we finish the job, though some few seem to work so well that we keep them and others begin to copy us, and soon the innovation becomes a standard part of our sociocultural inventory.

Certainly in the workplace, one need not be the classic self-employed entrepreneur to be a niche-creating originator of some good or service. The following is an example of entrepreneurial innovation. A waitress in Pittsburgh, having difficulty taking the orders of several deaf customers who frequented the bar where she worked, decided to learn sign language so customers wouldn't have to write out their orders. Students in the classes she began to attend were attracted to visit where she worked—especially when it became known she had persuaded the tavern owner to arrange for captioned TV. Word spread to other deaf people in Pittsburgh and today the bar is well patronized by deaf and hearing people alike. They go there not just because the restaurant offers special services to the hearing impaired but because, as one put it, "it's a place where you're treated like people, not just customers." Her innovation resulted in happy patrons and therefore less stress on the job; naturally, happier patrons are more generous tippers. But these were not the genesis for the innovation. The profit for this entrepreneurial waitress was her awareness that she had found a better way to do a job.

There's another explanation for change and innovation: they may occur accidentally. A sender, a receiver, or both may mishear, garble, or misinterpret some portion of the original message (i.e., "noise" becomes a factor in the transmission of information). One simply may forget to send some segment of the message; or the recipient may fail to recall the entire package; or some component may seem so obvious to the sender that it's not included. For example, every year, the Turkey Hotline receives calls from people who roasted supermarket turkeys without removing them from the plastic wrap in which the birds were enclosed—but who would think you'd need to tell someone to do that? Sometimes when the intended message becomes distorted, an innovative response will emerge that is considered quite adequate even after the error is discovered. Thus, around the turn of the twentieth century, a St. Louis brewer, having been told to move to the American Southwest for his health, selected Monterey, California, as his new home and brewery site. He left the travel arrangements to his wife—and the two found themselves in Monterrey, Mexico. The locale so delighted the couple, however, that they settled there instead.

We tend to think of innovations as major inventions—the printing press, the steam engine, the computer. But the majority of people make changes in ways of doing things in their personal lives without making much ado about it and without universal consequences. We may be pleased that we've discovered a better way to do something and send our innovation to a newspaper column called *Smart Tips for Shoppers*, *Hints from Heloise*, or something similar—or we may not. But one interesting note is that employees who are satisfied with their jobs are more likely to contribute ideas to the suggestion box about ways to improve performance, operate more efficiently, shave some costs, and the like. It appears, then, that making changes is part of the average person's life.

What we tend to forget, however, is that the cumulative effect of millions of such changes can, very gradually and almost invisibly, result in major shifts in lifestyle, for, in the words of an old song, "Little things can mean a lot." After all, as recently noted in *The Economist*, in the nineteenth century some great mind once suggested that, by adding an inch to the tail of each shirt sold to the Chinese, enough additional fabric would be utilized to keep the British textile mills fully operating despite an emerging downturn in demand. And so, one day, some event causes us to become aware that a great many things are no longer the same; we, along with others, begin to wonder, "When did they stop or start saying, doing, making, or behaving like that?" It may be a defining moment such as a teenage mass shooting at a local high school, a catastrophe that leads to a national examination of such questions as "What is happening to the family?"—"to civility?"—"to our children?"; or it may simply be a momentary puzzlement as to why we still say things like, "Dial the number you see on your screen" or "Hang up the phone," given that many in today's world have never seen a telephone dial and few phones still require hanging up (returning a phone to its cradle) to break the connection.

Indeed, one school of thought has it that some of the most significant and successful innovations are those that are perceived as major only after they have been initiated and spread out in the society. If we thought they did have revolutionary potential, most innovations would be delayed while people debated them, formed committees to study them, and set up research teams so they could be analyzed and subjected to an Impact Assessment Analysis. Groups would form and publicly demonstrate to prohibit them; there would then be a series of laws and regulations to monitor and manage their growth—and they might be rejected out of hand as unnatural or dangerous or, above all, carrying too many unknown risks. The resistance of the medical profession to the use of anesthesia, the current outcry against genetically modified (GM) foods, and the delay due to the refusal of the French government to use a new machine to test blood (which led to over one thousand AIDS deaths and several thousand HIV-infected hemophiliacs) are three examples of the resistance to change.

This raises an issue that needs to be discussed briefly: the emergence of the system of economic organization called capitalism. While production is often considered the key component of all sociocultural systems, this seems especially true in the case of capitalism. However, the Industrial Revolution brought with it the introduction of global capitalism. And global capitalism altered not just production but distribution/exchange and consumption as well. The shift in scale of these activities was so great that the massive sociocultural changes that accompanied the shift moved through the world's societies like a tidal wave.

Scale matters enormously. As a noted biologist has commented, a mouse as big as an elephant would no longer look like a mouse; a whole series of other structural changes would have to occur along with the increase in size. Since any change, no matter how small, will usually generate other changes, a shift in scale exacerbates the impact on communities. On the one hand, think of the consequences of a Wal-Mart superstore being set up in a small town on the prairie. The town's small businesses will lose customers and be forced to close down. As these small shops disappear, so do dentists, lawyers, and doctors, and the other families, taking their children with them and forcing the local school to close, along with the hospital. But as people leave, the superstore, finding sales are down, closes down—and, finally, we have a ghost town. On the other hand, one peddler, showing up in town with a pack on his back, is unlikely to substantively alter life for the local merchants or in the community generally (though even in this case the introduction of some new tools or weapons could prove, long term, to have a significant impact on social relations of the town's inhabitants).

The mediators between producers and consumers—call them what you will, middlemen, brokers, merchants, traders—also assumed a more critical role. They not only initiated major differences in consumer patterns but, among producers, became more pivotal figures in the quantification and regulation of production. Under the influence of global capitalism, their role as arbitragers—turning a quick profit by buying goods cheaply produced in one community and selling them in locales where they commanded higher prices—led to the extension of the capitalist market system to regions where labor was abundant and cheap enough to offset costs of moving the goods between the communities.

Long before industrial capitalism and still today, those who provide goods and services were not always merchants per se but also could have obtained their products by theft or force—as highway robbers, smugglers, pirates, even tribal chiefs, nobles or religious leaders. Whatever they were and however they obtained the products they moved into the market, they were all engaged in the same activities and had the same goal, profit making. In the pursuit of their search for stuff to exchange, they altered the daily lives of those from whom they obtained goods. Whether raiding villages for slaves or for the fall harvest, taking over towns and forcing their citizens to work in mines, or making goods for export, or offering desirable foreign goods as an inducement, their search for profit altered the daily lives of the inhabitants in substantive ways. (And, let me remind you, "profit" may be variously defined and, as with "benefits" and "costs" need not be quantified in monetary terms.)

Further, in societies where production for trade had not been the dominant theme, the intrusion of these go-betweens, no matter how infrequent, required those who were now required to produce for them to be persuaded (one way or the other) that performing such activities had benefits that outweighed costs of noncompliance. True, at least initially, some of the potential producers would not have worked in the regular and steady way the brokers demanded. They sometimes "voted with their feet" against the scheme and simply ran away. Some tried refusing to comply and met the attempts with violence against the newcomers. And, if all else failed, they performed their productive activities with such inefficiency that the attempt to introduce change was given up as too costly (e.g., "the local population is too simple-minded to understand what is wanted of them")—a tactic that is still employed by some populations today who reject the employment opportunities presented to them. They could have sabotaged the work process (again, something that still occurs today—as witness the subtle acts of destruction or outright havoc employed by workers to resist "the bosses"). Most of the time, however, in most locales, all such tactics only postponed the inevitable penetration of the market economy; for one thing, there were always a few—sometimes those with the most power authority—who saw the new ways as adding to their existing benefits or some who saw the new ways as offering avenues to obtain benefits not accessible via the existing sociocultural pathways. The ethnographic and historic literature is filled with examples of how those in various sociocultures did a cost/benefit analysis and decided that the costs of rejection (e.g., death or flight) were greater than the costs of compliance (a transformed life under the new production regime).

And note that we're now again talking about the cost/benefit model, which, many argue, is a distinctive product of industrial, capitalistic production. As already noted, however, the calculation of costs and benefits need not have been introduced to these sociocultures along with mercantile or industrial capitalism. Decision making doesn't require markets or money, any kind of formal bookkeeping (as we'll see later, people are capable of keeping surprisingly complex accounts in their head), or even the concept of profit or monetary gain. All that is needed is the "simple" idea that benefits are more satisfying than losses and that losses are much less satisfying than risking the loss of what one already has (see, for example, the old folk saying, "A bird in the hand is worth two in the bush"). Social accounting is constructed on the common hope of either getting something or, at least, not losing something, versus the equally common fear of having nothing. Indeed, there are numerous studies that show people measure their losses with greater emotional intensity than they measure their gains. Thus, to repeat for added emphasis the important claim made earlier: rather than having invented a new way of viewing the world as a result of their special concern with market dynamics, it's just as likely that, first, bookkeepers and, then, economists took a commonplace idea and used it to formulate an increasingly complex and highly technical explanation to account for the working of the market.

Similarly, although entrepreneurs have long been regarded as the product of modern capitalism, these risk-taking individuals have existed in many places and times.

Now, in all societies there are different types of people. No matter how homogeneous a group may seem, individuals differ. Nuns in a convent, for example, may live a rigorously regulated existence and one of their own choosing; one would suppose they would gladly follow the rules for living that they had sought out. Yet, within their ordered life they show what for outsiders seems a surprising variation in attitudes, practices, leisure activities, work patterns, and so forth. In any aggregate of humans, there are those who work hard and those who enjoy taking it easy, those who are always willing to help a neighbor and those who do it only if it's necessary in order to avoid ridicule or scorn. There are always some who deviate from the norm by being better at what they do and receiving social or supernatural approval, or behaving in ways that lead to the loss of resources, social approval, friendship, or (so it's claimed—and hoped—by others) supernatural blessings. Some individuals always do more than their fair share and some are freeloaders; some keep resources they are expected to share (hiding them away or consuming them in secret) while others use the resources extravagantly or invent new ways to "flaunt their wealth."

(Note, I've avoided using the word "traditional." No rule, norm, social structure, belief, and so forth is without a beginning—a time when it wasn't "traditional." Some of you may be thinking, "That's all pretty obvious," but, in point of fact, it isn't. There are many who, when confronted with two or more sociocultural variants, seek to identify which is "The Real Tradition," the one that existed in some timeless "before"—as in "before European colonialism," "before industrialization," "before money was invented." As the noted historian Eric Hobsbawm has stressed in *The Invention of Tradition* (1983), innovations can quickly attain an aura of longevity and this aura lends legitimacy to various acts and activities, many of which are only a few generations old.)

Few sociocultures lack individuals (sometimes even groups—as with young men of the warrior grade) who are more consistent risk takers and who—despite traditional rules or norms of what to produce, how much, when, and what to do with it—more regularly risk social disapproval. They innovate, create new ways of doing things, bend the rules, and somehow manipulate people or the system in ways from which the risk takers, the adventurers, derive some benefit. These benefits may be the aggrandizement of resources, power, authority, prestige, status, respect, a faster or less costly way of doing something, whatever. More important, they are frequently able to persuade others to become coadventurers, sharing both risks and profits—or losses. Entrepreneurs are innovators who depart from precedence, may risk fortune and reputation, and seek to reweave the social web in order to introduce changes that increase resources for themselves and, usually, some others as well. They may also fail and face the loss of their resources (whether these are material, such as goods, supporters, and friends, or nonmaterial, such as respect and social acceptance), leaving them to face ridicule, disgrace, or even exile. In some small societies, there may be times when no such individual is on the scene, but the larger the population, the more likely it is that you will find at least a few at any time. The entrepreneur, often labeled a magnate or a "Big Man," is an agent of change. Interestingly, the term "Big Man" (literally translated) turns up in languages as different as German, Chinese, and Kwakiutl (a North American Northwest Coast Indian group). Since these enterprising individuals diligently engage in ambitious and aggressive efforts to accumulate resources, archeologist B. Hayden (1992, "Ecology and Complex Hunter/Gatherers . . .") labels them "accumulators," but I prefer the term suggested by Clark and Blake, "aggrandizer." As Hayden puts it: "Such individuals seek to gain advantages for themselves by influencing community affairs (i.e., acquiring power) and through material gains" (p. 550 in *A Complex Culture of the British Columbia Plateau*, B. Hayden, ed.). In either case, the terms speak tellingly of the aims of such individuals and, as well, allows the comparable activities of women and even children to be addressed and included.

The classic entrepreneurs are individuals who talk up their ideas. They try to get others to become coadventurers and to support them by sharing in the risks, benefiting from the profits, or by spreading the costs, minimizing individual losses. They appear in ancient times—for example, King David of the Old Testament and, from Greek mythology, Jason and the companions he co-opted to seek the Golden Fleece. And the ethnographic literature also has a number of such individuals—not a few of them women.

Surprisingly, religious beliefs are often the motivation for innovation—even though many think of this segment of the sociocultural system as a force for conservatism and highly resistant to change. So, for example, both the Quakers and one of their breakaway offshoots, the Shakers, have been singled out as groups whose members were constantly thinking about new ways to do things and new ways of living. Historians have stressed the role that Quakers—already outsiders because their religious beliefs marked them as being outside the Establishment and the Established Religion (The Church of England)—played in advancing the Industrial Revolution in Great Britain. In North America, the Shakers were noted for their innovations in furniture and house design as well as techniques of farming and animal husbandry. In both cases, non-Shakers (even those hostile to the religious beliefs of the group) were willing to adopt their innovations after seeing how successful they were in increasing production while reducing costs. For example, the Shakers invented the idea of selling seeds in a paper packet and started a whole new industry geared to home gardening. Further, Shaker Sister Tabitha Babbitt came up with the idea of a circular saw while sitting at her spinning wheel, and this faster, more efficient way to cut boards revolutionized the lumber industry. Similarly, in an Alberta Hutterite community where religious beliefs prohibit the use of technology for entertainment (i.e., no TVs, VCRs, or radios), pig farmers are enthusiastically adopting both personal computers and small, handheld Palm III computers to keep track of vaccination schedules, the feed the pigs are getting, when individually numbered sows are ready to breed, and commodity prices. In their religious community, prestige is obtained through being "the best farmer"; when they are successful agriculturists or stock raisers while remaining true to the guidelines of their faith, God's pleasure is shown by the profitability of their labor. Thus, Hutterite farmers are more likely to be in the vanguard of adopting any technology that seems to them to underwrite the legitimacy of their religious beliefs.

Stereotypical aggrandizers are commonly individuals who have family connections to the elite, as younger sons or as poor relatives. Unable to rise in the system through traditional ways, yet enough a part of it to be tantalized by something so near and yet so far, they seek to create other avenues for attaining power, prestige, or resources. They may open up a new market for a product in another locale or bring back resources from those other places, creating a new market at home, adding value by bringing goods to the consumer.

The term "Big Man" or "magnate" was used, for example, in the city-states of Italy and Germany during Medieval and Renaissance times to designate people (often merchants) who, outside the usual path of inherited wealth or position, achieved respected and important positions. Today, we still talk about "the self-made man" or "Big Man on campus."

Aggrandizers usually make their initial moves by going outside their home community. First, it may be easier to innovate in a society where one is an outsider; one may be freer of various traditional constraints (e.g., pressure from friends and families to play it safe). Second, and more important, such locales may be used to accumulate an initial fund of resources. These resources are used to finance trading trips, to buy weapons, or to attract supporters who cooperate in helping them get more resources. Not uncommonly, even today, entrepreneurs gain their initial store of resources by raiding, robbery, piracy, or trickery and other shady practices, using success in such ventures to acquire more coadventurers, supporters, or followers. Often, success follows success—and, if all goes well, respectability follows success. The resources may also be used to bribe, corrupt, or otherwise buy (or marry) their way into the power elite of their own or an adopted locale. The story of David as told in Samuel I and II of the Old Testament is not atypical of how early leaders came to power. Modern-day robber barons of the nineteenth century, rumrunners during American Prohibition, and, most recently, drug lords and the new rich of the post–Soviet Union are also extreme examples.

More typical, however, are the entrepreneurs who operate on a more modest scale, bringing new products to the markets or managing to expand those that already exist by giving added value. The product may be cheaper, but it may also be more costly (e.g., designer jeans); it may be timely (as when Swanson invented frozen TV dinners and matched the emergence of TV with the desire to spend less time in the kitchen); it may be better or worse than what is already available (McDonald's hamburgers); it may be simpler or more complex (do you want a computer that does everything or simply a word processor and access to the Web?).

Whatever it is, entrepreneurs find (or create) a market for a good or service. I. M. Lewis, a British social anthropologist, has defined an entrepreneur as "an innovator who can turn a situation of unfulfilled potential demand to profit" (see Bibliography). He points out that besides being original and imaginative, entrepreneurs have a special genius for creating links among previously unconnected people, goods, services, processes, and so forth, preferably according to the entrepreneur's design. Lewis recognizes that there are barriers to innovation and that, in most societies, most of the time, people exert pressure on others to conform and (in current jargon) not push the envelope. Any innovator, but especially an entrepreneur, has to be willing to break (or at least bend) traditional rules—even "moral impediments." Lewis suggests that it is those at the top and the bottom of the society who, more than the great mass of average people, are most likely to be willing to go outside the rules. He chooses to illustrate his point by looking at Big Men in tribal New Guinea, individuals who become influential in their communities through their skill as accumulators and manipulators of resources (especially people). The profit such individuals seek is not material but social: The resources they acquire aren't hoarded or stored; they're distributed around the community. Aggrandizers manipulate "streams of generosity." New Guinea Big Men, says Lewis, are "the very epitome of entrepreneurs" and, I would add, so are people like Andrew Carnegie, Ted Turner, George Soros, and Bill Gates—all men who have fought to acquire wealth but in the process also have given it away in order to attract the resources that, ultimately, really seem to matter to most entrepreneurs: power and prestige and winning over others (in both senses of the phrase).

The need for aggrandizers to gain legitimate status in a society is based at least in part on the instability of their position until such legitimacy is attained. As long as they remain outsiders, they can never be sure they are secure from some kind of legal ploy that will permit others to seize their wealth and reduce their social standing. Jews in many parts of Europe, forbidden from engaging in many traditional occupations and activities, became adept at finding and creating unexploited niches that were not yet barred to them.

The situation is only slightly more assured in the entrepreneur's home communities. Aggrandizers can be a threat to the established leadership. First of all, they attract followers away from the more traditional decision makers—the established household, lineage/clan heads, the councils of elders, chiefs and monarchs—who, correspondingly, grow weaker as the number of those in their power base shrinks. Members of the traditional elite may find ways to confiscate or otherwise appropriate the entrepreneur's wealth, thereby ending the threat to their position (and, in the process, frequently adding to their own wealth). Since it is resources that attracts followers, the entrepreneur's loss of resources (in the case of the modern business entrepreneur, through the legal process of bankruptcy) usually leads to a loss of friends and supporters, and a swift decline in influence.

In various African societies, for example, the ethnographic literature abounds with cases where such individuals might be charged with using some form of magic, of being in league with evil spirits. How else, it would be argued, could the exceptional wealth and success they had achieved be explained, when the cattle or crops of others were not doing nearly so well? During a public trial, the accused might plead involuntary possession by malignant forces and would promise not to behave in ways that made them vulnerable to possession by evil spirits. They would get off with a fine (confiscation of all ill-gotten gain) and/or some other form of punishment. Some, however, refused to admit guilt, challenged the charges, and refused to change their ways. They hoped that their supporters would help them win the day; losing carried heavy penalties. In most cases, such individuals might be judged so far removed from the human condition, so irrevocably lost to human sentiments, that they were labeled as witches—and a witch, by definition, is inhuman. As nonhumans they lost any rights they possessed as members of the community, and they (and perhaps their family as well) could no longer lay claim to the resources the community normally thought of as basic and inalienable human entitlements—rights, as a community member, not to go homeless or hungry. As a witch, a nonperson, such "creatures," along with their families, could be and were sold into slavery—a sale viewed as the same as that of any nonhuman creature, say, a goat or a chicken. In some cases, they might be exiled, with consequences sometimes worse than that of slavery, for living outside of a community was dangerous, sometimes impossible, for what other community would accept a known witch? A long and hazardous trek to find some place where they were unknown and were able to start again was the best for which they could hope. In short, the life of the entrepreneur, for more reasons than one, was and still is precarious. What is surprising is that, in spite of such risks, entrepreneurs continue to emerge.

There are historical moments when conditions favor the emergence of aggrandizers and entrepreneurs, but because such times are periods of great general change, aggrandizers find they are targeted for attack and held up to the public as symbols of all that is wrong with the emerging New Order. Clergy and kings alike saw the citizens of the city-states during the European mercantile revolution that took off around the twelfth century as greedy, soulless adventurers who would challenge church teachings and established rule, who would deny their moral and Christian duties in order to trade with heretics, Christ-killers, pagans, whomever, if the price was right.

Similarly, those who led the Industrial Revolution were charged with destroying the natural order. The multifaceted Goethe (1749–1832), who watched a critical phase of that revolution emerge in his lifetime, viewed the dilemma from the dual perspectives of idealistic poet and hardheaded finance minister at the Court of Weimar. Seeing the potential of the new industrialized order to transform the world, he wrote the famous tale of Faust, a man who sold his soul to the devil in order to achieve his dream of designing a Utopia—a perfect world with perfectly happy citizens. A leading European economist, Hans Christoph Binswanger, sees Goethe as using the tale to present what Goethe himself saw as the trade-off between the choices offered by the Industrial Revolution. The famous "Faustian bargain" offered the possibility of a Utopian world but losing one's soul to the devil versus living in the imperfect world we know but retaining the hope of eternal life in a perfect heaven.

The entrepreneurs of today, no matter whether engaged in the IT revolution and the world of global capitalism or in the new agricultural revolution, are facing the same responses as Goethe had to the Industrial Revolution. An articulate and highly visible segment of social activists is warning the world that we are being presented with yet another Faustian bargain.

The Good News and the Bad News of entrepreneurial activity may be illustrated with the story of Andre and Blairo Maggio and is typical of such individuals. In western Brazil, there is a huge tract of savanna that until the 1970s was inhabited only by small groups of Indians and a few cattle ranchers. The latter were minimal in number because of the difficulties of moving their cattle 1,500 miles to Brazil's major coastal cities. However, in the last five years or so, more than a million immigrants, mostly land-hungry and poor Brazilians, have been drawn to this area to work farmlands owned by such multinational corporations as Monsanto and Cargill, by the Japanese and Chinese governments (the latter even presenting a proposal, which the Brazilian government ultimately rejected, to settle 60,000 Chinese colonists on a million acres in the region!), and by private individuals such as the Maggios. The region is now attracting entrepreneurs from all over the world—even from Siberia—are able to buy hundreds of thousands of acres so cheaply that, in the case of the Maggios, it is easy to afford to give away 1,200-acre tracts to any settler who agrees to purchase seeds from and sell their produce only to the Maggio Company.

The sons of an Italian immigrant, Andre and Blairo knew that having land and being able to attract people was not enough; to keep new arrivals stable, happy, and hardworking, settlers have to be provided with basic services such as houses, stores, electricity, recreational facilities, schools, and hospitals. The Maggios set about installing such facilities, sometimes charging settlers with some of the costs but allowing the farmers to pay those off over time against the prices they received for their harvests. The original major barrier to the Maggios' plans to expand was the same one that had isolated and protected the area from earlier intrusions: some way would have to be found to move the soybean over poor roads to major shipping ports 1,500 miles away. Blairo saw that until this problem could be solved, development would be impossible. He argued that a better routing method would be to truck the beans to a small, nearby port on the Madeira River. This drained into the Amazon River, and via this route, crops could be cheaply shipped to such Atlantic ports as Macapá.

At first, the Maggios were unable to find support for their idea. It was a foolish idea, said people in the government and in banks; the rivers were both too shallow and too rocky to permit any major riverine transport. But Blairo toured waterways around the world and came back convinced that vessels with satellite navigational systems and hulls like those of Baltic Sea icebreakers could do the job. His idea proved workable, and now huge vacuums fill barges with over two thousand tons of soybeans an hour; five to six such barges are moved by one tugboat downriver to the ports. The shipping system works so well that over half of the Maggios' annual revenues (about U.S.$300 million) come from other growers.

There have been unsuccessful attempts to restrain the Maggios. When the Federal government halted work on a public beach near the town that serves as the center of the Maggio empire, Andre Maggio, as mayor, merely annexed the beach to the town to remove it from Federal jurisdiction and went ahead with the beach project. Blairo Maggio, now a senator, admits to using his political position to promote support for various new savanna development schemes. Opponents charge he also uses that position to obstruct opposition, both from environmentalists—worried about plans to construct more new routes through virgin woodlands—and from Indian Rights activists who, among other things, are concerned about yet another scheme that involves raising soybeans inside an Indian reserve. The Maggios say their ultimate aim is to use their Amazon transport project to open up another 75 million acres for farming. As Matt Miffed and Peter Fritsch point out in their *Wall Street Journal* article (May 18, 1999) detailing the Maggio saga, this is an area as great in size as that of the total U.S. soybean acreage. For the land-hungry impoverished of Brazil, the Maggios are Good News; for the native Indians and for those who wish to preserve the habitat, they are Bad News.

The emergence and the success of many entrepreneurs is first due to their single-minded dedication and ability to find ways to acquire and increase their supply of resources—anything they consider useful in furthering the achievement of their goals. Second, there is a willingness to employ those resources to distribute goods and services—to give, at low cost or as gifts, land or houses; mundane, exotic, or prestigious objects; feasts, entertainments, or sexual services; bonuses or scholarships; jobs or holiday trips; schools, temples/churches, or sports stadiums; health services, arts centers; even children as spouses—in short, whatever will attract and keep supporters, followers, those with useful connections, or those already in high or powerful places.

In modern capitalist society, entrepreneurs rely heavily on start-up funds obtained from one or more banks, venture capitalists, or governments. But there still remains a need to convince others to become coadventurers, to share the risks through a collaborative effort, to enlist those with no money to use their labor as capital, working for little or even no pay other than the promise of some future bonanza (often by receiving stock or stock options in the venture). Entrepreneurs may also accumulate resources by tapping the wealth of many small investors who can be persuaded that risking some portion of their savings might reap them big rewards. None of these strategies are new. In the records of thirteenth-century Genoa, for example, there are lists that include people who invested small amounts (a baker, a sail maker, a dressmaker) to back those offering to undertake dangerous sea voyages to bring back exotic goods, and young men were willing to share trip expenses for the chance to bring back a portion of the valuable cargo as their own reward. At that time, Europeans viewed nutmeg as so valuable a spice that even a small share, the equivalent of a few ounces, might permit an investor to retire for life.

Just as frequently, however, initial capital was obtained by illegal activities: robbing, looting, smuggling, selling illicit goods, or, with a gang of coadventurers, becoming pirates or raider–warriors. Today, the list of illegal sources of income may also include laundered drug money, stolen information or patent infringements, even laboratory specimens. The history of the Normans in Europe is full of tales of noble dynasties built on the basis of the founder moving quickly from highway robber, to gang leader, to robber baron, to "protector of a city," and finally—employing a few judicious marriages as well—to prince or king. The history of such dynasties ranges from the Hohenstaufers, who ultimately became rulers of the Holy Roman Empire, to the Grimaldis, with their tiny, three-quarters of a mile principality of Monaco. (In an ironic twist of history, a Philadelphia aggrandizer of more recent vintage started out in the construction trade and used his entrepreneurial skills to accumulate the wealth that led to the marriage of his granddaughter, Grace Kelly, to the Prince of Monaco.)

The "warlords," still found in parts of the Balkans, Africa, Central Asia, and China, are modern-day examples of the rather anachronistic military entrepreneur. But there are also enterprising religious entrepreneurs (e.g., Jim Bakker) and political entrepreneurs—some of whom may be elected (one well-known U.S. senator, asked by a reporter to comment on charges of bribery, replied, "Son, I can be rented but I can't be bought"), but others prefer to maintain powerful positions behind the scenes—as with Joe Kennedy, who built a fortune during American Prohibition and rose to become ambassador to Great Britain under President Roosevelt.

In today's world, it's not at all unusual for entrepreneurs—John Rockefeller, Andrew Carnegie, Henry Fricke, Henry Ford, Ted Turner, George Soros (even, of late, Bill Gates) to distribute a portion of their wealth through philanthropic activities. As noted earlier, "generosity" seems typical of aggrandizers. But why give away the wealth one worked so hard to accumulate? Some who have studied present-day entrepreneurs maintain that the distinctive mark of entrepreneurs is their fierce dedication to and concentration on building wealth, in turning a profit—but, importantly, not necessarily just an economic profit. Indeed, one hears from such individuals, over and over, that it's not wealth but winning that is most important. They are determined to prove that their vision is true; that they can be movers and shakers; that they have been right to persist and others were wrong or, lacking the courage of their convictions, too timid.

Entrepreneurs sometimes create the consumer before production is really organized and a supply is available. Good examples are the origins of the markets in coffee, sugar, tobacco, and cocoa. Entrepreneurs encouraged aristocratic venture capitalists (including royalty) to invest in plantations for the production of such foods. They and their patrons then colluded to create a fashion for the consumption of such strange (and, at first, not always particularly pleasant) commodities. As the scale of consumption/production brought both costs and prices down, affluent urban commoners and, eventually, even the working classes followed suit. Canada's Hudson's Bay Company was an entrepreneurial venture that profited mightily by obtaining furs from Amerindians, for which the Indians received in trade such European products as guns, flour, sugar, and cloth. Typical of successful entrepreneurialism, the company founders created new consumers at both ends of the production-consumption-production chain.

As links between producer and consumer, aggrandizers in incipient market societies find or create a need which, in such societies, often involves organizing a number of people to produce in amounts that exceed their own needs. This is not always an easy task, since people don't necessarily want to labor beyond the need to satisfy their needs. The entrepreneur must find some inducement to turn a "self-employed" individual into someone who will work for others on demand. There may be persuasive talk about how such labor will make the future lives of children better, or make life for the producer less risky than at present, or offer an opportunity for whatever kind of advancement is culturally desirable. Often, as just noted above, the producer has to be enticed with the potential of being able to consume certain goods, obtainable only by regularly producing the goods required by the entrepreneur who in turn can obtain the goods desired by the producer (as in the case of Amerindians trading furs for European trade goods or in the case of factory workers laboring for wages).

Sometimes, of course, people are simply forced or tricked into becoming producers of commodities—initially because they somehow become subject to the manipulations of their new overlords, for example, colonial rulers or, as in the case of the many who immigrated to North America as indentured servants, become indebted to someone who paid their passage. Even today, we still have prison labor as well as sweatshop operations that use immigrant workers (often living illegally in the country), where people labor for little more than a minimum amount of food and a place to sleep.

Still, even in the world of literal or wage slavery, there were and are always a few hapless victims who, against all odds, are able to become entrepreneurs by doing some work on the side (e.g., prison entrepreneurs who conduct thriving business both inside and outside the prison walls), independently of the demands of their owners or bosses. Women seem especially adept at this, becoming midwives, healers, and moneylenders; making beer, running houses of prostitution, providing street food, and otherwise engaging in what at first is very small-scale market trade—but is capable of developing into very prosperous enterprises. Even slaves could sometimes engage in activities that, ultimately, allowed them to buy their freedom. They often went on to acquire their own slaves or start their own sweatshops so as to continue to pursue their profitable activities.

Peasants are often labeled conservative and reluctant to adopt new ways. Yet, many of those who have studied peasant communities give good evidence that, when they have an adequate risk fund and calculate a reasonable chance of success, peasants are just as capable of innovating and becoming entrepreneurs as any street-smart urban dweller.

Donato Tredicine is one such person. A former peasant, sometime in the early 1960s he left his small village in Abruzzi and moved to Rome. Using the names of other family members as well as friends, Tredicine started to accumulate vendors' licenses, allowing him to set up street-corner stands where one could purchase roasted chestnuts. Today he has a near monopoly on Rome's chestnut stands, owning over thirty of them. Masolino D'Amico has recently noted that only tourists, not local Rome residents, buy from the *caldarroste* (roasted chestnut sellers). The reason is simple: tourists like to buy at such stands because it makes the visitor feel part of the local scene. Residents don't buy the product because the chestnuts are so outrageously expensive that "only a foolish tourist" would buy them. After all, when for 5,000 Lira one can buy about two and one-half pounds of raw chestnuts at the local market, why buy from the caldarroste who charge 5,000 Lira for a bag of five chestnuts—1,000 Lira each? Nevertheless, Tredicine has created a niche, a tourist attraction, and has exploited it. Now an old man, he and two Pakistani helpers still appear each day at one of his stands on the Via Frattina.

Tredicine's other stands are operated by immigrants from emerging economies and, despite the deliberately quaint appearance of the stands, there is nothing old-fashioned about Tredicine's operation. When supplies of the caldarroste run low, they use their cellular phones to order more, and vans deliver the already roasted nuts in a few minutes. The iron braziers of the street stands no longer roast the chestnuts but only serve to keep them warm—and add atmosphere for the tourists who continue to flock to buy a bit of "authentic Roman street life." If each stand, over the year, averages one hundred bags a day, the thirty stands can gross 15 million Lira a day, a comfortable entrepreneurial niche indeed.

Entrepreneurs, because they're innovators, have little past history to guide their decision making. That brings us to the major problem of entrepreneurs: how to make good decisions when uncertainty increases risk. Of course, decision making always involves the factors of risk and uncertainty. To get a sense of the magnitude of the problem, take the game of chess. It has thirty-two pieces and a small number of places fixed by the rules as to where each may go. Yet, there are more moves in chess than the universe has atoms. What, then, are the risks an entrepreneur encounters when attempting to predict the outcome of the multitude of decisions that feed into a global economy—an economy made up of another multitude of activities and choices made by the multitude of those enmeshed in the global village?

Of course, most of us most of the time think we know more than we do, and that's a major problem. For example, until recently most medical research was done on males—females often being deliberately excluded because of concerns about the effect of investigations on the potential childbearing capabilities of women. Recent research, however, has shown that women have specific immunities as well as sex-specific susceptibilities to various health problems (because of the extra X-gene in females, for one thing). Further, their reaction to drugs also frequently differs from that of males and, as well, will differ depending on when the medication is taken in their monthly cycle. Despite this, most physicians still believe they are able accurately to diagnose illness in women by relying on medical and pharmaceutical research in which women were not part of the test sample. Such confident ignorance can be wasteful and dangerous. For example, Dianne Hales recently noted that in an 1889 report of the U.S. surgeon general, 51 percent of operations for the removal of women's ovaries were performed because almost all medical practitioners of the nineteenth century believed that these uniquely female organs accounted for "female hysteria"—as most mental disorders in women were then labeled.

In several recent (1998, 1999) studies, primary care physicians were shown what they didn't know were staged films of male and female white and African-American "patients." Individuals from each of the four categories were given matching ages, matching symptoms, and matching medical histories. The findings: A significant percentage of physicians diagnosed and treated "patients" differently, depending on their sex and race. For example, when chest pains were described by white males, it was far more common for the diagnosis to be cardiac disorder and the recommended treatment be a surgical procedure (e.g., bypass surgery). White females, African-American males, and African-American females were, in that order, decreasingly recommended for such surgery—and there was an increasing likelihood that their chest pains would be diagnosed as symptoms of stress rather than be cardiac-related.

Of course, medical misconceptions are not limited to sexual or racial dissimilarities; as late as the 1940s, whole sets of perfectly healthy upper and lower teeth were being removed because some physicians linked arthritis to teeth exerting pressure on various nerves.

Similarly, entrepreneurs don't believe they are risk takers par excellence. Indeed, they see themselves as individuals who are no more inclined to take risks than other people. However, they are more convinced of what they know and are more inclined to believe their choices are based on an accurate assessment of the weight of the variables involved in each choice. *The Economist* (July 19, 1997:56) reported on a study by Lowell Busenitz and Jay Barney published in the *Journal of Business Venturing* (Vol. 12, 1997), which involved asking 124 entrepreneurs and 95 managers a number of questions with two possible answers (e.g., "Which cause of death is more frequent in the United States: cancer or heart disease?"). Though entrepreneurs and managers scored approximately the same in the correctness of their answers, there was a marked difference in the results when members of each group were asked to estimate the level of confidence they had in their answer. Not only did entrepreneurs show greater confidence in the correctness of their answer, the more incorrect the answer—that is, the greater the differential between the correct and incorrect answer—the greater the degree of their confidence. The researchers concluded that, relative to the managers who run the businesses for which entrepreneurs had both the idea and the initial drive to find money to finance the startup, entrepreneurs are more confident of their ability to know what they need to know, more willing to generalize from a small amount of information, more inclined to minimize potential risk, and have a greater belief in being right.

As already shown, such high degrees of confidence are not unique to entrepreneurs. Most people seem incapable of accurately assessing the extent of their knowledge or ignorance. One hundred percent of students, when asked to identify anonymously what they expected their grade to be at the end of the semester, answered in the upper 50th percentile. Also in violation of all statistical laws, a well-known study in Sweden showed that 90 percent of drivers believed their driving ability placed them in the upper 10 percent of the skill category!

While attending the prestigious Davos World Economic Forum (1999), one noted entrepreneur, Michael R. Bloomberg, spoke to a reporter from the *Financial Times* (London) about innovation. He noted that the major danger to innovators and innovation was short-term unpredictability. This is not surprising: related research shows that the longer the time frame in which a decision and a goal are set, the more likely it is that the choice will prove to have been a good one. But in innovative situations, a decision maker may have only seconds and rarely longer than a few months to make crucial choices. Further, as Bloomberg noted, running a business requires planning. However, in the startup phrase, especially, when given a choice between being involved in development or planning, entrepreneurs are more likely to choose development. Indeed, it's not uncommon that, long past the crucial initial development stage, entrepreneurs remain unwilling to devote time to management, preferring to focus on making decisions concerned with issues of growth, expansion, a bigger (even monopolistic) market share—and bigger profits to fuel more growth. The crux of the issue seems to be that entrepreneurs are concerned with winning, but managers need to be good at negotiating and building consensus.

What about the entrepreneur's need to make decisions? How best to reduce risk and uncertainty? In an innovative world, how can there be "tried and true" predictive tools? In a contest of innovation, how can we know what tools are best employed? Bloomberg's response to this question, though insightful, was less than helpful for the would-be entrepreneur: "Innovation," he said, "was a religion, not a science."

It's not only the initial startup phase that is uncertain, however; studies show that the more successful a business is, the more unpredictability it faces. For one thing, an entrepreneur is going into uncharted territory. Further, each new success increases the universe of choices—and, again, there are few precedents to guide decisions. It becomes increasingly difficult to tell whether particular decisions will lead to things getting better and better or, often quite suddenly, getting very, very bad. In either case, what's the entrepreneur to do? Bloomberg's response to this question was the pronouncement that what really mattered was ". . . to keep the fire in your belly and plough ahead," an answer that is both profoundly banal and remarkably right.

One of the difficulties for entrepreneurs (or anyone else for that matter!) is the confusion in most people's minds about the difference between risk and uncertainty. Economic theorists see an important distinction between the two. In both, a number of possible outcomes may occur as the consequence of any particular action or path. Risk, however, is identified as a situation in which one can determine the statistical probability of the outcome. For example, if I toss a coin, I can say there's a 50 percent chance it will come up heads and a 50 percent chance it will come up tails. Uncertainty, on the other hand, is what will be the outcome when I ask my boss for a raise. There are a number of possible outcomes. She could say "Yes," "No," "Maybe next month," "If you want more money, plan to work somewhere else," "Don't ask me; I sold the company yesterday," and so on.

Despite what seems to be the greater precision of risk, there are areas of fuzziness. What is the difference between "necessary" and "unnecessary" risk? Perhaps one of the most intriguing perspectives on risk comes from the famous Italian industrialist, Giovanni Agnelli, whose comment on the subject was featured in a full-page ad in the *Financial Times* (London, January 4, 1999). It consisted of two brief sentences: "It's impossible to take an unnecessary risk. Because you only find out whether a risk was unnecessary after you've taken it."

As with most of us, economists feel more comfortable dealing with a theory of choices under conditions of certainty, a situation labeled "riskless choice." According to this model of decision making, (a) each choice has a single, known outcome; therefore (b) individuals should select the choice that they perceive will lead to the most desirable (or least negative) outcome. This surely is a world that, in our more rational moments, we know exists in formal models but rarely in everyday life. The problem, of course, is that in the real world there are no conditions of riskless choice or absolute certainty. There are only situations or scenarios that, "all things being equal" (i.e., staying as they are and allowing for no intrusive innovative conditions), the decision maker will *perceive* as "a sure thing."

Take this example: I can choose to increase my contributions to my pension plan (and, all things being equal, have a greater income in retirement) or I may buy or lease a car and allocate the same amount of money on monthly payments (deriving the current pleasure of a new car). I know that increasing my pension contributions by $500 a month now should allow me to retire at fifty-five with an income large enough to enjoy life while I'm still "young and active," so I opt for the pension plan. But then I stop and reconsider: I'm concerned that my car will start getting expensive to maintain. If I put the money into the pension fund and my car dies, I can't take the money out of my retirement plan without a severe penalty for withdrawal. I can't be without a car. A bird in the hand is worth two in the bush. I opt to buy the new car. But wait a minute, are these conditions certain? What if the market crashes just as I am ready to retire and takes sixteen years to return to the level it was before the crash (as it has on one previous occasion in this century); what if I have a heart attack and die at age forty-eight? Or on the other hand, why should I worry about my car having maintenance problems? It's been running perfectly and I'm conscientious about keeping it up; it has plenty of good mileage left. But then what if. . ., or if. . .? If one allows for perturbation, glitches in the system, new inputs—in short, a future where conditions change—it's difficult (I really want to say impossible, but that would be a certainty to which I'm reluctant to commit myself) to come up with a realistic example of riskless choice.

So, it's not the certainty of the results of choices that is involved in decision making. People act in terms of their expectations and make choices by weighing the utility (achieving desired wants/goals or avoiding unpleasant consequences) of probable outcomes against what they and others believe is the probability of their occurrence: How likely is a market crash, and could it last a decade or more, and could I end up a bag lady? Could I die of a heart attack? Will my car start needing major repairs before my next raise brings the money I need to replace it? Could my company downsize and leave me out of work? What if the government doesn't approve licensing of the new drug my company has developed?

The risk and uncertainty that accompany change are what lead individuals and the aggregates in which they cluster to try to limit the decisions they make to what they perceive as "manageable amounts" of risk and uncertainty. If, as Lewis says, entrepreneurs are innovators "who can turn a situation of unfulfilled potential demand to profit," then (though usually in small ways) we are all, at some times in our lives, entrepreneurs. After all, in the anthropological eye, profit is not solely economic, nor are entrepreneurs limited to financial ventures. As noted above, there are various types of entrepreneurs—political, religious, whatever—and profit may be counted in terms of influence, power, happiness when achieving a goal, joy at seeing one's children realize their aims (especially when the aims are consonant with one's own), or simply the knowledge of a job well done. The bottom line would seem to be that, since the only world that doesn't change is a dead world, despite risk and uncertainty, it's not such a bad thing to have to make choices; after all, the alternative is not having any alternatives.

Chapter Six

Distribution and Exchange

Property as the Missing Link

Distribution and exchange are central to being human and for staying alive. As with reproduction, distribution and exchange require a minimum of two. In reproduction, there is exchange between male and female, then exchange between a caregiver (not necessarily the mother or even a female) capable of providing sustenance for the infant. But more than that, the large brains of our species require us to produce offspring capable of passing through the birth canal but so immature at birth that the young of our species are, for years, incapable of surviving on their own. Our trade-off with nature means that the brains that make it possible to "invent culture" as our primary adaptive tool also require our young to go through a long period of dependency on adult caretakers. It is a period critical for human development. As shown by studies of lost or abandoned children who survive in the wilderness as feral, so-called "wolf children" must be at least about age seven when they start out alone in the wilderness or else they simply die.

Our dependency on others, the ability to communicate our needs and wants, and our cognitive capacity to remember the past, relate that past to the present, and project imagined scenarios for the future, all combine to make humans the animal that, above all others, engages in distributing and redistributing resources. For one thing, we humans carry virtually every animate and inanimate thing from one location to another. Other animals, plants, insects, water, rocks and soil are transported to places in which they do not occur naturally. Further, we build canals, channel rivers, redesign shorelines, dig out tunnels, and mine for minerals. When our settlements grow too crowded, we push our young people out and tell them to colonize some new locale, and whatever the reason for our movement, we carry our sociocultural baggage with us. When we come in contact with others, we usually exchange some of our ways (and genes) for some of their ways (and genes).

Again, distribution and exchange have formed the basis of one of the selective pressures in the evolution of our species. Study your hand and note how useful it is to pick up, grasp, and move things about. Pay attention to all the activities you perform by opposing your thumb to another finger—and try picking up a pin and discover how useful it is to have fingernails. Because we need only two of our four limbs for locomotion, our arms and hands are left free to do other things. That same bipedal posture also allows us to stand upright for long periods of time and permits us to see over long distances. This ability, combined with our optical skills, allows us to see things in depth and, because of our body design, also allows us to turn our heads to scan a wide visual field. If we spot danger, that body design also lets us stoop, climb, crouch, run, crawl, and engage in a number of evasive actions that protect us from animals that are bigger, faster, and frequently more powerful than we are.

This combination of visual ability, upright posture, manual dexterity, and (above all) the brain allows us to invent tools to enhance the natural abilities of our species and carry these artifacts and mentifacts around with us until we need them. We're the only species capable of preparing materials from which we then create clothes, with sleeves or pockets to carry things, or make slings and backpacks, to transport young infants, leaving our hands free to carry weapons to defend ourselves and our young. Further, those weapons—rocks, spears, guns—can be accurately employed to attack as well as to defend.

Humans also have the unique ability to trap and train other animals, birds, or aquatic life so that these other species become subject to our usage of them. They can help plow, carry loads, haul goods in carts, provide food on demand, and have their skins utilized for clothing, shelter, boats, and decoration. They may also be used as gifts or objects of exchange. Because they can be kept alive until we're ready to use them, they provide a storage fund for the future.

All of this points up the fact that humans are disposed to alter the natural distribution of resources. We are continually relocating plants, animals, people, ideas, artifacts and mentifacts from the places where they first occurred to new locales. Though much of this is deliberate, a surprising amount is involuntary, as when we carry disease, viruses, small critters, such as rats, mice, or zebra mussels, as well as lice, fleas, bedbugs, and the like. Unknowingly, we incorporate them into our patterns of mobility.

Production is basic to survival, and the aim of production is to be able to use or use up what we produce. But without a distributional ability, humans would be as vulnerable as other living things to the natural carrying capacity of their various econiches. Like other living things, we would have few responses to environmental changes or to the entry of other predators into our territory. Our population fluctuations would be sensitive to conditions over which we had little or no control; as with other animals, whole regional populations of our species could be wiped out before natural selection or mutations had time to throw up defenses.

However, the most important and unique ability of our species is our capacity to carry sociocultural stuff around in our heads to distribute to others. As with most mobile people who don't want to be hampered in their travels by material items that have weight and bulk, the earliest humans began being human by developing ideas and selecting information to store and retrieve that informed them about the world they inhabited. Information about our surroundings isn't built into our genes. Nor are the languages that we had to invent to talk and think about in this natural, social, and super-natural world. We know how difficult it can be to learn a foreign language. Imagine having to invent one from scratch! No wonder we used the same material tools for so long; we were busy enough trying to invent ways to perceive and think about the space in which we lived. We had to work out that the sun and moon were different and that they rise and set (and why this might matter); why the weather changes over both long and short stretches of something that we had to conceptualize and name. We had to find ways to transmit information about, say, techniques of hunting or gathering; what was good/bad to eat and what was good/bad to do; ideas of how people were related and might be organized to do things as a group that couldn't be done by a single individual (such as hunting large, dangerous animals that were good to eat). We also took time to invent games, riddles, songs, jokes, stories, dances, myths, and so on.

In short, everything we think about, from the most commonplace to the most metaphysical, somehow had to be thought about before we had the components of language with which to think about them. (We've all, at one time or another, gone through the frustrating experience that often leads us to exclaim, "I know what I want to say but I don't know how to say it!") No wonder humans took so long to change from being the most primitive of tool makers to the complex technicians, inventors, and thinkers we are today. The task of inventing language (and the entire universe of stuff we can think about today) had to be accomplished first and was infinitely more difficult than attending to inventing some new artifact for food getting. We can't dig up the physical remains of these activities, but they must have been developed early in human history because they exist in all societies. There are no barriers to their possession, regardless of age, sex, technological level, or education. Despite their diversity from one socioculture to another, they have such underlying similarities that we all recognize a song, dance, or riddle when we encounter them in other sociocultures.

Humans also have long-term memory and are able to invent ways (not the least of which is language) to store, recall, and distribute mental stuff to newcomers who transfer or are born into our group. Thus, for example, the rock art that first appeared some thirty-five thousand years ago is thought to carry such information as what animals were hunted at the site, perhaps at the last time the hunters visited the locale (possibly giving those who later viewed the art the ability to differentiate these bones from those bones) and how the animals from which they came were obtained as well as how to butcher them. This rock art may contain yet undeciphered information. Even before rock art, humans may have used other ways to record useful information for future use, information now lost to us because the materials used have long decayed. It may be, for example, that early humans invented ways to map out travel routes, perhaps by using twigs tied with grass, and adding pebbles to mark significant landmarks—much the same way the ancient Polynesian navigators recorded sailing routes, including information on prevailing winds and currents, as they explored the Pacific islands. All that would remain today of such charts would be a seemingly random scatter of pebbles that even the most dedicated archeologist might overlook.

Human memory is even more useful than rock art or charts; combined with language, we humans are able to store and retrieve an infinitely greater amount of information than other species are able to control. If, for example, a drought caused customary water holes to dry up, shared language would enable the elders to tell younger group members not to keep heading north (however they had marked such a direction) because they recalled that long ago, at another time when water became scarce, the group went that way. But, after traveling a distance of "two hands of sunrises," all had nearly died before the survivors reached water. And if, for whatever reasons, north was their only feasible option, at least this time the group would have been forewarned to carry extra food and water (or at least remember the discovery that sucking on pebbles helped relieve their thirst).

All of this may seem terribly simple, but no other species comes even close to possessing such a complete package of these kinds of survival skills. Once invented or discovered, the uses to which such skills may be put are expanded beyond the need for immediate survival. They're employed for recognizing future risk and uncertainty, trying to avoid them, and making preparations to cope with them.

On the one hand, another thing that we humans may have learned very early in our history is that while we can gain the resources that others possess simply by seizing them (as one animal seizes another's meat or mate), the consequences of such attempts can be unpleasant. On the other hand, our ancestors also learned that it is possible to work out arrangements where we can offer to exchange and share goods and services. We came to accept that if, for example, we cared for animals, our gods, our children, our incapacitated elderly or ill, our neighbors—those animals, gods, children, elderly/ill, and neighbors were usually able to reciprocate by providing us with something useful in return. Lacking something possessed by another individual or group, we could fight for it, take it by stealth—or we could arrange an exchange. Thus, while distribution and exchange didn't always eliminate conflict (and could even occasionally create it), techniques for utilizing them reduced its potential considerably.

Because exchange and distribution can themselves generate conflict, and there are always rules to manage the way they're done. Indeed, sharing and exchanging within a specific group have been suggested as one explanation for the invention of nonkin-based groups, that is, associations of one sort or another that create new groups with new loyalties. Groups with a membership and loyalties that cut across household or kin lines have, at the least, a potential for defusing disputes and conflict among households or different family lines (consider clan feuds). Members of such nonkin groups often undergo a series of rituals—rites of passage—that help cement bonds among them. Rather than limiting cooperation and sharing to their own households and kin, members of such groups will also cooperate, share, and exchange resources with other association members, and this also helps to minimize or cut across lines of potential cleavage and conflict. In short, by recognizing that family self-interest can be destructive of a broader social aggregate that offers benefits unavailable to those in minimal, isolated households, humans have invented social structures and processes that encourage cooperative distribution and exchange within nonkin groups.

In any case, determination of the "who, what, where, when, and how" of distribution and exchange is never haphazard, casual, or random. Goods and services are always channeled through various pathways that have signposts, for example, rules, norms, secular laws, conventions of etiquette, statements of ethics or morality, supernatural directives. These determine or guide distribution. Obviously, all of these also have an effect on both production and consumption.

Distribution and exchange make up a complex system that is so important for humans that, for both economists (such as Kenneth Boulding and Amartya Sen) and anthropologists (e.g., Cyril Belshaw and Raymond Firth), the process of flow of resources among people was and is at the very heart of human socioculture. When this movement is flawed or breaks down, there are always grave consequences. Sen (see Bibliography), for example, has argued that famine need not exist in the modern world. There is, he maintains, no scarcity of food for humans, only inadequacies in the food distribution system; for example, prices make it difficult or even impossible to afford food (and the market does not provide goods where there are few, if any, buyers). What follows is an attempt to dissect the systems of distribution and exchange so that we might better understand how to address some of their problems.

There is a popular model that presents the circulation of what people produce as being of two major types. First, there is the distribution of goods and services produced within a narrow group of individuals who cooperate or are in some way practically linked in producing the resources they use for their own day-to-day living. Second, there is the distribution of goods and services that are produced for the purpose or expectation of exchange. Thus, we have a distinction between goods and services whose value is based on use versus those whose value resides in their potential for exchange. An alternative model argues that goods/services produced for exchange also have "use value" for the producers; they produce something in order to receive something in exchange that is of equal or greater use to them than what they produce.

In either case, when we produce something, both we and our product enter into a chain of dependency. We want something, but the only way we can obtain it is by entering into a relationship with other producers. Goods and services may be viewed as either stationary or circulatory, either remaining in the context in which they are produced or becoming subject to a centrifugal distribution pattern. In the latter case, goods move beyond their point of production and link the original producers to others in a chain with an almost infinite capacity to keep extending outward. Producers become linked with at least one other person or group who may be the final consumer or, very often, are simply links to still other producers, distributors, or consumers—and so on, ad infinitum.

Now, it's generally accepted that the transition from stationary to circulatory production was well under way no later than some five thousand years ago (probably first in the Near East but occurring independently in other places as well). And there's evidence for the circulatory exchange of exotic trade items as early as the Upper Paleolithic, some 25,000 years ago. Whenever and wherever this first occurred, production for exchange became an increasingly important component of sociocultural systems. As is usually the case with human innovation, the reasons for this shift vary, and it's difficult to describe the circumstances because there are many gaps in the information available to us. Trying to describe the process is somewhat like trying to determine what a completed jigsaw puzzle looked like before someone lost 90 percent of the pieces.

The production of goods and services for exchange presents a far more complicated situation than producing goods for one's own use. Even though we've studied only a small percentage of all the human societies that have existed and have uncovered only a rather scanty amount of information about the ways people move things around, we still find ourselves confronting a bewildering array of ways people have invented to distribute and exchange goods and services. In order to understand patterns and processes of distribution and exchange we need to know the properties of what is being transferred, namely, property itself.

One of the most important and certainly bewildering concepts playing a major role in distribution is embodied in the term "property." Before anything is distributed and, especially, before anything is exchanged, allocated, or given as a gift, there is a need to establish precisely what is being distributed (e.g., if you hire the services of a secretary, do services include making coffee?) and, once it's been distributed or exchanged, what the recipients are allowed to do with it. Are they expected to return it (with interest)? Redistribute it to some other(s)? Are there certain restrictions on its use? Did the giver have the legitimate right to distribute or exchange it away? And even so, do others still have some residual rights to it at some future time (e.g., do grandparents have visitation rights to see their grandchildren despite having "given their daughter away" in marriage)? Are there some goods or services that can never be transferred? What kinds of tangible and intangible stuff is considered property? Indeed, do we even have any kind of definition of property that is general enough that we may talk about property cross-culturally and cross-temporally? The rest of this chapter will discuss these issues.

Problems surrounding the idea of property probably have a greater impact on our daily lives than any other issue because many of them touch on the question of what to do about the market, that economic abstraction that addresses the way that production, circulation, and consumption are affected by price—and how price is affected by them. At the root of the debate is what to do when the market fails, that is, when the balance between demand and supply get out of kilter, resulting in resources priced so that people don't want them, can't get them (because it doesn't pay a producer to make them available), or can't afford them. Many economists argue that, left alone, the law of supply and demand will establish a balance that allows the market to work to the best advantage of both producers and consumers. But just as many economists say this is hogwash. What if, for example, too little demand produces unemployment? What if demand, price, and the desire for maximum profit lead to reckless disregard for the welfare of workers or the unwise use of natural resources? What if, in an attempt to meet rising prices, workers seek higher wages, which leads to a vicious cycle of higher prices, leading to higher wages, leading to higher prices, and so forth, with the result being runaway inflation that erodes the purchasing power (and, worse, the savings) of the public?

Now, there never has been and never will be a totally unmanaged or free market. People have been tinkering with both marketplaces and the more recent market system for several thousand years. People with ideas about how to guide or manage the market when it fails to work in its ideal way fall into two main camps. One camp argues that such failures are only short-term, that over the long haul the aggregate of self-interested producers and consumers whose collective behavior constitutes what we label "the market" will respond in ways that allow the system to self-correct and return to working as it should, performing beneficially for everyone. It does no good, they argue, for governments to intervene by providing incentives for businesses to provide jobs, establishing price ceilings or subsidizing producers so that prices to consumers are affordable, or using public resources obtained through taxes, tariffs, and the like, as well as using its regulatory capabilities to guide or manage both the market and the provision of resources (jobs, health care, housing, etc.). To date, the noninterventionists argue, there is little evidence that the people in government who make such decisions have either the correct incentives or the necessary information to be any more competent at fine-tuning the system than those who make up the market itself.

In the other camp are those who argue that it is the role of government to work to resolve certain problems of its citizens. We all depend on government to do the job we pay it to do, mainly, to offer ways to deal with and protect us from the multitude of crises and catastrophes that can lead to great suffering and intense personal tragedies. People want assistance now, not in the long run for, as the famous economist J. M. Keynes pointed out, "in the long run we're all dead." Sadly, some may be dead sooner than others.

We humans like to think that one of the things that differentiates our species from others is that most of us, most of the time, appear to care about the ills, woes, and suffering of others, that even when our lives are comfortable, we are distressed by and empathize with the problems that other humans cannot manage on their own. So, for example, those of us with jobs worry about the unemployed; those of us who are healthy are concerned as to how the economically marginal will meet the high costs of medical care. We who are well fed will try to find ways to help feed the hungry, and those of us who have secure lives will feel compassion for and try to assist those forced from their homes by natural catastrophe or war. Even those dedicated to the idea of a free market—people who believe that the self-correcting (so-called invisible hand of the) market will ultimately balance supply and demand—are not immune to the demands of their consciences and the pull of their emotions to step in and do something to help others—now.

Unfortunately, "the devil is in the details," as the old saying goes. How exactly can we intervene in the market without risking the possibility that the intervention will lead to still more imbalances, more catastrophic consequences? A popular technique these days is to bring together a variety of people with varied interests and points of view to negotiate a consensual solution. Economist Ronald Coase (see Bibliography) has won the Nobel Prize for his Coase Theorem, considered by many to be the best intervention solution to date. It requires a variety of people with a stake in settling a problem to sit down and arrive at a mutually agreeable contract. If all agree on how to address a problem, they will be willing to help make it work. How, Coase asks, can people with sharply contrasting, even mutually exclusive positions about the distribution of resources arrive at common ground? His answer: Let the negotiations begin with property rights to the contested resources being clearly assigned. Let us carefully specify particular contexts and then identify, for all involved, what property rights they and others have within that context. This will be sufficient to create a rational market, one in which the final settlement allows all to attain the best or most "satisficing" outcome.

This is an interesting idea, but in many if not most cases it is difficult to operationalize. Take, for example, the issue of managing the New England coastal marine resources. Who are the people who believe they have rights to these resources? Even a brief listing will have to include commercial and recreational fishery users; those who buy and process commercial fish; shipping interests; conservationists; marina owners; those who provide recreational boating services (e.g., whale watching and sports fishing rental vessels); retirees who own beachfront property; sand dredging companies; offshore mining interests; the National Park Service, the U.S. Coast Guard, and the National Marine Fisheries Services (Federal agencies that speak for the public at large); shore-based businesses that provide goods and services to those who pursue the fisheries; and tourist interests. How would those within each group reach consensus? There is a wide diversity of opinion among those in each category. Next, how would we price both the resources and the rights to them? With a crisis (even a catastrophe) upon us, do we have, as one poet has put it, "world enough and time" to undertake what is sure to be lengthy and drawn-out negotiations? What would be happening to the resource (as well as those dependent on it for their livelihood) while we worked to resolve the issue?

Thus, Coase's suggestion could work, but he has more faith in the reasonableness of humans than I do. All negotiations operate under time constraints. Crucially, most decisions must be made before the crisis takes a new turning and the terms of the issue shift. When this happens, the old questions and information pertaining to them often become irrelevant; the playing field has changed while attempts to resolve the problem were going on. Thus, for example, federally appointed and diverse members of regional fishery councils—negotiating arenas designed to address the issue of declining fish stocks—took so long in hammering out who had what rights (including the very contentious question of whether a specific resource was owned by everyone or no one) that years dragged by without any workable resolution. Meanwhile, the stocks of certain species were so heavily fished that stocks declined to the point where they became threatened with extinction by the 1990s.

Examples like this lead to the conclusion that we have reached a point where we must become better informed at a general level about such issues. Despite the wide variation in the what, how, who, and where of the kinds of resources being addressed and the complexities that surround the various rights, duties, privileges, and responsibilities attached to each, relative to access to and use of them, we must increase our capabilities for having some kind of consensual understanding of the basic components of the debate. Otherwise, the problems will continue to overwhelm us. The evidence to date is that our lack of knowledge about such things will, in particular negotiating contexts, lead us to waste valuable time trying to settle things from positions where, too often, we go around and around simply in an effort to find common ground from which to *begin* negotiating. A fundamental problem is that all involved can be unaware of the unarticulated (and, we must assume, equally legitimate) premises that underwrite another's position. The result, not uncommonly, is that people believe they have settled on a position only to be told at the next meeting that "You never said that," "We never agreed to that," "That hasn't been brought up before," or "I assumed you meant . . ."

So what follows is an attempt to increase our understanding of why we take so much for granted and how much we just assume "everybody knows that" or "that's just ordinary common sense" when, in reality, everybody doesn't know it and much of what we believe is neither common nor, by the standards of others, sensible.

First, the phrase "private property" is really an oxymoron. Property is never private—if by "private" one means that some resource, currently in the possession of an individual or corporate group, may never be removed from the control of whoever presently possesses it and, more significantly, if that "private property," property that is "owned," entitles the owner(s) to do with that property what they will.

Second, whether distributed (transferred) or destroyed (consumed, burned up, torn down) and whether tangible (as in a piece of land, water, or artifact) or intangible (as in my labor energy, your idea, a song, a formula—e.g., magical, ritual, or chemical—a copyright, a scenic view, or clean air), we must identify just what is leaving our possession and what we retain. Not only do specific sociocultures categorize different resources differently, but there is wide variability among groups as to what can or cannot leave our possession and how that may occur.

Third, anthropologists have taken the idea of property and have argued that it makes more sense to see the vast array of resources that we may label as property as best defined as any resource to which we attach a bundle of assorted rights, duties, privileges, and obligations pertaining to utilization.

Take the "simple" case of land. Despite an emphasis in Euroamerican society on private property, it's obvious to all of us that land may be held as private property or as public lands. Private property is ours to do with as we will—or so we tend to believe. Public land belongs to all the citizenry and is under the stewardship of our legitimate government, whether an individual city or at the national—and, these days, even the international—level.

However, if you look at the three points made above you will see how, for example, there is a wide range of rules that differentiate the distribution, use, alienation, or destruction of land, public or private. These rules have changed over the centuries. When Europeans first colonized North America (and other parts of the world as well), the concepts they then held about land created much of the dissention that took place between the Amerindians already in place and the invaders. For one thing, Europeans believed that any "proper" society was organized with a monarch at the top and various ennobled individuals who held their lands as a result of assorted arrangements between the monarch and themselves. Commoners, those who were not landlords, were at the bottom of the hierarchy. The very first European arrivals saw few such rulers, and even when they did (as in the case of the Aztec and Inca empires), they subordinated the rulers, as well as their subjects, their wealth, and their lands by right of conquest.

Since, in the eyes of the Europeans, groups that lacked governmental and ecclesiastical hierarchies were primitive, childlike, or savage and, at the least, "undeveloped," such sociocultures were made subjects of and subject to countries with "civilized rule, civilized law, civilized religion." For the native people, this arrangement was both nonsensical (it violated their rules of common sense) and, to understate the case, a tad irritating (until the point was forcibly explained with superior weaponry).

The Europeans arrived with charters signed by monarchs of their own governments, bits of paper that entitled the newcomers to settle the land and gave them the rights to leave such land to their heirs or, if they chose, to rent or sell it to some other approved individual. Such private property rights didn't mean that the European monarchs who issued the charters saw themselves any less the real owners of the land, and the owners in the first instance. Settlers had various duties and obligations; for example, they were expected to pay taxes and band with others of their group to defend the territories of their monarchs from seizure by representatives of some other monarch. As in Europe, some rights relating to the land were retained by the community or the government back in Europe. Certain individual trees, for example, tall, straight, hardwood trees critical for making the spars of sailing ships necessary for the European merchant and naval fleets, were marked as Crown property. In some locales a King's Ranger could, on the spot, try, convict, and execute for treasonous behavior anyone caught cutting down such trees—even if the tree cutter was on his own land.

There were, of course, people who believed themselves to be honest, decent, and God-fearing. They didn't simply seize the land from the previous inhabitants by killing, enslaving, or otherwise ridding themselves of them. Rather, they sat down and negotiated with those they believed were leaders, empowered to negotiate the exchange of the land. Although the price paid for the land was far below European figures, the Indians seemed willing to accept the amount given (e.g., gifts of beads, cloth, and assorted trinkets). The colonists bought the land by what they considered fair and square, honest and aboveboard marketplace dealings. We must forget, for a moment, that there were serious gaps in the knowledge that each group had of the other's culture (including its language). Further, as anyone knows who has ever tried to read legal documents relating to real estate sales, the legal technicalities can make things difficult indeed, especially for those who have never before encountered such concepts, exchanges, or negotiations. We now know that information began to be circulated throughout various Amerindian groups that something very strange was happening as a result of their dealings with Europeans. Word began to spread that negotiations—especially any that involved the establishment of settlements and access to the land and its resources—were proving disastrous for the native inhabitants.

Scholars are now finding evidence that shows how, initially, the majority (perhaps all) of the Indian negotiators believed that they were giving gifts or were bartering use rights to resources in return for, say, muskets or cloth; that all that was going on was an exchange that would permit the newcomers to settle peacefully in the region and use the land as well as its resources to house, feed, and clothe themselves. That the land itself could (or would) be transferred by any other means than the right of conquest was totally alien.

At first, when peaceful exchanges were concluded and the Whites settled in, the Indians expected and continued to do what they had always done on such lands: they hunted, fished, collected, cut down trees, and moved through them on trading or war expeditions. European settlers, however, saw such actions as an outrageous abrogation of the treaties and bills of sale that made these lands the "private property" of their new European owners. "The savages were trespassing." To teach them a lesson about the sanctity of property that civilized law had brought them, to teach them that "a deal was a deal," trespassers were beaten or, worse, killed (as horse thieves were killed right up to this century). Indians were to be taught, one way or another, how important it was to honor contracts.

True, some Amerindians soon began to sense that Europeans thought they actually had, somehow, gained control over the earth itself. Europeans, they came to realize, did not simply see the land as a surface on which to settle or move through, or from which to take resources. They controlled the actual earth itself. When, at first, a few suggested this in tribal council meetings, their comments were received with bewilderment and even some degree of amusement. It was all really beyond understanding: "Do the White men plan to fill up their baskets and carts and haul the earth away with them when they move on?" It took some time before the Indians fully grasped the concepts of just what property rights they had lost and the extent to which they had alienated what, for them, was as incapable of being "owned" as it was of being "alienated." Imagine, for example, if you were told someone wanted to purchase the air you breathe. Incomprehensible! How can anyone own the air? How can one buy or sell it? Many once said the same of water, but in the 1990s in some parts of the world, a gallon of water now costs more than a gallon of gasoline.

Eventually Amerindians grasped the European concept of the world. They realized that, while they understood about bartering goods and services and about producing goods and services for exchange, the Whites had discovered a way to make the earth itself a marketable commodity. Again, to get some sense of the Indians' confusion, remember that in most of our textbooks we learn that a commodity is usually defined as "something produced for exchange." This being so, how then do we explain how one can "produce" land? It's not surprising that, regardless of whether the land was transferred by treaty, bought, or simply taken as today urban squatters take over uninhabited buildings, for the Amerindian all such transfers involved theft of or disregard for their rights. Any transfers were illegitimate because rights had been transferred that (a) did not exist and (b) therefore could not have been transferred, and thus (c) had never been alienated. Conclusion: If such rights were imposed after contact, any contracts based on earlier Amerindian law were rendered invalid and would have to be renegotiated now that both parties were in agreement as to what rights were involved and that these were transferable.

If you're still having problems understanding the Amerindian point of view, try this: Imagine, for a moment, that John Smith buys a piece of property on your block, the last empty lot on the street. But instead of building a house, the next thing you know, there's a constant stream of digging equipment, and dirt is excavated to the depth of twelve inches on the entire lot. Dump trucks carry away the soil and then nothing more happens. The lot of land and the earth removed were the new owner's property, but you and your neighbors now have a deep hole on the block, ugly and a risk to children. Was the owner within his rights? How do you react? What responsibilities do you think he has? What rights do you have?

Another problem (and a very real one that appears in today's news): When you buy a burial plot, how far down does your ownership extend? Could someone buy a second or third plot above or below yours? What do you think of a cemetery owner who parcels plots into, say, ten plots of 3' each, down to a depth of 30'? This is actually happening and most people are incensed by the "unethical" behavior of the seller. But how different is this from a crypt in a crematorium where boxes (for ashes of the deceased) are stacked row on row?

The private property concept can get even more fuzzy. You buy a piece of land and it's yours to do with as you will—you think. But let's say that instead of hauling away the earth, you want to build a gas station. Will you be able to get a building permit? Is the property zoned for business? These and a host of other conditions indicate that, despite the land having been bought and paid for, owners can't do with it as they will; the public has rights in that "private" property. In many towns in North America and in Europe, owners are prohibited from doing any external remodeling that will "violate the historic integrity" of the community. For example, in Santa Fe, New Mexico—a town that the Spanish invaders built when they entered the region in 1620—no one is permitted to install, say, a bay window in their home; it's been mandated that this feature would contaminate the "traditional Indian and Hispanic architectural roots" of the town. Similarly, Lunenburg, Nova Scotia, appeals to a growing tourist trade because the town still preserves the appearance it developed during its peak period of prosperity as a fishing and shipping port. But at least some townsfolk resent laws that prevent them from building homes or making architectural changes that reflect their own taste. They argue that the laws deny the reality of how their town, like any other, has changed with the times. "It's like being on exhibit in a museum," grumbles one inhabitant.

Try covering the front of your house with subway-type graffiti; try letting your lawn go unmowed and creating a wilderness; announce that you've decided to donate your home to an organization that will use it as a halfway house for recovering addicts. You'll soon find out what rights and duties you have. These days, if you're a fisherman in New England, don't take it for granted that you may continue to stack your several hundred lobster traps on the front lawn, as fishing families have done since the early eighteenth century. Urban retirees, now active in town affairs, may like the ambience of a "quaint fishing village" but don't like a pile of dilapidated traps, nor do they want the smell of dead fish to disturb the quality of their afternoon cocktail hour on their "sun deck with ocean view." So, this traditional right is now being phased out in many coastal communities.

And there are covenants, some legal, others illegal and imposed covertly. These are rules that identify certain restrictions which, at time of purchase, are attached to your use or sale of your property. The way such restrictions are operationalized may be subtle; real estate agents simply don't show the property to some categories of would-be buyers ("not our kind")—despite the fact that such discriminatory marketing practices could be successfully challenged in the courts; or, at an open auction sale, the neighbors will band together to outbid "the wrong sort." The latter, the closed-sale technique, is practiced in some locales in rural Northern Ireland. While not all covenants are geared to racial or religious discrimination (they may address uses to which the land can be put), the *Wall Street Journal* (L. E. Wynter, May 5, 1999) has reported economist Stephen Ross's claim that any such agreements result in neighborhood segregation that not only limits housing choices for the targets of the discriminatory acts but in the process limits their labor-market choices, and thus their labor-market opportunities. Says Ross,

"You don't take a job if you can't find a place to live."

There's more: Everyone knows that if you fail to pay the taxes on land that's been in your family since, say, 1867, the property will be taken for those unpaid taxes, no matter how long you've owned the property or how long the taxes have been being paid. But consider: These taxes could be viewed as a kind of land-rent to the real owners—the city or county (representing the citizens as a whole)—and thus, the land is not really "your private property." This may seem similar to the case of you going to a bank and borrowing money on your property—failure to repay the loan allows the bank to seize the property; ditto the pawn shop when you leave, say, a $1,500 Rolex watch as security for a $150 loan for ninety days. However, a moment's thought will reveal how different are taxes from loan pledges. Note, too, that for centuries, land sale contracts have often excluded mineral rights or sometimes (in the public good) exclusive access rights to the water. Private property? Just try burying your cat (let alone your grandfather) in the backyard of the family home.

But what about those public lands held in trust for all the citizenry—of which you're one? Even though they "belong" to you, you need a permit to use most of them. Try driving your car without paying a fee for a license plate on it—even though it's your car and your tax dollars have been used to provide public streets. Further, in the United States, a portion of the Fifth Amendment of the Constitution states that ". . . private property [shall not] be taken for public use, without just compensation"—but note that provision merely insures you "just compensation" (to be determined by the government), not that the property is safe from being taken. In addition, public use is whatever government says it is; it may be an urban renewal program, a highway—or a football stadium. And another thing: Those public lands—for example, our national park system—may be closed indefinitely to the public for various reasons, such as preserving an archeological site, protecting an endangered species, or respecting an area that an Amerindian tribe has claimed as sacred grounds. Blue Lake, part of Kit Carson National Forest in northern New Mexico that is sacred to the Taos Indians, is one locale off limits to park visitors. In this latter case, although Indians and non-Indians are all American citizens, some citizens have more rights than others.

On the other hand, there are many types of "stuff" that we assume are in the public domain and are free for general use—but they are not. The song most of us sing to celebrate a birthday was written in this century and, not too long ago, had its copyright renewed. When used commercially, a fee is owed to the heirs of the original composers. As with an individual's genes, there are patents, copyrights, and a maze of regulations and laws now constraining activities that just a few generations ago were neither private nor a general public good; they were, if you will, "unthinkable" property, never considered capable of having property rights assigned to them.

Here's another example of a lost property right. Monsanto, one of the world's largest chemical firms (but now identifying itself as a "Life Science" company), has begun producing a potato called "NewLeaf," genetically modified (GM) to include a bacterial toxin—an organic insecticide known as Bt—that will make the potato resistant to potato beetles. But the potatoes also include another genetic characteristic in the altered DNA of the product. This second gene has been spliced into NewLeaf DNA in order to permit a Monsanto representative to identify a NewLeaf potato on the spot. Now, in the traditional scheme of things, one grows another crop of potatoes by planting eyes from the current crop. NewLeaf potatoes are still capable of being reproduced in this way, but this form of reproduction is legally prohibited. Monsanto has patented the NewLeaf, and when the farmer purchases NewLeaf seeds from Monsanto, a contract stipulates the buyer will not utilize any of the current crop for future plantings. Rather, next year, the farmer will have to go back to Monsanto and purchase new seeds. And the next year, and the next year. . . .

And it's not just potatoes: Currently, the Federal Court of Canada is hearing a case involving a farmer, one Percy Schmeiser of Saskatchewan. Though he's refused to use such seeds, he is being sued by Monsanto because they discovered GM canola growing in his fields. His claim: Some of the material must have entered his fields accidentally, perhaps blown from trucks that pass by his farm, carrying the seeds. Question: If the courts support his position, will he be entitled to countersue Monsanto for contaminating his crops? The case is being carefully tracked internationally because, as Mark Nichols reports Schmeiser as saying (*Maclean's*, May 17, 1999), ". . . where do Monsanto's rights end and mine begin?"

In one way, GM crops are something new. Rather than spraying crops with insecticides, the DNA of the seed will be modified to make the crops resistant to insect and disease infestation. However, in order to receive a return on the research and development costs, Monsanto (and the U.S. Department of Agriculture, which has cofunded the research) jointly hold patents that prohibit anyone unlicensed (i.e., buyers of Monsanto's seeds) from taking the seed and using it for next year's crops. Not only do the seeds' DNA contain genetic features that protect it, they also contain an identity marker and a terminator gene to prevent a black market.

Monsanto argues that GM is simply a variant of the cross-breeding that humans have long employed to modify a plant's or animal's genes. As for sterility, well, when you buy a mule, you don't also buy its (re)productive rights; mules (the result of cross-breeding a horse and a donkey) are naturally sterile—just as the eggs you buy in today's supermarkets are not capable of producing chickens.

In June 1999, however, the Rockefeller Foundation weighed into the debate on the side of those who wished to stop further research in this area. Rich with financial resources, politically influential, and with powerful international connections, this foundation's action led Monsanto to announce in October 1999 that it would not commercialize the terminator gene. This was the first sign by an American firm that it was taking the general outcry against GM crops seriously.

What we can say as a result of this review of the diversity of and confusion about the rights, duties, privileges, and responsibility relative to the distribution of goods and services is this: all sociocultures identify some sorts of property—and private property at that, though those private rights may be exercised by a corporate group rather than an individual. We also are able to note that the history of property is as marked by trends to limit rights as it has been to expand them. What once was open access to any who wished to utilize it has gradually become surrounded with a variety of duties and responsibilities that put limitations on use. The concept of "the commons" emerged as a way to manage and preserve resources. Further, as populations expanded, a broadening range of people were deprived of use rights; the individuals or groups who occupied the social positions that gave access to certain resources became increasingly limited—only particular families, clans or lineages, religious groups; only native-born members of the community; only free citizens but not slaves. Members of a certain class or caste, women, even occupation groups, might be excluded. For every property right that has been broadened, there are many more that have been curtailed or lost.

Take, for example, the information and knowledge as well as the kin, friends, and work contacts you accumulate through the years. Most people think of all these as their resources, weightless baggage that can be carried from place to place. Nowadays, however, it's not uncommon that, when individuals join or leave a company, they are required to sign a contract agreeing not to utilize any information, knowledge, or contacts acquired while in the service of their current or previous employer. This, of course, may impose serious limitations on an individual's employability—if for no other reason than because a potential employer might be loathe to risk lengthy, expensive, and highly publicized legal battles. But a resource that can't be utilized is, by definition, no longer a resource. Is this a legitimate limitation on one's traditional property rights—or have such barriers to portability always been an obligation accepted by mobile workers?

It seems obvious that one's career is a kind of property, but recently, as growing numbers of women have built up their professional employment histories, the differential career property rights of spouses are becoming a point of marital conflict: Both spouses are being required to decide how to balance individual career rights against the traditional rights and privileges, as well as duties and obligations, in the relationship established or implied in the marriage contract. Divorce settlements may include monetary transfers centering around career costs incurred during the marriage.

Anthropologists have grown increasingly aware of the subtleties in identifying property cross-culturally and cross-temporally. However, just as buyers in a flea market may not be aware that the merchandise they have just purchased is not legally owned by them (because the seller was offering goods obtained by theft), we often discover it's easy to be deceived. Indeed, the difficulty of dealing with "stolen property" is particularly interesting, not least because, as in the case of the Amerindians discussed above, a subjugated population or oppressed minority may argue that the original taking was what constituted the theft. It's not unusual for conquerors to create laws that legitimate their usurpation of the resources of those conquered, all the while criminalizing attempts by the victims to reclaim their property. The subordinate group will first (a) deny the legitimacy or the laws ("it is only legalized theft") and then (b) set out to liberate their stolen property. Thus, for example, (the possibly mythic) Robin Hood stole from the Norman conquerors who made themselves both ennobled and rich with the property and loot they seized from the Anglo-Saxon inhabitants. Denying the legitimacy of Norman rule and law, Robin and his band "took from the rich" (Normans) to give to the poor—that is, they snatched back what they saw as illegally seized properties in order to return them to their rightful owners. The "merrie band" established themselves as "free" forest dwellers and gleefully accepted the tag of "outlaws" to proclaim their ability to live outside and in defiance of the "illegitimate Norman legal code" that had been imposed. Ironically, in one of the more popular versions, Robin Hood is a Saxon nobleman, deprived of his land and position by the Normans. Yet the Saxons were themselves invaders who in earlier times conquered, stole from, and ennobled themselves at the expense of the Angle residents.

Similarly, wherever there were slaves bound by laws made by slave owners, one wonders how anyone with common sense could believe or expect the slaves to accept the legitimacy of the slavery laws.

Finally, there's scarcely a locale anywhere in the world where people do not invade the legal property rights of others because, they argue, underpayments, overcharges, misrepresented or flawed goods and services for which they paid full price (and a host of other rationales) allow them to claim retaliatory rights. For example, students steal books from or cut articles from periodicals in university libraries and claim the theft is justified by "exorbitantly high" fees or various restraints that they claim deny them their right of access. Students also point to faculty who steal information and ideas from their students—who may also be charged with having stolen ideas and information from the faculty. Both groups offer some sort of claim to a legitimate right to the resource. Employees take home office supplies; conduct personal business on company time; take sick days to go shopping or to attend a ball game; extend coffee and lunch breaks; or use a public agency vehicle for personal travel. These resources are appropriated because, for one reason or another, the employees feel entitled to compensate themselves. However, not a few employers consider these activities a form of theft.

Certain forms of behavior by officeholders and public or private employees are labeled "theft" or corruption by their colleagues, the company, or the citizenry. Individuals so charged are accused of having taken advantage of their positions to acquire resources (material or nonmaterial) illegally. Not uncommonly, those accused (if they admit to such acts) justify their actions in various ways. Thus, in 1999, charges of bribery and corruption were laid against some of the members of the International Olympic Committee that determines what city will be selected as the site for the next Olympic games. Several committee members had children who received college scholarships or were placed in high-paying jobs in companies headquartered in potential sites. The individuals charged denied the accusations, claiming that although such gifts were accepted, it didn't influence their votes. This may have some truth in it; the same committee members received gifts from a number of cities.

Similarly, there was an uproar in the press when it was discovered that a number of members of the European Parliament put in for reimbursement for first-class air travel between the locales they represented and the meeting site of the Parliament—but had actually traveled by car or train. Some few admitted to this but claimed it was justified, since other legitimate Parliament business had to be paid for out of their own pockets because of what many believed were irrational or misguided bureaucratic rulings.

It's notable that use rights to food and shelter are among the most basic of human rights. All societies recognize the rights of those they designate as "members in good standing" to have access to those fundamental necessities for survival, the resources of food and shelter (though there is a marked degree of variability as to what constitutes good standing). What is available under such access is not necessarily equally distributed among all members, but there is, at least, sufficient accessibility that, if other members have food and shelter, all members collectively and individually have some degree of responsibility to make these resources available to all other legitimate members of the group.

I must issue two caveats concerning the above generalization: First, in a few and relatively rare cases of sociocultural breakdown—as Colin Turnbull has recorded for the Ik of Africa—these rights along with other ethical, moral, and normative guidelines can be left in disarray. The onslaught of invading groups and the collapse of life as it was once lived can leave the members of a socioculture so convinced that the world is in chaos that they come to believe that nothing they held true any longer prevails or makes sense. Historical records provide evidence of such behavior among native peoples whose lands were invaded, whose people were slaughtered or enslaved, or who, like many Australian aborigines, survived as remnant composite groups in ecologically marginal regions. There are similar data from interviews with those who struggled to survive in Nazi concentration camps or in the Soviet Gulags. These kinds of evidence tell us how people respond to what they see as a world gone mad, forced to discard their rules for living that once made sense and left with nothing to put in their place—except, perhaps, with cruel irony, the rules of those who brought the chaos and destruction in the first place.

The second caveat is evident in the phrase "members in good standing" that was employed above. Recall the aggrandizers and others who were labeled witches or, as with Jews in medieval and Renaissance Europe, charged with practicing diabolic rituals. Witness Captain John Smith's edict for the settlers in the Virginia Colony that, "Those who don't work, don't eat" (a sentiment currently being revived in some U. S. states relative to rights to welfare). Note, too, the treatment of strangers, aliens, foreigners, and vagrants or rebellious groups. In all such cases, those who are not "in good standing" are often considered as not entitled to protection and care. Yet, it is often the scarcity of resources that causes both the activities that lead to the loss of one's good standing or (and here again we may face the chicken and the egg problem) leads the group to tighten up the rules of eligibility for access.

However, in all sociocultures, members (or at least those who have the authority to do so) make exceptions to the rules governing property rights at various times and for various reasons. Let me give two examples from modern Euroamerican society.

For many in Euroamerican society, both abortion and the death penalty for certain types of crime deny the general premise that all humans have a right to life; indeed, in the United States it is a right enshrined in the Declaration of Independence by the words, ". . . the right to life, liberty, and the pursuit of happiness." The death penalty for certain criminal acts, it is argued, denies that "inalienable right." People who commit such acts are surely mad and not responsible for their actions—but, as such, they still deserve to live and have their illnesses treated. Though some supernatural agent may impose death or some other ghastly form of punishment, no human agency has the authority to impose "cruel and unusual punishment."

Others take a position similar to those African societies mentioned earlier and believe that some crimes are so heinous, so inhuman, that those committing them have surrendered their claim to being human by failing to act in a humane fashion. Proponents of such a position will often sum it up in such phrases as, "Only an animal could have done that."

The abortion issue is even more problematic because the terms of the debate are based on a variety of ideological convictions (could Coase's model be successfully used here, do you think?). Unlike the debate over the death penalty where there are two opposing positions, the abortion debate involves a continuum. At one end, we have those who hold that from the moment of conception there is life, a special creative act that must not be stifled. Those in the middle hold that abortion should be permitted up to the stage where the fetus has reached a level of biological development that marks an infant capable of surviving when deprived of the mother's support system. At the other extreme of the continuum are those who maintain that so long as the fetus is an integral part of a woman's body, she has the right to do with her body as she will. In other sociocultures, the argument is that infants are not fully human until, for example, they utter their first cry, they are given a name, or they have lived one full year (during which time it is believed they acquire a soul that gives them truly human standing).

The complexities are manifold: Are humans so privileged as compared to other living things—threatening wild beasts or animals that are destroyed in the course of medical experiments; cows, chickens, or fish that we eat; flies that we swat; viruses that we spend millions in attempts to destroy? Do malignant tumors have a right to life? More to the point, should someone hired to be a surrogate mother be allowed to abort a fetus that she has conceived through artificial insemination? If your body is your property, should suicide and euthanasia be an approved form of self-determination and an exercise of one's property rights? If so, at what age is one deemed old enough to make an informed decision to exercise that right? Is the fetus as much property as, say, blood or internal organs that can be sold or given as a gift?

There is currently a hot debate about the desire of some companies to patent certain human genes. The basic question is whether such genes are an inalienable possession of the individual of whom they're a part. However, if fetuses are a woman's property, does a male have no property rights in the genes he contributed and, thus, in the fetus itself? If so, does a woman have the right to destroy the genes of the father? Does he have no rights but only responsibilities for and obligations to support the child if the woman gives birth? Could the grandparents argue that they, too, have rights in a fetus since they, too, contributed their genes? At what point, if ever, does a fetus obtain civil rights as a person and, as some argue, become entitled to protection under the constitutional clause that forbids "cruel and unusual punishment"? (However, it would seem that, logically, this law only pertains to and protects those found guilty of a crime; how can a fetus be given protective rights from excessive punishment when it cannot possibly have committed a crime?)

Further, are children the property of parents? Can they legally be sold, mistreated, or even (as has been the case in some societies) killed if the parents so decide? And do children have any property rights/obligations in their parents? Finally, if life is life and death is death, why do many people who support the right-to-life position also support the death penalty, and why do many who oppose the death penalty support the pro-choice position?

The answer to these questions is yes—for some sociocultures during some period(s) in their histories. This doesn't mean that there may not exist—somehow—some moral absolutes or imperatives. It is possible that such do exist but that only some sociocultures have recognized or discovered them. It does mean that, given the diversity, no one can be sure that it is *their* socioculture that possesses the absolute truth of all things.

Let me hasten to say that I'm not trying to persuade readers as to the legitimacy/illegitimacy of one or the other position. These questions are raised only to illustrate how many aspects are involved when we deal with concepts involving property rights (not leaving aside the additional complexities raised by including privileges, duties, and obligations). The problems are especially acute when we examine the property rights that the State, as the community writ large, has over people. I've tried to illustrate that the terms of debates over resources—and people are a resource par excellence—may among other things, (1) vary in consistency, one resource to the other; (2) vary depending on the resource being discussed and the condition of the resource (e.g., does what you discard remain your property, and are you protected from people searching through your trash to obtain information about you?); (3) shift the resources that may be classed as property (e.g., human life, genes, fetuses); (4) shift ground so that at one time relative to one resource, one has both/neither rights/responsibilities, at other times rights without responsibilities, and at still other times responsibilities without rights.

If this sounds complicated and confusing, it is. That's the point. If I've been able to show how even in our own socioculture the terms of the debate about resources and property are riddled with fuzziness, contradictions, and lack of consensus, you may have a better grasp of what it's like to try to make sense of (let alone genuinely understand) the way humans have treated a multitude of resources in a multitude of places at a multitude of times under a multitude of circumstances. My aim is not to lead you to throw up your hands in despair but to illustrate that such issues permit no simple answers and to emphasize why, despite our growing technological capabilities, dealing with the most important human questions is exponentially more difficult than finding a cure for cancer or putting a human on the moon.

Let me conclude by raising a few more questions about resources and property rights to consider. All of the cases are actual geopolitical situations or conflicts that exist today.

Case 1. A river flows through countries A, B, C. The headwaters of the river are in Country A. Country A decides to build a dam to prevent disastrous floods and provide irrigation water to its farmers. The dam, however, cuts the flow of water reaching countries B and C. Do the latter two have rights to the water? Are these rights more basic than Country A's right to build a dam on its own sovereign land?

Case 2. Country A has a large oil field. Some oil from the field seeps into Country B. Country B drills a well on its own land and the well begins to produce oil that, claims Country A, belongs to it, since the oil is being drained from its deposits. If the wells are not closed, Country A says it will bomb the oil installations. Does Country B have a right to oil it recovers from wells drilled on its land despite the location of the origin? Does Country A have a right to protect its resources?

Case 3. Country A has prohibited the internal sale of a certain automobile on the grounds that government tests have shown the vehicle to be unsafe by its legal safety standards. Country B has no laws or agencies that deal with such matters. Does Country A have the responsibility to prohibit the export of these autos to Country B if the latter is aware of test results but chooses to admit the cars anyway?

Case 4. Country A has strict guidelines to regulate the labor of individuals under the age of fourteen. Its citizens and governing officials see it as their duty to end the exploitation of children by prohibiting the import of goods manufactured with such labor. Country B encourages children between the ages of eight and fourteen to work in factories because the products exported provide much-needed foreign currency to help improve, among other things, weakly developed educational and health care systems. Country B has given a pledge that 20 percent of all export-derived funds will be allocated to expand, especially, educational facilities so that eventually there will be no need for children to perform such work. Country C neither encourages or discourages child labor but maintains that, since other countries have no right to dictate to its government what laws it should apply to its own citizens, any restrictions that another country imposes is a violation of the World Trade Organization Agreement as well as a new form of colonialism and economic imperialism. If Country A will not allow imports from Country C, the latter simply will ship to those who will take them. What options does Country A have in working out a consensual agreement (say, along the lines of Coase's suggestions), and what trade-offs might it make?

Chapter Seven

Exchange and Distribution

Routes of All Evil?

For all the flaws and inequities of the market economy, few people, when given a choice between access to it or living lives of "affluent poverty"—meeting basic needs and satisfying a few modest wants—choose the latter. Ironically, some of the very anthropologists who are least comfortable with (or outright hostile to) global capitalism, also encourage and help arrange for members of nonmarket societies to produce crafts for sale in nearby cities, open up their villages to ecotourism, or assist in setting up organizations that encourage "the natives" to produce local products and then use that same system of global marketing to encourage Euromerican consumers to buy, for example, "organically grown, natural rain forest products." Their aim, of course, is to produce commodities that, when traded, will enable such marginal people to obtain resources that will improve their quality of life. They are, in short, opting for the "route" of all evil, global capitalism, in order to obtain the "root" of all evil, money.

But this is a choice we all have to make: to what extent are we willing to take the Bad News with the Good News? My exploration of this issue is intended to provide some insight into how such choices emerge and how better to make the decisions that, in the long run, will seem to have been satisfying. Most of us already know that there's no free lunch, but, on the other hand, few of us want to have a costly meal that leaves us unhappy with our choice of restaurant or meal. The desire to get what we've paid for is what makes for restaurant critics; when deciding between alternatives, each of us wants to be as well equipped as possible to measure the potential costs and benefits of each.

However, in another of those paradoxes that are becoming more and more common, even as computers and improved analytical models make it easier to gather information and make some sort of sense of it, it's becoming increasingly difficult to understand what's happening or predict what might happen. You and I—and most of the world—live in what is commonly labeled "the new Global Economy," a world in which Thomas Friedman (*The Lexus and the Olive Tree: Understanding Globalization*) observes a barefoot cigarette vender in Bangkok checking her stock market investments, while large investment firms may speed billions of dollars (though in all kinds of currency) around the world every day. It's a world, Friedman argues, in which the local and traditional (the olive tree) is being overwhelmed by the global economy (the Lexus). One might think that in an increasingly homogeneous and interdependent world, and with the growing sophistication of our tools, decision making would become easier. Yet it hasn't, and at least part of the reason is that although some parts of the global economy are becoming unified, others remain stubbornly local. For all the talk about, say, the McDonaldsization of the world, consumption still shows marked differences, one area to another, one generation to the other, one socioeconomic group to another. More interrelated, but still showing distinctive variations, is production. For a variety of reasons (e.g., geography or national infrastructure), different regions still have different competitive advantages over other regions. Currently, it is distribution that is showing the highest degree of homogenization and integration. But even this statement needs to be used with caution.

Before examining why, let's think for a minute about that convenient but deceptive phrase, "global economy"—deceptive because, despite increased interdependency of world production and the presence of global-market brands such as Coca-Cola, despite the growing presence of online suppliers (wholesale and retail) who are conducting a growing amount of trade in cyberspace, there is yet to exist a single, fully integrated economic system with, most important, any centralized tracking or regulatory unity (indeed, as I plan to show, with good planning and luck, such a system will never come to pass). Rather, all the available evidence indicates there are multiple, albeit overlapping, regional and sectorial economies. Though each is sensitive to activities and events in all the others, they still maintain a surprising degree of independence from each other. As just indicated, this is probably A Good Thing: In a truly singular global economy, all sectors, regions, and countries—as well as their institutions (and not only those marked as specifically economic)—would be so intermeshed with all other parts that even a relatively small (let alone a major) disturbance in one component would create a chain reaction, and such interdependency would carry a high-risk potential for disaster on a global scale. We would, to use an old phrase, have all our eggs in one basket. Who would or could we trust to help restore the system's equilibrium? Who would be capable of bailing out the region(s) in trouble if all regions were affected? How could we balance risk by distributing it in relatively independent sectors? How could we, even with the most sophisticated models and computers, make informed decisions that discerned the important from the trivial in the deluge of information pouring into the central data banks of such a system? And if our decisions were flawed, how would we deal with the escalating scale of the disaster? There are other, equally compelling, reasons to reject the concept of a global economy, but it will have to do that a cautionary note has been sounded about taking its existence for granted and, as well, working to attain it.

Certainly, however, as just noted, of the three components of economic activity—production, distribution, and consumption—distribution is the most globally homogeneous and the most integrated. This is in large measure due to the Internet. In a few short years it has revolutionized both the structure and process of distribution, not just at the consumer level in which so many of us participate and take note as we order books from Japan, music from a Finnish rock group, even virtual sex services from southeast Asia. In addition to bringing new questions about, say, property rights, trust, and contracts, the cybermart is having an impact on both production and consumption. For example, ranchers once raised cattle that were sent on the hoof to a central gathering place (say, Kansas City) where, after purchase by meat packing firms, they were transported to some locale (such as Chicago) where meat packers butchered and processed them before distributing them to retail outlets. Now, a new Internet firm, e-Auction Global Trading, will shortly initiate the first real-time livestock auction via the Web. The company will integrate information about the market, allow customers to learn about goods and services within the commodities sector, and link sellers to buyers. Auction house agents will inspect and grade cattle before the auction, and these assessments will be used to provide information for potential buyers who will also receive schedules for auctioning of the lots. The company will provide assistance with transportation, arrange financial settlements, and sort out such problems as foreign currency exchange rates. A report by Scott Morrison in the *Financial Times* (London, April 29, 1999) notes that these types of auctions will allow sellers and buyers to save on infrastructure and transportation costs. Where cattle once lost as much as 10 percent of their weight on cattle drives, this shrinkage cost will be reduced, allowing ranchers a greater profit per head sold. One important efficiency of this new system is a reduction in service costs: the present system allows one hundred people to sell some twenty-five hundred head of cattle in thirteen hours; the new system will allow three people to auction the same twenty-five hundred head in ninety minutes.

However, a major concern today is whether the growth of the cybermart is occurring so rapidly and is creating such dramatically new structures and processes that established guidelines, rules, and laws are being bypassed and undermined in ways that are increasing risk exponentially.

Many of these rules have a long history and are deeply rooted in the sociocultural system. The anthropologist Scott Cook (see Bibliography) has distinguished distribution from exchange by noting that social norms, rules, laws, and values guide distribution while exchange is grounded in individual decisions to use what is distributed to each in order to obtain what is personally needed or desired. In line with this distinction, it's clear that in all human societies, over time, guidelines, rules and laws have emerged to help eliminate some of the uncertainty and risks in decision making, making it possible to initiate exchanges (as well as set out socially acceptable rules of distribution) with some degree of surety that each party gets what is expected in the relationship.

When the first marketplaces emerged, it was then, as it is now, important to keep the peace of the marketplace, to eliminate potential conflict and hazards by offering some protection, some kind of warranty to insure that exchanges with strangers and outsiders would be as reliable as those made with friends and kin. Indeed, that some marketplaces were better than others at managing, monitoring, and inventing protections was probably a major determinant for some locales to grow at the expense of others. In short, it was good business to protect those who came to trade, buyer or seller—and it still is. Fundamentally, the modern market system, with all its rules, protections, restrictions, laws, trades, and trade-offs, though more complex, addresses the same kinds of issues, using similar tools to accomplish tasks and achieve goals similar to those of the earliest marketplaces.

But, in addition to these externally created protections, humans take other tools to the marketplace. Buyers must, for example, decide on the seller with whom they'll transact exchanges. One such tool is, of course, using a cost/benefit model to evaluate potential rewards and risks of making a particular exchange with a particular other rather than someone else. As has already been noted, this is a controversial model for examining how human choices are made. Unquestionably, there are different lenses that we could and, indeed, have used to understand human behavior.

We could, for example, look at competitive play as a model for human interaction, noting the way in which game strategies are both planned in advance and adapted or scrapped when two competing teams are actually playing out the game on the field. In this framework, we would see people distributing and exchanging in a context of rivalry. The seller and buyer are competitors and haggling is an important part of the strategy that determines whether the exchange ends in a win, loss, or draw—and for whom.

We might have chosen the complementary relationships and distributional patterns among the members of a household production unit. How are production, distribution, and consumption decisions made relative to the productive input (or lack of it) of household members? Do age and gender play a role in who gets what when or in who makes the critical decisions about production and distribution? In times of hardship, what are the triage criteria for determining who suffers first or last, most or least?

Perhaps we might choose as our model the way any child, anywhere in the world, learns by about the age of five how to produce a language and becomes capable, for example, of grasping the difference between "I see you" and "You saw me," or "I saw the dog" and "The dog sees me," or "You may have a cookie" and "Can I have two?" How is it we've learned all those sounds and worked out the socially approved way to put them together in words and sentences, in the process employing grammatical rules for singular and plural or past, present, and future tense or agreement between the singular/plural noun and the correct verb—as in "I run/he runs," "you say/he says," "the book is on the table/the books are on the table," and "a book is on the table" but not "a books are on the table"? How does the young child learn how to say things, if we adults don't teach children to speak by explaining the rules but by simply correcting the child—when, indeed, few of us are able to explain the rules though we may speak a reasonably standard form of the language most of the time?

These and other models have been utilized to explore the ways humans learn the rules by which they interact. The different perspectives they each offer can address some important issues. But, on the whole, the cost/benefit model seems to have a more general applicability and, as well, appears to have a greater potential for giving rise to a wider field of more interesting questions being asked.

What are the conditions that lead to some societies having rules that stress cooperation while, on the other hand, others (or even the same society at a different time) encourage competition? What determines what resources are distributed through cooperative networks or authoritarian hierarchies whereas other resources are exchanged in a competitive but egalitarian context? Whatever the case, there are rules. But we know that no amount of rules, laws, norms, styles of etiquette, and the like will inevitably determine what real people in individual cases will do. If this were so, there would be no need to decide how to deal with people who violate the rules. It is not simply conflict between buyer and seller in the marketplace: Whether we look at adjoining villages or nation-states, we find examples of groups that previously had been exchanging resources peacefully, now breaking off trade as they go to war with each other—a conflict that is, not infrequently, created by what one or the other claims are "unjust (or unfortunate) resource allocations or unfair trade practices."

Viewed in the aggregate—that is, using statistics to bundle or separate individual behavior into various categories—the elaboration and growing interdependency of such rules (as well as the social relations they create) seem to emerge as the unintended consequences of individuals following a bare handful of such rules.

Why should people obey the rules? Why don't most of us cheat or even ignore them? The answer is that sociocultures need to operate in ways that allow members to receive a sufficient degree of satisfaction in their interaction with others so that the aggregate can continue through time. Rules provide the basis for our expectations of what will occur when we interact with others. These "reasonable expectations" in turn form the basis for the trust that must exist if people and groups are to cooperate in carrying out the daily affairs of everyday life.

There are, of course, people who break or bend the rules—not just very occasionally (we all do that)—but habitually and as a regular part of a sub-rosa lifestyle. But they live lonely lives unless they win the approval of a significant number of others who also break such rules. In this latter situation, the rules may change (laws will be rewritten or norms will gradually alter as more and more accept that the rule is honored more in the breach than in the observance), or a subterranean society of rule breakers emerges. Criminal gangs or "families" who make up organized crime groups are an example. But people who break rules do live lonely lives, whether they operate alone or with accomplices. As rule breakers they are forced to accept that no one can be trusted to keep the rules any more than they do. Indeed, they often end up betrayed or dead.

Thus, individuals recognize that while they might get less for themselves by obeying the rules, there's a high probability they'd lose much more by ignoring them. The benefits derived from satisfying the needs of others are judged to be greater than the social costs and losses of other resources that might be incurred if the rules were violated.

Whatever the case, it's clear that long before the market system or capitalism emerged, people distributed and exchanged things and entered into transactions, at first among the family; then among family and neighbors; finally among family, neighbors, and outsiders. Putting aside theft (secretive, open grab-and-run, or raiding/warfare), many transactions (even with family and friends) require covenants (redistribution) or, in the case of exchange, trust—especially that even what are only implicit contracts will be honored—and an acceptance of responsibility that the goods and services exchanged will be as represented. As early as five thousand years ago, the very earliest city-states kept records concerning the transfer of land through inheritance or sales, the inspection of animals to make sure the number of animals was accurately represented for, say, tax purposes (one such record shows 1,380 sheep received from taxpayers in a single day), the arrival or departure of goods, or conditional promises to deliver certain resources if a precondition was satisfied (e.g., "Hamrab promises that he will give five sheep to the temple if his prayer is answered").

There were also tablets that recorded laws governing rules of marketplace transactions as well as accounts of legal disputes that arose because one party to a transaction believed he was cheated. All societies show a concern with fair exchange practices, whether between individuals or between institutions (such as government or religious organizations) and individuals. Thus, we may have expectations that the rules will be followed, but these expectations are violated with sufficient frequency that every socioculture has developed ways to try to prevent rule violations and, as well, deal with actual, suspected or potential rule-breakers. And then, of course, we have to come up with more rules that say what to do when rules are violated.

Sometimes it is very difficult to make rules governing distribution and exchange that satisfy most of the people most of the time. Anthropologist Raymond Firth has pointed to at least one distribution issue that is especially difficult to resolve. Take a situation where a large number of people cooperate in the production of a resource, for example, an entire village cooperating on a flood control system. This requires a coordinated productive unit whose members engage in a wide range of activities such as managerial ability, heavy physical labor, creative or technical skills. In this fairly common situation, sharing rewards equally may be viewed as inequitable. Does one who engages in backbreaking labor deserve more or less than someone who sits in the shade and "manages"—especially if it seems that all the latter does is sit and even manage to find time to gossip with a few friends? Do the individuals who spend sleepless nights worrying about how to manage production deserve more or less than those who simply put in their eight hours and go home to relax and drink a few beers? Do the women who laugh and chatter with friends as they sit in the shade and pound corn into flour deserve as much as the men who clear, tend, and harvest the fields? Does the record keeper of a cooperative food store (who spent several years doing unpaid labor acquiring the necessary skills) deserve more, less, or the same proportion of the profits as the unskilled clerk who services the customers? What about slackers?

All of these concerns have existed for at least several thousand years—and still exist. Despite some arguments to the contrary, so does the extent to which the rules and the ethics of the market are as embedded in social relations, kin and friendship, associational ties, and the like as they were and are in any premarket society. It is part of the human imperative that, as social animals, we live in groups whose members are interdependent. We need to cooperate and exchange, and we surround that cooperation and exchange with protective rules—ethics, morals, rules, and laws—secular, religious (cf., taking an oath on the witness stand to tell the truth "so help me God"), and the distinction among civil, criminal, and contract law. Such protections, whether negotiated by councils of elders or the village priest, or written into law and enforced by governments and courts, underwrite the requirement that distribution and, especially, exchanges should be accepted by all participants as having been grounded in fair practice.

This universal concept underlies all exchanges—even those between humans and the supernatural—as witness the ancient concept of the covenant between God and the early Hebrews, or the still-current practice of burying and replacing local patron saints who appear to have violated the implied contract with the villagers ("In return for the honor and deference you give me, I will help you in times of need"). Just a few years ago, several villages in southern Italy and Sicily took this step when their prayers for rain went unanswered: "Fail us and we'll find a new patron saint." It didn't rain, and the villages *did* oust their former patron and adopt a new supernatural agent.

Even in the markets of today, people have a preference for buying from merchants they believe they can trust—even if it means paying higher prices. Surveys have shown that consumers say that an important consideration for selecting one provider over another is their level of confidence that the merchants or professionals are trustworthy, competent, and will "stand behind" their goods or services. This is an important factor, whether shopping at companies as diverse as Sears, Wal-Mart, L. L. Bean, and Tiffany's or when making decisions as to which local business to patronize—which car dealer, plumber, physician, or lawyer. Indeed, it may be that in today's impersonal, far-flung economic networks, trust and reliability among those transacting exchanges are more important than they ever were in a small village or town where the untrustworthy, incompetent, or unreliable were more likely to be quickly discovered and their behavior punished. People in a small town may point with pride at the degree of honesty and trust that prevails among the inhabitants; but they often add remarks such as, "Besides, everybody knows what everybody else has or hasn't and what they do and don't do. It's hard to get away with anything in a small town where everybody knows your business."

We can then begin to look at exchange in terms of what seem to be universal assumptions as to what is necessary for fair trade: (1) Exchanges will be equitable in the sense that each party receives what was negotiated; (2) all societies can avoid conflict if they establish safeguards against and ways to correct transfer failures; and (3) all parties are aware of and accept the specific rights and responsibilities that accompany the transfer of a good or service. As we saw in the preceding chapter, the last assumption is the one that is most risky, the most contentious, and the one that gives rise to the most conflict.

Beyond these few conditions, however, there is a wide range of variation through time and across sociocultures. To try to bring order to this variety, I've identified six factors that are used in various sociocultures to identify distributional formats.

Transfers—whether distributions or exchanges—may be viewed as: (1) reciprocal, (2) conditional, (3) allocative, (4) involuntary, (5) incentive, and (6) benevolent. It is rare that transfers are driven by one and only one compelling reason. Transfers involve multiple actors, each of whom sees the transfer from a different perspective—the motivations of the individuals or groups involved, the utility of the transfer, and, not the least, whether one is a giver or a taker/recipient. It would be self-defeating to focus on the action—the actual transfer—while ignoring the actors, who are differentially situated both in the transfer and in the sociocultural system at large. For instance, the government expects me to pay taxes because those in the government require resources to meet the costs of governing. I, on the other hand, give a portion of my resources to the government because, given that government has both the power and authority to coerce me to do it, I fear the consequences of noncompliance. Further, I also accept the benevolent argument that I have the responsibility to contribute from my resources to assist those who rely on government to answer their needs (as, for example, entitlement programs or a legal system that guarantees contracts and allows redress from shady business practices). In another situation my charitable contribution may be identified as a benevolent transfer, but I view it as a coercive transfer, since the sole reason I contributed to this particular charity was because I knew that upper management expected to achieve 100 percent participation from the employees—or else. If I tithe—give 10 percent of my income to my church/temple—this is both allocative (because the church assesses me a specific proportion of my annual income) and benevolent (because I wish to further the good work of the religious institution with which I'm affiliated). Finally, what I call a bribe and identify as coercing resources from me may be viewed by the recipient as reciprocal ("You should be happy to reward me for doing something that goes beyond my job description requirements") as well as an incentive (". . . and I'm doing it with extra care and attention as well as in a more timely fashion"). Thus, these six categories are best viewed as factors that let the actors and observers identify the rationale for the transfer.

Let's look at the six in more detail.

1. *Reciprocal transfers.* These involve exchanging or trading one thing for another—for example, impersonal marketplace exchange: wages, of course; contracts; barter; the market system. Many such transfers are heavily dependent on agents whose primary or sole function is to oversee the movement of goods and services in a process of circulatory exchange—a key component of market capitalism.

Just as producers may produce something in order to distribute it, buyers often buy simply to sell it (or even transfer it as a gift). Thus, A buys wheat and sells it to B, who turns it into flour so that it may be sold to C, who makes bread that is then sold to D, a restaurant or a supermarket (and may even be sold again to E, who packages stale bread so that visitors in a park may feed the birds). Exchange is the primary motivation and each *link* in the system engages various factors of production—the *land* on which the wheat is grown, the location of the factories where wheat is turned into flour and bread or where a store or restaurant is sited; the *labor* for growing/harvesting the wheat, transporting it to where it can be turned into flour, the baking of the bread, the work of store clerks or wait staff; and *capital*—the money needed to purchase the farmland as well as the machinery to harvest the wheat, the trucks or railroads (as well as the tracks, highways, and bridges) used to transport the product in various stages, the granaries in which the wheat is stored, the mills and their machinery to mill the flour, the physical plants and the ovens for baking the bread; the stores or restaurants and their equipment.

2. *Conditional transfers.* We may (a) shift the location of a good without a change in ownership—for example, I hire you to take charge of moving goods from point A to point B, for which I pay you a fee but retain ownership of the goods. I may hire a shipper to move goods for me, or I may ask someone to act as an intermediary in the transfer of resources. Brokers may take goods on consignment, a situation in which ownership is retained by the consignors who, (1) if the goods are sold, receive a specified price while the brokers earn a commission for their role in the transaction; (2) if the goods are not sold, receives them back; or (3), if the goods are lost (say, because a ship carrying the goods goes down at sea), may receive nothing.

We may also (b) assign temporary care-taking rights/duties to another but either retain the right to call back the loan or stipulate that a certain event must occur for any property transfer actually to take place. Examples of this latter situation are: lending a lawn mower to a neighbor or sending a player under contract with a major league team to their minor league farm team, both done with the understanding that the recipients have temporary use or holding rights but with the agreement that what was transferred must be returned on demand; bank mortgages in which ownership rights are retained by the bank until the mortgage is paid in full and that allow the bank to seize the property (regardless of how much has already been paid to the bank) if some regularly scheduled payment is not made; gambling debts, where one offers an IOU or jewelry, for example, as security for the loan of gambling chips. In a similar way, it should be noted, pawn shops still perform an important function in many societies or for segments in given societies. Here the debtor retains ownership rights to the item pawned until the due date for the loan (plus interest) arrives—in which case the creditor assumes ownership. In Chile, for example, the government has a monopoly on pawnshops and some five thousand people a day (approximately 1.8 million loans a year) rely on these shops. For one thing, a Chilean's "rich aunt" (as such places are nicknamed) charges only 2.13 percent interest; second, the very poor rely on pawn shops because they lend small amounts, usually no more than $40 (as compared to consumer finance companies that won't lend less than about $160). Given the worsening condition of the Chilean economy, the government expects that the number of 1999 pawn loans will increase at least 15 percent.

Conditional care-taking rights are often part of a relationship between debtor and creditor in which the links established as a result of the debt are more important than the debt per se. The relationship between debtor and creditor can be complicated: Sometimes creditors deliberately encourage the creation of debt in order to obligate the debtor to deliver more important benefits than the payment of the debt itself. Even if the debt is paid in full, the creditor will remind the debtor that something more is owed simply because of the lender's willingness to make the loan in time of need. Similarly, a debtor may incur a debt in order to obtain other benefits while the debt is outstanding. Consider the obligations that debtor nations incur with creditor nations or the lending agencies that are funded and controlled by particular countries with particular economic or foreign policy agendas. On the other hand, some may seek to become indebted deliberately in order to receive additional, future benefits from the creditor. Thus, if a leader of Country X arranges for a foreign loan, it is often the case that the government that requested the loan must remain in control to help insure the loan will be repaid. Further, future loans must be made in order to protect the previous loan and save the country from defaulting on servicing the loan (i.e., paying the interest) or declaring bankruptcy and cancelling the debt. In cases such as these, there's much truth in the old saying, "If you owe the bank $10,000, you have a problem; if you owe the bank $10 million, they have a problem."

An interesting variant has recently emerged among the marginally poor who, because of age or poor health (e.g., AIDS or terminal cancer), are unable to obtain life insurance. Yet they wish to provide for their funeral expenses, meet certain current expenses, leave some sort of wealth to designated heirs, or simply do something they always wanted to experience before they die but could never afford. The strategy involves going to a bank and borrowing, say, $10,000. To qualify for the loan, applicants need only to have an income deemed sufficient to meet the monthly repayment schedule. They must also be willing to pay a few dollars a month for debt insurance. Whatever they choose to do with the $10,000, they have been able to obtain the insurance otherwise denied—and at a very modest price.

3. *Allocative transfers.* This is a form of distribution in which some individual or group assigns various portions of resources that are to be transferred either to them from a defined source or from them to a specific group of others. The amounts to be allocated (not necessarily equitably) are not only determined according to some preexisting plan but often have some specific goal in mind. Common allocations include inheritances to a group of heirs; religious tithes; licenses required of anyone who wishes to engage in certain activities or make certain transfers. At the most simple level, I may take a pie, count up the number of people to whom I wish to serve it, and divide the pie into the appropriate portions—with someone I know is dieting receiving a slightly smaller portion and my teenage son receiving a larger portion.

In some cases of licensing, for example, it may be that only a certain number are issued and, once gone, one must wait for someone to die or find someone who has a right of transfer from whom to purchase it. A scarcity of licenses can create a secondary market, but those willing to transfer the license often will demand premium over the official cost of the license. In Boston, where cab medallions (licenses) are auctioned periodically, no new medallions have been issued (except forty for handicapped-accessible cabs) since 1934. The lowest qualifying bid for a court-ordered auction was U.S.$139,000. In other locales, however, the way to get a license in a closed market is to go through a broker who will attempt (for a fee) to find a current holder willing (for a premium) to make the transfer. For a substantial number of current medallion holders, it's the future benefit of transfer—say, at retirement—that represents the major value of their investment.

Another example of allocation is found among small-scale New England fishermen, where crews usually work for a share in the catch profits rather than a fixed salary. After trip expenses are paid, the money received is allocated among the crew, according to the following formula: Two shares to the captain, one share to the owner of the vessel (who may also be the captain), one share to each crew member, except the cook, who, between cooking duties, is also expected to do deck duty but usually receives only half a share.

A budget is a system of allocation that apportions specified quantities of a resource. It may be the national budget (a monster of an annual document, running thousands of pages and allocating so much for defense, education, research, etc.) or your personal budget. In the case of the latter, say that your weekly take-home pay is $465; from that you allocate so much to rent/mortgage, food, gas, credit card payments, telephone and other utilities, insurance, and any other fixed costs that must be met. What's left is your discretionary fund, income that may be used as you desire, say, for clothes or entertainment and other forms of recreation. When you're surprised by an unanticipated or overlooked bill, you usually transfer funds from one category to another or, as the saying goes, "rob Peter to pay Paul."

A budget is based on self-rationing. Most people believe that if they just made slightly more money they wouldn't have to ration themselves so stringently or wouldn't be forced to forego some pleasurable benefit to pay for some necessary but dull resource: "If I made more money I wouldn't have to ration my entertainment when the car insurance bill comes in." Since choosing to pay the car insurance surely does not bring as much pleasure as going to a concert, doesn't this refute the rational choice model? Well, which will give you more pleasure: your own transportation whenever you want it (without insurance, you won't be able to drive your car) or the concert that lasts a few hours?

4. *Coercive transfers.* B has the power (or authority) to coerce A into transferring goods or services to B. B may threaten to or actually employ force (e.g., war booty, blackmail, or theft) or may have the authority to impose certain forms of punishment (imprisonment, a fine, confiscation of resources, or all three) if the good or service is not transferred (e.g., taxes, tribute, duties, tolls). B may hold some resource as ransom, as in a kidnapping, or may hold A as a slave or chattel and thus control the latter's resources (in some societies—and even in parts of Euroamerican society up to this century—women and minors were considered chattels of the male household heads, who had the right to use the resources of such chattels as household heads willed). Not uncommonly, coercive transfers are resented and, often, resisted. History is full of events labeled slave or peasant revolts, and all of colonial history is evidence for the willingness of people to die rather than submit to such forceful takings.

5. *Incentive transfers.* These are transfers that may be negative or positive. Negative incentives identify actions to be avoided while positive incentive transfers indicate socioculturally approved activities. Promotions, high grades in school, bonuses, and so forth give evidence that one's performance is favorably viewed; demotions (or transfers to unfavorable locations), low grades, and the lack of a bonus or raise indicate behavior that is disapproved or unsatisfactory. The market system of today is a powerful incentive tool, transferring wealth to a producer when consumers approve of a good or service, withholding wealth when the product is not favored. Examples are: Discounts for regular customers or those who buy in large amounts; gifts or rewards received once a certain amount is produced or purchased; evaluations that give information about a product or performance (as with free supplies of a new medication or software program during test periods); free samples to acquaint individuals with a new product; bribes either to motivate the recipient to provide special services or to avoid the possibility that the recipient will work to block some process; awards given in recognition of some special achievement; rewards given in return for a particular good or service.

One variant of a positive incentive is the subsidy that governments provide to help attract businesses to a certain locale, start up new firms, or provide (supposedly) temporary support to some ailing company. The usual rationale for investing public tax dollars in a risky investment is that the subsidies serve a public good, such as providing jobs, preventing the loss of them, or ensuring that the State will not become forced to rely on uncertain foreign suppliers to satisfy national strategic needs.

6. *Benevolent transfers.* Resources may be transferred to support some future activity whose purpose is general; the donor is not expected to announce any claim on or expectation of anything in return. A benevolent transfer may also be made to recognize some activity that has already taken place, the transfer being a "privileging" mark, for example, a tip or intensified thanks—as in the case of the supernatural when we offer thanksgiving. Benevolent transfers also include true gifts, inheritances, religious offerings, charity, or philanthropy.

A great deal of exchange and distribution takes the form of gifts. They can range from the exchange of a smile for a special service, or the exchange of "a round of drinks" ("Hey! It's my turn to buy!"), to obligatory gift-giving that occurs when friends, relatives, or important others (such as coworkers or bosses) marry; have birthdays or anniversaries; undergo a religious rite of passage, such as a bar- or bas-mitzvah or christening/confirmation; celebrate a job promotion, a retirement, a move into a new home, the arrival of a baby, and so forth. The gift giver appears to receive nothing in return, but the gift may be made because the donor received similar gifts in the past or the recipient is expected to reciprocate by acknowledging similar events when they occur in the life of the donor. When the gift is made because a counter-gift is expected, such "anticipated reciprocity" transforms the true gift into an incentive.

Charity and philanthropic gift giving often involve an interest in furthering the aims of some group. One makes contributions to one's religious group or a special interest group; campaign donations or donations to a group that lobbies in the legislatures for bills that favor the aims of the group; as well as donations to activist and advocacy groups whose work one supports—animal welfare, starving refugees, anti-/pro-nuclear power. It's difficult to find something that does not have some organized way of soliciting support and monies. I belong to the Slow Food Society, a society dedicated to resisting the growth and spread of fast-food consumption.

Charity and philanthropy may be distinguished from each other on the basis of the scale of giving and the purpose of the gift. The distinction can be fuzzy, but perhaps a cynical friend was not too far off the mark when she noted, "Philanthropists are rich, give lots of money, and support the arts and other elite concerns; charitable givers worry about paying their bills but drop a quarter in the tambourine, a dollar bill in the plastic bubble at the check-out register, or send a $10 check to a wildlife preservation fund." (However, those who contribute to or work within the organizations that are dedicated to such activities have very different views on the subject, and the reader is advised to search out their views.)

Gifts are important for those who solicit funds for philanthropic and charitable work. But, again, we must question whether the gift is a true gift. Lisa Gubernick recently reported in the *Wall Street Journal* about the way in which museums, ballet companies, symphonies, and opera houses—that once claimed to invite the old monied elite and the newly rich to become part of their board of directors on the basis of their standing in the community—now flat-out inform those invited as to the amount they are expected to contribute in the form of what is variously called a "gift," "mandatory contribution," "donation," "pledge," and a "tithe." Across North America, the annual minimum contribution expected from board members is about $10,000, the average is about $25,000, and the top exceeds $100,000. And one must add to this the assorted "invitations" board members are required to "accept" (though not necessarily attend) to balls, cocktail parties, dinners, art exhibits, auctions, or gala theater performances, the admission to each requiring an additional sizeable contribution. Sometimes there is an explicit donation figure spelled out (e.g., $1,500 a couple, $5,000 for a table of six). Is this benevolence? Gubernick suggests it is not—and neither side in the equation is deceived about it. For the old elite, it is part of the way they maintain their position and exercise power (signalling their gatekeeper function through controlling who is invited to join); for the new rich it is a sign of "having arrived" and the opportunity to signal this to others by dropping the names of those with whom they now mingle. For those whose museum, ballet, or symphony is supported, it's cash on the barrelhead, money in hand that they need to continue being paid. Indeed, Gubernick even notes that some large institutions "have two-tiered boards, with the lower tier typically having looser requirements and conferring less power."

Whether as philanthropy, charity, or gratuity, there are often "suggested levels of donations" (as when etiquette columnists tell one to never tip less than 15 percent and, "in a fine restaurant, leave 20 percent"); sometimes (as in the dishes that sit on washroom counters where an attendant hands you a towel), there is a minimal quantity of money, giving a clue as to the amount expected as a tip for such service ("minimal" and frequently checked because washroom attendants report such "tickler tips" are often pocketed by the patrons!).

Charities have found that even unsolicited (and often unwanted) items sent to prospective donors are an incentive for the recipient to reply with at least a token amount. I have no idea what the donation return rate is for such gifts-by-mail, but it must pay off; the number of such mailings has increased to the point where, in the month of January alone, I received four boxes of "mixed greeting cards," three each of calendars and key chains (that would bring my lost keys back to me), and sixteen sets of gummed labels with my return address (four with my name spelled incorrectly). And if you give to only one, your name goes on a list that may be "shared" with (i.e., sold to) other charities. Your name and charitable persona have now become a commodity, priced by and circulated in a particular market segment.

In the everyday world—and this has doubtless been true ever since humans began sharing their lives together—the expectation of some benefit or the reduction if not negation of some cost or loss has provided the essential for all distribution. Benevolent transfers are no exception. More than other transfers, this type of transfer (and, again, especially gifts) creates linkages grounded in indebtedness. This sense of indebtedness becomes a component of a relationship between giver and receiver; thus, there are changes in the relationship once even one (perhaps especially if only one) party thinks the debt is paid. When Jane informs George that she's decided not to marry him, does she return the engagement ring? Was it a symbol of a relationship and necessarily returned if Jane breaks the relationship, or was it a gift from George to Jane and as unlikely to be returned as for Jane to reimburse George for all the dinners and entertainment he gave her when they had a date? Are any of us obligated to return a gift when we break our ties to the donor? Certainly, we expect that those who give wedding gifts are entitled to have them returned if the wedding is called off. However, most people don't expect them to be returned if the marriage ends in a divorce—yet what if valuable family heirlooms from the bride's grandparents were given to the couple? Does the husband have no property rights in them and does the wife automatically get to keep them?

An interesting example of the complexity of classifying gifts relative to some other category—say, bribes in which one expects reciprocity—comes from the recent (April 1999) ruling of the U.S. Supreme Court that, though limits remain in effect as to the types and monetary values of gifts made to government officials, Justice Department investigations must show that gifts accepted are tied to specific official acts performed by the recipients. It's predicted that a number of officials found guilty in the past will now appeal these earlier verdicts.

Further complicating the identification of a true "gift" is the fact that sometimes there is a long delay, years even, between the original transfer and a return gift. Indeed, among the Trukese of Micronesia, to return a gift too soon is insulting to the original donor; prompt return signals the original gift is being classed as a trade object rather than a token of generosity between friends. In any case, in many situations where goods or services are transferred, an observer, seeing no *immediate* reciprocity, may assume greater altruism on the part of the donor than is the case.

Another problem of classification may arise when a charitable donor refuses some good or service in return for "offering" (as when I turn down a loaf of bread baked by a religious organization that calls on me at Christmastime for a contribution). Not uncommonly, however, benevolence requires an inequality of transfer because that very inequality is crucial to maintaining a relation. Employers are expected to be generous with gifts and rewards; employees, however, are less compelled to give gifts and are rarely expected to give rewards to their employers. Recently, a situation that made national headlines involved an employer discovering in the company trash bins some of the Christmas gift turkeys given by his firm to his employees. It's moot as to whether this was due to simple disdain, lack of interest, or (as the use of company bins as a discard site leads me to suspect) a way to send a message to the employer that the workers considered this an unacceptable reward for their labor. Occasionally, employees do make transfers to employers but, as in the case of kickbacks from one's salary demanded by an employer as a reward for hiring an employee, it is illegal and considered a form of coercion.

Again, though parents may reward children for performing household chores, most are expected to give their children allowances. Is this a benevolent gesture, a bribe, or their parental responsibility? If there's any reciprocity involved, there is usually a long delay in any return on the part of the children (if at all). Certainly, most children and parents would reject the idea that children will love their parents less if they're not given an allowance. On the other hand, is it any more satisfactory to argue that in return for what parents have given them, children have a responsibility to "repay" their parents with love—or, at least, respect and obedience?

Business firms often will give "good measure" to special customers, adding additional goods and services over those made to other clients or customers. This is considered a goodwill gesture—not quite a gift but more like a "thank you," similar to the tips we give waiters, hairdressers, and so forth, that supposedly represent an intensified expression of our thanks for their service.

We know, however, that in every society gifts present complications. It's not unusual for a recipient to reply to a gift by responding with a counter-gift that has a value (or price) that is less or more than the good or service that was the original gift. What is interesting is that, in either case, the relationship will be sustained because of this inequality: someone is indebted to someone and the debtor bond is binding.

Gifts, especially when they are commodities—when they are produced solely for the purpose of exchange—often have the paradoxical ability to increase resources when they are given away. While donors diminish resources with one hand, they accrue them with the other. Services offered may consume time and money given may reduce wealth, but prestige, power over the recipient and the ability to call for reciprocal services at some future time are usually increased, often beyond the value of the original gift. (It should be noted, however, not all sociocultures see benevolence as entailing a response to reciprocate, be grateful or obligated to the donor.)

Businesses today will use gifts to introduce recipients to a commodity and thus hook them on the product, much as the drug dealer will give free drugs initially to create an addict. Seeming "benevolence" is actually self-serving. Several years ago, the global company of Nestlé in Switzerland became targeted worldwide by activists who charged the company with malevolent intent behind their generosity in distributing free baby formula powder to women as they left the hospital with their newborn infants. It was pointed out to Nestlé that many recipients were too poor to afford the formula without a trade-off in some other family expense, that poor mothers often diluted the formula to make it go further, and, as well, frequently lacked access to nonpolluted water. The claims then were that poor women were substituting expensive powdered formula for free and nutritious mother's milk; that the powder didn't build up the infant's disease immunity as would natural milk; and that these purchases (as well as additional medical costs for children with lower immunity) were an additional economic burden on the family. Eventually, Nestlé responded to the bad publicity (and the drop in sales figures worldwide) and stopped the practice.

One more point about benevolent transfers: They are a major reason for the discomfort with, if not downright rejection of, the cost/benefit model. That model denies the possibility that there is such a thing as a truly altruistic individual. That, however, is an argument separate from the utility of the cost/benefit model in the study of benevolent transfers. Even assuming there are true altruists, they, too, have to make choices between one good and another. There are always limitations of resources such as money or time. Do you volunteer at the Crisis Center or as a Big Brother/Sister? Do you give funds to refugees, to the homeless in our own society, or to an animal welfare society? Deciding among these choices requires utilization of a cost/benefit model even for those truly rare individuals, altruists—assuming they do indeed exist.

One may arrange the alternatives in terms of preferences and do a standard cost/benefit analysis, but what if you don't know very much about any of the programs—might you end up postponing a choice till you had more time to check into them all, and end up doing none of them? And how do you handle multiple "first choices"? If this last situation was the case, you could employ the triage approach: (1) weigh alternatives in terms of urgency, (2) review the practicality of utilizing available resources (e.g., since you know that you could not plan a regular number of hours contributed per week, you try to determine which program offers you the greatest flexibility or suffers the least from erratic input on your part), and (3) try to find out the success rate of programs relative to each other.

Let's look at the position that claims there are few, if any, genuinely and purely altruistic acts or gifts, that is, gifts that carry no expectation of some kind of return. Some argue that any transfer that is made because the donor derives benefits (even if it is the satisfaction and self-congratulations one gives oneself for being such a good person) is no true gift. If, for example, I give a gift to my various job superiors in order to increase my social credit with them, does this expectation make the gift more of a bribe than a gift? Similarly, if I make an anonymous donation to charity in the belief that God will note my good works and reward me in the hereafter, or because the anonymity makes me feel especially virtuous (given that I earn no social capital for a good deed that goes unnoticed), are these not benefits I receive?

A common counterargument to using a cost/benefit model rests on a position that gives rise to such questions as: "What about those who sacrifice their lives for strangers?" This must, it's claimed, be proof that humans commit genuinely altruistic acts since a cost/benefit model must result in preserving one's life; being alive brings greater benefits to the actor(s) than dying to save some stranger—who, for all we know, might be a despicable individual. From an anthropological perspective, however, nonmaterial benefits are just as valuable as material benefits and do not exclude those values or beliefs, those guideposts to life and the yardstick by which we measure our own worth and that we know is used by others to measure it. There is nothing in the anthropological model that excludes the possibility that individuals or groups can make decisions that place a higher value on ethics, morals, religious beliefs, or even the fear of being branded cowardly, rather than living with the knowledge that they made some base trade-off. Such a decision might be made to avoid the risk that, for the rest of their lives, the choice would corrode their sense of the value of their lives, that they opted for staying alive as more important than having lived lives that were true and meaningful. The cost/benefit analysis may have been made out-of-awareness or occurred so quickly that the action seemed instinctive, but it doesn't preclude making a choice that validates one's existence. As Levin, a character in Tolstoy's *Anna Karenina*, puts it: ". . . my life now, my whole life apart from anything that can happen to it . . . is no longer meaningless, as it was before, but . . . has an unquestionable meaning of the goodness which I [now realize I] have the power to put into it."

Whether production, distribution/exchange, or consumption, economic activities inevitably affect and are affected by social relations, creating new ones or destroying, intensifying, extending, or contracting those that already exist. Thus, for example, no matter how brief, any exchange involves two or more people in a relationship; those who join, say, the Rotary Club form both business and social ties with fellow members; bitterly divisive family inheritance disputes tear a family apart; existing clients recommend their goods/service provider of goods to others; and once a child reaches a certain age, a pediatrician loses a patient.

That the relationship matters can be seen in tracking the most ordinary and seemingly impersonal of market exchanges. There are times that we choose to buy or not in one shop or another because of the salesperson, the shop's ambience, the neighborhood, and so forth. You hire John Smith rather than Paul Brown to work in your office because Smith seems likely to be more pleasant. Sometimes an ethnic, racial, or religious component, assumed or real, attracts/repels us to the point where the seller has little selling to do, is given much trust on initial contact—or is avoided and no transaction can be initiated (e.g., there have been complaints by African-American males that some non–African Americans will not allow them into their homes as, say, plumbers or painters). Some males who apply for jobs at child care centers report that interviewers seem to suspect such applicants might be child molesters for, as one day-care director told me when I questioned the lack of male staff, "What kind of man would want this kind of work?"

When we focus on the kinds of relationships established specifically within the context of exchange, we find a variety of patterns that signal various types of relationships. Individuals or large firms may (1) *compete* and vie for each other's customers or engage in a price war. However, (2) they may also *collude*, for example, work together behind the scenes in a cartel to agree to fix supplies and/or prices. Traders may also (3) *cooperate* (e.g., sharing common membership in a trade association) or (4) atomistically *aggregate* in some geographic locale such as the garment district of New York, Silicon Valley, or a flea market, and, by the very fact of such aggregation, attract more consumers than each could in isolation. Distributors may (5) *share* resources, seeking to create a situation where differences complement each other and create a greater potential for growth than any could achieve separately (as with Centers of Excellence or when universities agree to form a consortium that collectively shares library resources with all faculty and students). Alternatively, distributors may (6) *exploit* others in the distributional network (see, for example, the role played in the illicit system of drug distribution by so-called mules—carriers of drugs who, since they are at the lowest level in the chain, are considered expendable and receive relatively low pay, and whose participation commonly results in their arrest or even death). Distributors may form dyadic links in which each of the two members (7) *reciprocates* when given goods and services by the other (e.g., two oil companies agree to supply each other's gas stations when supplies are short). Contrariwise, one member of the dyad simply (8) *appropriates* the goods or services of the other—for example, the master-slave relationship.

In sum, as with distribution, exchange is a basic part of life and we learn how to trade even as infants, parents and baby rewarding each other with smiles and loving gestures or with frowns and harsh voices in exchange for one or another activity—or the lack of it. We trade smiles with friends, handshakes with strangers, kisses with loved ones, apologies when we bump into someone, a "thank you" in return for someone saying, "God bless you" when we sneeze. The economically marginal are very dependent on exchanges as well as distributions: They help each other by sharing necessary goods and services, trading useful information, and bartering a great deal amongst themselves. They also barter "good behavior" (as defined by the various bureaucrats with whom they have contact) in return for eligibility to receive State entitlement distributions. Learning about exchange is an active part of the lives of small children. Watch the trading that is carried on among them—marbles, baseball cards, Beanie Babies, lunch items at school, and, of course, just like grown-ups, information. However, it's surprising how much we still have to learn about the way children acquire trading skills.

Dr. Joyce Brothers recently wrote (*Wall Street Journal*, June 5, 1998) of the amount of "floor trading" she observed among a group of children engaged in the secondary market in Beanie Babies; the original $5 cost being pushed as high as U.S.$3,000. She tells of hearing from children not yet teenagers, such phrases as, "I have a feeling the market is peaking," and "the median market in the U.K. is much lower than the median market in the United States right now." She writes:

> The children's market is extremely sophisticated. They advertise Beanie Babies on their Web pages. They get paid by check or money order but prefer the latter "because a check can bounce, and besides I don't have a bank account" says one. . . . They have their own newsletters or magazines to keep up-to-date with the current prices. . . . I asked my fourteen-year-old granddaughter what she would do with her collection if the entire Beanie Babies market crashed. "Don't worry, I will sell out at the right time," she replied. How will she know that time has come? "I have been watching the trends carefully. I'll know," she answered.

What bothers Brothers, as a psychologist, is that the toys are no longer toys.

> Children are buying them, trading them, hoarding them, collecting them. But . . . they are not playing with them. If the tag attached to each animal (with its birthday, name and a poem describing its unique personality) is missing, their secondary market value evaporates. . . . "Loved" Beanies are looked down upon; young collectors don't dare take the Beanies to bed, pet or hug them. They can only count them like a miser his gold. . . .

A final question: What's the difference between trading and sharing? Here's an experiment: First, picture (*really* create a mental picture of them, put clothes on them, and even give them names) two children trading cookies, "One of mine for one of yours"; now picture two children sharing sandwiches from their lunches, each offering the other half of theirs.

In each scenario, what were the children's names? What sex were the children—were both boys, both girls, boy and girl, boys in the first case, but girls in the second—or the reverse? Because some maintain that males "trade" but females "share," I loaded the dice by talking about "trading" in scenario one and "sharing" in scenario two.

There has been little study of the exchange relations of children: Do boys distribute more/less frequently, among a wider/more narrow network than girls? Do boys and girls trade different things? In different ways? Is it correct to claim that boys trade but girls share? Does the good or service being exchanged determine whether we trade or share? When there is boy–girl transfer, who is more apt to make the overtures to initiate the transfer? Do boys and girls start to trade and/or share at the same age, and do the gender-marked patterns remain constant through adolescence? Which sex—if either—is more likely to exchange services rather than goods ("I'll show you how to do the map if you show me how to divide fractions")?

And if we can't answer questions like this, what more don't we know?

Chapter Eight

Consumption

Give Us This Day Our Daily Bread

Of all areas of economic behavior, consumption is the one that humans do the most and understand least. Despite all the attention given the matter by economists, religious leaders, politicians, psychologists, philosophers, marketing experts, sociologists, anthropologists—not to mention lawyers concerned with clients wishing to collect debts or wishing to file bankruptcy—we really understand very little about why people consume, how much they consume, when their consumption intensifies or declines, how it is that consumption preferences alter, why some societies encourage it and others decry it, and so on ad infinitum. Why, for example, do many people go on a buying spree when they're depressed? How is it that, if we delay purchasing something, we seem to lose the compulsion to obtain that object that, as briefly as a few hours earlier, seemed so irresistible? And what does it mean to "consume"? Do we really consume cars or clothes the way we consume food and drink? Last, but not least, do we consume because we produce, or do we produce in order to consume?

Let me begin with the last question and emphasize that, while production, distribution/exchange, and consumption are often identified, separated out, and analyzed as if they were separate, sequential phases or components of an economic system (as the arrangement of the chapters here suggests), the three are part of a single, mutually interdependent process. As with other texts on the issue, I have tended to treat them as distinctive units because each has its own distinct structure and processes and, at least for initial analytical purposes, must be separated in order to dissect these various distinctive components.

Of course, one can't consume something that doesn't exist, but it might be profitable to ask why we produce in the first place. (Admittedly, this question is somewhat like the famous philosophical puzzle of "Why is there something rather than nothing?"—i.e., why do galaxies, a universe, and life itself exist—indeed, why anything at all?) A reasonable answer seems to be that, especially among humans, we produce because living things have a prime directive to consume. While this seems to suggest that consumption takes priority over production, a position that not a few would find disturbing, it may be noted that current research shows that even what seems to be the productively pointless activities of fidgeting or doodling are necessary production generated by the need to consume energy. Boredom is the cognitive recognition of nonproductivity, and when we face enforced inactivity, we begin drumming our fingers, swinging our legs, moving our eyes about, flexing our toes, twisting a strand of hair, tapping our fingers, scribbling, doing anything that allows us to consume what is often labeled restless energy. Thus, without the interdependent process of consumption-production-consumption—one of the most basic being a mother providing milk for her offspring—we would die.

Further, some would argue that the items we put in those boxes so neatly labeled as production, distribution/exchange, and consumption are actually rather problematic. For example, a number of anthropologists have argued that most consumption, even what we eat, is a way of communicating information to ourselves and others about who or what we are. The goods and services we select to consume or not to consume are not just ends in themselves but convey or conceal information about how we view the world. Thus, for example, we frequently buy certain goods and services, produced a certain way and sold at certain prices, solely in order to display them. They are symbols as well as extensions of ourselves—our taste, our place in society, our educational background, as well as our ideals, goals, inner longings, and states of being that we may be too shy to express or incapable of articulating.

Building on this idea, Michel de Certeau has suggested that when we consume we actually are engaging in what he calls "secondary production." Whether goods or services are imposed on us or freely selected, consumers produce new uses and new meanings for them, creating or imposing uses and meanings unintended by the original producer. We may even actively subvert the intent of the original producer. When, for example, subject colonial people were forced to buy certain European trade items or particular religious goods and services, they often used them to mock, revile, or invert the intended purpose of such items. They might use European clothes in festival activities, dressing characters in the European mode to make them look foolish and subject to ridicule via a secret code Europeans didn't know. Forcibly converted native people often used Christian religious objects in ceremonies that actually honored the old gods rather than the God or Jesus of the missionaries or colonial administrators (e.g., statues or paintings of the Virgin Mary might be addressed and revered as the precontact fertility goddess). Similarly, the automobile's primary purpose is transportation. Recall that earlier I took issue with the economists for arguing that purchases reflect consumer preferences. Preferences, however, never stand alone; one has bundles of preferential criteria that continually are reordered according to specific factors operating at the time of purchase. In the case of a car, I may weigh affordability, reliability, gas mileage, safety, and (the main factor for many) the image it communicates of who I am to me and others.

Anthropologist Mary Douglas, with economist Baron Isherwood, produced a provocative and brilliant study of consumption, *The World of Goods* (see Bibliography). In it they explore the depth of meanings that acts of consumption convey. We are given the example of the mundane process of selecting kitchen tools and asked to note how the size, color, or specific design of such ordinary items as toasters, coffee makers, stoves, refrigerators, mixers, pots and pans, and so forth, are selected as much if not more for the statement they make about us as for their function in the kitchen. Certainly Douglas's claims are borne out by the current absurdity of the countless number of North American and European consumers who redecorate each year or remodel their homes for no other reason than that they wish to be in fashion or are bored with living with the same old thing. Redoing one's kitchen is currently the focus of much such activity in North America, and one of the hottest items is the kitchen stove. Pick up any home decorating magazine and you'll see ads and articles touting the latest in such appliances. Stoves are now designed to be elaborate, multipurpose (e.g., warming ovens for dishes, three or more ovens with each having a specific function, modular in order to scatter the various segments around the kitchen "for convenience") and very expensive. Among the affluent (or those who wish to be judged affluent), the most desired are European imports. These cost an average of U.S.$10,000 to $12,500 (plus tax) and set the standard. Articles about consumers who have recently purchased these kinds of stoves often have the owners laughingly admitting that it was somewhat of an extravagance since, as one couple admitted, ". . . we usually eat out and, really, neither of us even knows how to cook."

Lest you think this is proof of female irrationality, move next to the growing assortment of high-tech barbecue grills, an artifact that, in North America, is in an almost exclusively male domain. In order to grill hot dogs and hamburgers or, in gourmet circles, chicken, steaks, or vegetables, one may spend as little as U.S.$20 to $30, but among the affluent it may mean spending as much as U.S.$5,000. This doesn't, of course, include the necessary add-ons that often accompany the purchase of a single commodity (think of the add-ons the purchase of a house spins off). There are barbecuing tool sets, serving carts, a place to store the monster in those seasons when it's not in use. In short, one may spend as much as another U.S.$3,000 to $5,000 for the extras, which are, of course, viewed as essential rather than "extras." Each year, these tools for "informal and casual living" grow increasingly high tech. Some of the equipment is now so complex that I've seen catastrophes (or near ones) because, despite considerable use, the chef du jour is still not quite sure of his mastery of the instructions for getting the grill flame started. Yet, for thousands of years (and even today), people have been able to achieve the same end with a small pile of wood or charcoal. If Douglas is correct (and most who study consumption agree with her position), what message does the grill user think he is sending, and why are such senders usually male?

In the midst of all this competition to keep up with the Joneses, to stay in fashion, to buy the latest of whatever, what happens to the old stoves, kitchen appliances, home furnishings, clothes, cars, and all? In what strange way can we be said to have "consumed" what is now being discarded? And this brings us to the question asked at the beginning: What do we mean by "consumption"? Surely people don't consume stoves, clothes, cars, and the like in the same way they consume food. Any standard dictionary tells us that *consumption* means something like "to eat, to use up, to waste." Are nonedible goods and services "used up" in the way that term usually implies, that is, are they reduced to a state where they have no further utility? Not usually, though in certain physically or mentally demanding jobs and in the case of those who provide entertainment (e.g., sports figures and rock stars), perhaps we can say that when these individuals lose their ability to provide their services at the demanded level of performance, we have "used them up" or they are "wasted." But, as we'll see in the next chapter, identifying "waste" is equally problematic.

Certainly, there is a close relation between the idea of consumption as a form of eating and consumption as the act of using up. While eating is one of the most necessary activities of human existence, one of the similarities that links us to other animals is that individuals of all species spend much of their lives in the food quest, looking for something to consume. Food and drink aside, many of the goods and services that we consume are not used up or wasted; indeed, even food and drink are not totally consumed; they produce human waste. But, in many societies, human excrement is not waste; such material is drained from privies or cesspools for use as agricultural fertilizer. So, ironically, the human elimination of waste is a valuable act of human production and is transformed into capital when it is used to produce more food for consumption. And so the cycle goes. But, for the moment, let's put the question of the leftovers of consumption aside and return to the question of what we mean by "consumption."

Here again we anthropologists (along with much of the general population) are in disagreement with economists about what belongs in what neat little boxes we invent to talk about the world. It's a truism in science, in statistics, in accounting, and in most of the real world that what you measure is what you get: what you identify as a category, what you decide belongs in that category, and how you decide to measure the "stuff" in that category will determine what you get. Say, for example, that you want to measure robbery; then, make another decision that leads you to collect data on street and house robbery but not, say, embezzlement or investment scams; next, decide that you will include information on the ethnicity of the perpetrator; you will discover that the ethnic groups most likely to be involved in robbery are quite different from your findings when white-collar crime is included.

What are we measuring and what kind of information are we getting when we create the categories of "consumption," "saving," and "investment"? Those who buy a new outfit to make a good impression on a job interview, or a computer on which to learn new skills in order to increase their employability, view such purchases as investments. Economists, however, label such purchases as consumption though, again, we don't "consume" computers or clothes. To further confuse things, this same average person labels things like retirement plans, stocks, bonds, or mutual funds as investments. As a friend recently put it, "My savings are the money I put in the bank; it can't grow the way my investments do." Economists, however, label her collection of "investments" as "savings." Money is only "invested," they argue, when it is put to work, to buy new equipment or to expand the plant, when it is allocated to research and development, or used to hire more labor. That is, it becomes an investment only when a capitalist takes your savings and uses it to invest in machinery, labor, and other means of production—when it becomes a resource-producing resource. From this perspective, a farmer who sets part of this year's harvest aside to provide seeds for planting the following year is simply saving the seed; it isn't until the seeds are planted that they become invested and are now capital. Similarly, when Jim White's wife entertains her husband's clients at a dinner party in their home (a home that, together with its furnishings, is designed to provide a context for White's business activities), the home, the furnishings, the hostess gown she wears, the purchases she makes at the supermarket and liquor store are all placed in the "consumer" box by the economist. But the restaurant dinners Jim buys for potential clients (the prices of which are based on the restaurateur's building, its furnishings, the labor, as well as the uniforms and their laundering for the service staff, and the food) are all viewed as expenses of doing business; items that produce figures that go in the "investment" box. Now, the fact that economists offer excellent rationales for their categorizing only makes it difficult if not impossible for all of us to break free of the mind-set that makes for the difficulties we encounter when attempting to understand consumption, particularly in that cross-cultural and cross-temporal framework commonly used by anthropologists.

What makes all this important is the role such concepts and categories play in guiding decisions and making choices. Such decisions are most crucial when they are governmental decisions made about entitlement allocations in the national budget, when they form the basis for shaping laws dealing with bankruptcy or taxes, and myriad other things that have an impact on the lives of most citizens. Among policy makers and shapers—economists, civil servants, politicians, financial overseers, and so forth—there is growing concern about national consumption patterns. Washington worries that the American consumer is going into debt on the promise of inflated HT stocks; Ottawa complains that "Canadians are spending more than they are earning, accumulating debt they can't possibly hope to pay"; Tokyo worries because its citizens aren't consuming enough and the Japanese economy is in trouble.

In the United States many academicians who spent much of their adult lives doing research that had to be squeezed in between classroom teaching, student conferences, committee work, and bureaucratic paper work, look forward to when, retired, they have the time to pursue their scholarly activities (limited only by their inexorable movement toward a possible decline of their mental and physical capabilities as well as their inevitable demise). They're shocked to discover that the government has transformed these same activities into "a hobby." Where once subscribing to journals, buying a new computer, attending learned conferences, and doing research—to mention only a few items—were considered (tax-deductible) capital investments in order to maintain one's job and/or earn a salary, they are now classed as non-tax-deductible purchases made to enhance our leisure. Yet only a few scholars earn any sort of income from their research (not only are they unlikely to write books that make the best-seller list, but scholarly journals—unlike popular magazines—do not pay for articles and may even charge page costs). We might, of course, make an abrupt transition to this leisured existence, taking up golf or bridge or spending our "golden years" roaming the country in oversized mobile homes (complete with bumper stickers that announce "We're spending our children's inheritance!"), but this is hardly what we planned. True, we enjoy doing scholarly work but where is it written that one must find life's work painful drudgery? Some of us wish to continue to make productive (and very cost-effective since they are free) contributions to our professional and civil communities. What it boils down to is that the simple fact of earning a salary has led to the same activity being transformed from a productive enterprise—requiring purchases the government labels "investments"—to some form of play in which the same expenditures are now considered items of "consumption."

Consumption presents other problems to governments. Politicians in every country worry about the demographic issue produced by the concern that, as the number of nonworking elderly grows, there will be a declining proportion of working producers (taxpayers) relative to the growing number of elderly (tax consumers). How will we pay the bills presented by this leisure class of elderly idlers? Another problem: If too many people consume too much, the government may have to address concerns about inflation. On the other hand, if too few people spend too little, there will be an economic slowdown and the government will become concerned about unemployment. Finally, economic and political unrest in other parts of the world lead to a drop in the consumer spending of those regions—and this leads to a decline in our exports and so to a rise in our unemployment. In sum, patterns of consumer spending, investment, and savings change according to the dynamics of the larger society; similarly, the dynamics of the larger society, even the global society, lead to changes in national, regional, and local consumer spending, investment, and saving. It is vital that we understand how all of this fits together. Equally important is to understand how they shift and change in response to micro and macro events.

Clearly, as the goods and services purchased change, so do the rationales behind spending, investment, or saving. For example, thrift and the avoidance of conspicuous consumption used to be encouraged in children by giving them piggy banks at a very young age and issuing such homilies as "a penny saved is a penny earned." Long before the current emphasis on recycling appeared, our parents, grandparents, and generations before them were urged to "use it up, wear it out, make it do, or do without." Children were often made to sit at the table until they "cleaned their plates" and were (supposedly) shamed when reminded of many starving children in whatever country who "would be glad to eat their vegetables." (This admonition may be one of those rare cultural universals: Friends from China tell me they were advised that there were many starving children in India; those from India tell me they were told to think of the starving children in China; Argentinean children are currently reminded of the starving children in Brazil, but, in my day, it was the starving children in war-devastated Europe.) Of course, in many North American households today, it is considered unwise to force children to eat what they don't like. Further, even quite young children shop for and prepare their own meals—unless, of course, they follow the increasingly common pattern of eating out.

Moreover, in today's world, cautions about consumption and waste are more likely to be framed in terms of health or environmental issues. Rather than insisting children consume all the food on their plates, parents are more likely to be given and provide elaborate psychological arguments as to why they shouldn't force their children to eat, are advised to give smaller portions but, when necessary, simply to discard whatever is left. (However, particularly among the less affluent, I often watch parents, especially mothers, consume what children have left behind, confessing to me with a sheepish smile that they just can't bear "letting all that food go to waste.")

Here is an example of how generational and socioeconomic differences create variations in consumption patterns and how it is that, in all societies, achieving what is socioculturally defined as "the right levels" of consumption or nonconsumption (whether saving, investing, or wasting) is tricky. There are subtle rules that govern staying within the approved boundaries between consuming too much or too little. Consume little and save much, wear clothes until they wear out (fashion go hang!), limit your children's expenditures, work hard and build up a risk fund, and you risk being labeled stingy, unfashionable, a workaholic, money hungry, or bad parents who don't provide their children with the things they need to mature as healthy individuals with all the social graces and necessary learning abilities. Consume too much, support innovation, tip underpaid service providers lavishly, and you face scorn from those who label you a slave to consumerism, are liable to have your tax records examined by the government, become a target for thieves or revolutionaries—or get fat. Consume conspicuously and people grow suspicious about the source of what you spend; consume inconspicuously and people wonder where you've hidden your wealth.

Among the world's societies, charitable or philanthropic acts have often been viewed as having the dual character of both saving and investment. Charitable gifts usually entail some constraints or even sacrifices in consumption. But the act of sharing or distributing resources to help others may allow them to make a productive contribution to the socioculture at some future time. And this is a social benefit that you receive. Thus, for example, if a scholarship fund is set up to assist in educating those who would otherwise not be able to avail themselves of educational opportunities, the fund is contributing to the future productivity of the society; it is an investment in the future of the individuals and the group. Though this would be an example of enlightened self-interest, there are sociocultural mandates for encouraging such activities. Thus, for example, in the Old Testament book of Leviticus, the "Law of the Corner" directs that, when reaping a harvest, one should leave a portion in the corners of the field untouched, leaving some of the grain, grapes, or olives for the poor, widows, orphans, and the needy stranger (19:9–10). And still today, members of most Christian congregations are expected to tithe, to give to the church a tenth of their income annually. Similarly, even among the most secular and least observant of Jews, studies show there is an explicit awareness of and deeply felt need to obey the ancient Judaic injunction to share even the most modest supply of resources with others.

The desire to accumulate and the desire to consume might seem to pull individuals and groups in opposite directions. But there are occasions when these seemingly conflicting desires become complementary, namely, when they lead individuals or groups to make attempts to accumulate the resources of others (through robbery, raids, and warfare) in order that they may increase their own consumption at the others' expense. It may be that the conflict produced by combining these two aims accounts, at least in part, for such sociocultural rules as the biblical injunction, "Thou shalt not covet thy neighbor's goods," one of the Ten Commandments that constitute the basic rules for community that God gave Moses. These are held to be a divine message by Jews, Christians, and Muslims alike. This moral precept is grounded in the very practical aim of maintaining a community's peace and stability. Envy of the resources of others, especially when it involves trying to keep up with the Joneses, is a powerful motive for expanding production in order to increase consumption. Despite much of the current attack on excessive consumption, such a motivation is not necessarily "evil." Without it, numerous human innovations and inventions with the capabilities of relieving human distress would not have occurred. In the Euroamerican world, the Industrial Revolution, despite initial excesses, helped to eliminate slavery and, as well, released servants (so-called free labor) from the frightful living conditions that many were forced to endure in the middle- and upper-class homes in which they labored (even Marx's household, despite his claim to poverty, usually had at least two servants). Though for more than a century, the trade-off, that is, life in the nineteenth- and early twentieth-century factories, was just as bad if not worse.

However, the desire to consume also has the potential to create malcontents who, never having enough of the resources they believe will insure The Good Life, are willing to bend and even break the rules (remember the corrupt and professional thieves—but also remember the entrepreneurs and their potential for introducing the potential chaos of change). Unfortunately, if things are going well, this often leads the less affluent to run as hard as they can in order to catch up—only to discover that the Joneses have also become more affluent and are still ahead of the Smiths. To some extent, this accounts for the common charge that "as the rich get richer, the poor get poorer."

Obviously, then, an increase in wealth leads to an increase in consumption: Houses grow in size, the number of things in them (as well as outside of them) increases along with the prices paid for them—and the number of people that must be hired to take care of the bigger houses, larger grounds, and expanded guest lists of those we must invite to display our wealth; there are more closets and more clothes, bigger garages and more cars, swimming pools are larger (in 1999 diving boards were out, but grottos and waterfalls were in). All of this sets new levels for the less affluent and, in subtle ways, for those who are concerned with consumption equity. As a current ad for a European car puts it, "Do the rich have more children? Do they deserve more comfort when they drive? Are they more entitled to safety?" But, as the bar rises, average consumers (i.e., those neither impoverished nor "seriously rich") in affluent countries find that instead of feeling richer they must pinch here and shave there in order to be able to afford a constantly changing and growing list of things they feel they must consume if they are not to fall behind. The philosopher Thoreau (so popular with environmentally concerned individuals these days) maintained, "A man is rich in proportion to the number of things he can afford to let alone." However, given the extent to which he relied on his family and friends to provide him with necessities, one is led to wonder if he mentally added ". . . leaving others to produce what he needs to consume." After all, the land where he built his house in the woods near Boston, Massachusetts, was provided by his friend Ralph Waldo Emerson, who paid the taxes on it, and his mother made weekly visits to bring food baskets and take away clothes that needed laundering and stitching.

Indeed, you often have to keep running harder just to stay in the same place. Watching their fixed expenses rise while their fixed income doesn't is forcing retirees to take part-time jobs simply to maintain their standard of living. Numerous studies over the years show that regardless of income, North Americans always fix on a figure roughly 10 percent above their current income as "what would be sufficient to have enough," "to be able to relax and be comfortable." Oddly, when income increases, the need to have "just 10 percent more" remains fixed; make $20,000 and another $2,000 or so would be enough; make $50,000 and another $5,000 will do it—make $250,000 and just $25,000 more will mean no more pinching, no more chasing the buck.

It would seem, then, that long before Marx, or Freud, or Rachel Carson (and her clarion call to address environmental issues), early leaders understood the negative potential of fixing your stare on those who have more—resources of any kind whether it is rich, productive farm land, money, or political power. While playwrights, poets, and painters have depicted the consequences of poverty, they have long been equally concerned with the consequences of overconsumption. Shakespeare, in *The Merchant of Venice*, reminds us that those who stuff themselves with too much can become just as sick as those that starve with too little. Religious leaders, particularly, have tried to redirect the gaze of those who grumbled, whined, or were thought to be cheating to the needs of those who have less. The underlying moral claim is that one should be grateful for what one has, that focusing on what you lack relative to what others have will always leave you feeling relatively poor because, no matter what you possess, you'll always experience a sense of relative deprivation.

Thus, the emphasis that most sociocultures put on tending to the needs of others, of sharing, not only produces acts that lend to social solidarity and makes for a more harmonious society, it also lends itself to encouraging members to count their blessings, to see themselves as fortunate in comparison to some others. The Bad News here is that such a stance often impedes useful innovation, not the least being acceptance of the control exercised by those who already occupy favored positions in the allocation of resources, as for example the feudal lords and other elite in Europe who resisted the attempts of those in the trade-oriented city-states to break the feudal system.

However, generous giving and sharing is based not only on the willingness of persons to obey an important religious teaching, it is equally important if you wish to be liked, respected, even honored. Not living up to the expectations of others, whether friends, coworkers, or business associates, failing to use your resources in socially approved ways usually creates serious social handicaps and often affects your access to future resources. These can be either material or social: for example, material might be getting a contract for a job from those whose view of you as a business partner is often based on their respect for you as a person; social might include having sound relations between you and your children, who respect you as a role model, or maintaining the social networks in which you and your family participate.

Similarly, governments expect people to contribute some of their surplus to the general welfare. In early societies, this contribution was in the form of corvée labor, energy contributed to work on community projects, or as service in the religious and civil portions of the governing system. In ancient Athenian and Roman society, the excellent citizen was honored by being asked to serve (without pay) in public office. Indeed, in or out of office, affluent citizens were expected to make generous gifts to the people—for example, paying for the costs of celebrating a festival; of building a stadium, a magnificent fountain to provide water for one or another neighborhood, or public baths; or of erecting a statue of one of the gods.

In Europe, between roughly the sixth and nineteenth centuries, the Christian Church (as well as Jewish congregations) and members played an important role in taking care of the needy—abandoned or orphaned children, the elderly, poor, ill, the homeless, and the maimed. Bequests in wills and regular charitable contributions were often obtained by using both the carrot and the stick: give and we will offer prayers in thanks so that you will receive a reward in Heaven; deny the obligation to be charitable and you'll suffer with the damned in Hell. Individuals were encouraged to contribute portions of their resources to the Church to care for the less fortunate. Mary Douglas points out, however, that such bequests not uncommonly exceeded the resources left by the deceased; however, by making their intentions of such bequests known, the potential donors at least received certain rewards and honors in their lifetimes (the fulfilling of such bequests was a problem left to the executors of their wills).

But, all in all, consumption is an action situated more in the present than in the past and even the future. Indeed, not a few are inclined to let the future take care of itself. We eat too much and say, "We'll start getting rid of our surplus flab tomorrow." We buy too much and periodically "clean out our closets" to make trips to the charitable thrift shops, or the city dumps, or have garage sales. We spend too much and find ourselves in a never-ending cycle of revolving credit charges.

And the curious thing is that few of us have any realistic sense of "where the money goes." Equally if not more curiously, those who make it their business to manage such things (will governments please make up their minds whether they wish consumers to buy more or less?) or track such things (will economists define realistically the difference between consumption and investment?) seem to be equally at sea.

There are a number of things that we are just beginning to identify as consumption items and, as well, items whose costs must be calculated in order for us to know the real price we are paying for them. The growth of the tourist industry is making us aware of the value of nature, of traditional and unique lifestyles, of escaping from crowds whether in art galleries, on beaches, or in historic venues such as Venice (which is being forced to consider rationing the number of tourists admitted each day to the city). And, of course, we are becoming more and more aware of not just the social value of consumption but, as well, its social costs.

So, life is difficult—and getting *more* difficult—even as many claim it seems to be "getting better" (though they are hard put to explain what they mean by that phrase). Even the events of shopping present problems. What do we say when asked, "paper or plastic?" If we try to pick a vacation spot, we have to question whether we want to preserve a wilderness that may have to exclude us if it is to stay a wilderness. How much is uniqueness worth to us—especially when that very originality makes it difficult to evaluate its fashionability value? When I eat or drink, smoke or ski, how do I put a cost on potential consumption risks? In a world where the latest fad is everything, is durability worth paying for? Should I purchase the more costly item that carries a ten-year guarantee or the cheaper item with a one-year guarantee—if previous purchases in the same category were discarded after a season or two? If I purchase something for its potential heirloom value, can I be sure that my children will value it too; or will they instead donate it to a church sale—or perhaps even put it out at the curb for the trash collector?

That brings us nicely to the important question of how consumption needs and wants result in our need to grapple with the risk fund of surplus and the wealth of garbage.

Chapter Nine

Surplus and Waste
An Embarrassment of Riches

It might seem that a modest level of consumption, that is, a lifestyle that practices thrift and avoids waste, would be A Good Thing, since, for example, it reduces personal stress and it conserves environmental resources. But the fact is that modest consumption combined with the human need to be productive can result in a surplus. And it isn't uncommon for surpluses to create as many (if not more!) problems as scarcity.

For one thing, most sociocultures frown on surpluses simply sitting there, accumulating, doing nothing or very little that is productive and useful. Indeed, there are some groups that strip away the superfluous, aim to eliminate excess, and delight in the diminution rather than the enlargement of scale. Let me suggest that one example might be Japan, where minimalism and miniaturization constitute important underlying cultural themes. This may have historical roots. Soon after emigrating to the Japanese islands from the Asian mainland, the new arrivals seem to have decided that they had reached the edge of the world: there was nowhere else to go and they must learn to live with what they had. The need to limit growth became a cultural imperative because there was limited living space.

There developed a fundamental value—aesthetic, secular, and spiritual—that less is more. *Bonsai* (the art of creating tray-planted miniature trees) is an apt symbol for this cultural leitmotif. To maintain bonsai trees requires constant attention to eliminating portions of roots, branches, and leaves. Bonsai gardeners work passionately to constrain growth, to manage nature, to reduce a tree (pines, junipers, and maples are the most popular) to what is defined as the essence of its nature. Cultural tools and techniques as well as knowledge of nature are used to control the natural tendency of the tree to expand and grow. As an artist tries to capture the truth of nature through accentuating or deleting particular aspects of a landscape being painted, those who mold bonsai trees seek to shape and portray nature according to their understanding of it—and, always, with an eye to subjugating any tendency to expand.

This outlook permeates other basic Japanese life components: not only are house types as well as the furnishings lean and spare, the number of children and how they are raised, relations among the family, and the ways in which communication of ordinary things as well as emotions are expressed all stress controlling exuberance and growth. So, for example, as with bonsai trees, parents tend to their children carefully, watch them constantly, and show a constant concern with the need to prune and control what we, in the Euroamerican world, would consider the natural expansiveness and creativity of young growth. This sociocultural directive to constrain and refine, to deny the willfulness of anything—plants, children, innovative entrepreneurs, the household, poetry, and so forth—that could expand and exceed its "appropriate" limits—seems to pervade Japanese life.

In most societies for most of the time, however, growth is preferred over nongrowth and surpluses are preferred over insufficiencies. The data indicate that, through much of human history, unplanned and occasional surpluses simply were ignored and left for other predators or to rot. If groups underwent erratic cycles of feast versus famine, these may have been the impetus for inventing ways to provide for future scarcity by preserving and storing current surpluses of food (as, for example, my earlier suggestion that the basis for human cooperative sharing stemmed from recognition that one could provide for future needs by "storing" food in a neighbor's belly). Some groups, fortunate enough to live in locales with a relatively stable food supply, never bothered to organize the social networks, invent managerial positions, and work to discover ways to preserve or store food.

If, however, a planned community surplus does emerge, a new problem may appear (a typical case of the good news/bad news scenario). The question then arises, "How much of a surplus is enough of a surplus?" and people begin to worry that the surplus could go to waste: Rats or rot might destroy grain before it is needed; raiders might hear of the stored resources and attack the village to seize them; individuals might die before they benefit from their labor to create the surplus; and, nowadays, tomorrow's inflation will reduce today's wealth. Further, the very presence of a substantial risk fund might lead people to begin to squander current income. So, for example, in 1998, for the first time, Americans began to spend more than they earned. As the rise of the U.S. stock market has caused the (future) paper wealth of many Americans to soar, people are continuing to spend beyond current income. They are taking on debt because they feel rich enough to afford the risk of such debt. They are assuming a future in which all things will be equal to or better than the present. An abundance (even a perceived surplus) of present wealth is leading to an increase in current consumption and future debt. Thus, to the question, "Can we have too much of a surplus?", if history is a guide in this, the answer is "Yes."

In working to encourage community members to accumulate a surplus, the community managers of ancient times had to face various rationales for resistance. In any community and however the contributions to the general welfare fund are extracted, at a certain level people begin to complain they've done enough to contribute to a community surplus. Just as present-day taxpayers, when the government announces that it has a budget surplus, respond by saying, "Well, then, cut taxes and use the surplus to let us enjoy, *now,* more of those goods or services that we need or others we would like," members of earlier communities also asked for a lightening of their tax burden: a decrease in the amount of corvée labor or the number of baskets of grains of rice; a call for a halt in the building of still more granaries (that they had to keep building to store the growing surplus); a reduction in defense spending; a more austere lifestyle for the bureaucrats, and so on.

Initially, people tend to accept the wisdom of those who urge them to work a little harder than they require for their daily needs. They can be persuaded to expend extra labor in order to produce a surplus for a risk fund. They've all experienced what life is like when, for a variety of reasons, resources decline or even disappear.

But when people begin to perceive that the costs of security are outweighing any benefit, they begin to balk. Even when they support the uses to which the taxes are put, they complain about them and begin to work out ways to avoid paying them. Canadians, for example, often say that the main difference between Canada and the United States is that Canada is a more generous, caring society. The symbol of the difference is, for the majority, comprehensive and, especially by U.S. standards, very generous entitlement programs. They especially point to their more comprehensive health care program. However, in the early 1990s, there was a sharp increase in the number of Canadians visiting the United States, and thousands of Canadians began crossing the border weekly to buy U.S. goods and smuggle them home; they were angry about a new 7 percent General Sales Tax (GST) that the federal government had put on goods in 1991. Residents from Ontario, Canada's most populous province, were especially outraged because they were already paying a 7 percent Provincial Sales Tax (PST) and saw goods become 14 percent more costly. With the PST and GST, a C$30 shirt in Ontario cost C$34.20. With a 7 percent sales tax in, say, the border city, Buffalo, New York, the cost was U.S.$32.10. In the United States, however, the majority of shop owners, struggling with lagging sales, took Canadian currency at par, dollar for dollar, despite that currency markets evaluated C$1.00 at U.S.$.89. This, of course, lowered the U.S. price even more. It took several years and a series of complex events for the anger to subside and the rush to cross-border shop to end. What makes this example noteworthy is that despite a strong national commitment to the social welfare programs that these taxes helped support, Canadians resisted the tax rise and began voting with their feet. A similar revolt has occurred in Germany where, in response to the government's attempts to collect taxes on bank savings, Germans have taken to "hiding" their money in Luxembourg. Yet, Germans, too, are proud of and dedicated to their very generous entitlement programs.

From time to time, certain goods and services provided by governments are viewed as an unnecessary "negative surplus." Despite that the usual rationale for building up a surplus is that it serves as insurance against catastrophes, people will present arguments that the elimination of certain underused, unused, or obsolete programs would allow the resources to be directed to more immediate and pressing needs. Such a redirection would transform the surplus from "negative" to "positive." The military faces this problem in every society during peaceful interludes and, when the Soviet Union imploded in 1991, there was an immediate burst of discussion as to the best ways to utilize what was labeled "the Peace dividend." The general public (and perhaps a few governments as well) believed that, with the Cold War ended, countries could cut back on defense spending (a more comfortable term than "aggressive capabilities") and put the resources to work for productive rather than destructive ends.

The resistance to governments' consumption of their citizens' resources can take many forms. Some people are unhappy with the consumption patterns of government personnel: "They spend too much on the military," or "they waste money on political boondoggles." Others complain that there are too many people who don't pay their fair share, for example, "the rich," "the big corporations," "the lazy welfare cheaters," "illegal immigrants," "religious institutions." Almost everyone has a pet target. Some citizens may add (as an excuse to cheat on their taxes) that such unfairness justifies shaving a bit here or adding there. Despite that North Americans are judged to be among the most compliant taxpayers in the world, there are always those who complain about the "freeloaders,"—the people who take but don't give—some real, many mythic. In not a few countries around the world, the most common complaint is that the public budget is a dining table at which a corrupt elite and civil service gorge themselves.

In countries where the level of taxation allows for adequate, even generous entitlement programs, there are people whose personal cost/benefit analysis indicates they're better off not contributing to their entitlement programs through various payroll deductions. Although it may be because they're undocumented workers (illegal immigrants) who fear that the paper trail left by paying taxes will lead to their discovery and expulsion, the majority of those who work outside of the official economy do so because they have been persuaded that, in the affluent industrial countries, the level of taxation and the availability of a wide range of safety nets makes it more worthwhile to work in the so-called informal economy. These types of workers pay no income taxes, nor do they directly contribute to health care programs or other forms of social security and, by working off the books, lack the protections offered those working in the formal economy, protections such as laws dealing with safety and healthy job conditions, overtime pay, minimum wages, and compensation for job-related accidents or health problems.

Though firm statistics are hard to come by, what evidence we do have indicates that the majority of those active in the informal sector have few if any other employment options. Workers may, for example, lack the knowledge of the dominant language; they may be considered too young for certain kinds of work; or, as is the case for people receiving other entitlement income (e.g., social security, welfare, health benefits), they wish to escape having those entitlements reduced or eliminated by reported earned income. A large segment are self-employed (e.g., street vendors unable or unwilling to obtain licenses), and, though all such work is identified as illegal, some are engaged in criminal activities (e.g., drug smuggling).

However, not a few of those in the informal economy argue that the deductions from paychecks earned in the formal economy would be a waste of their money. They calculate that, whether they contribute to it or not, there are alternative safety nets in place that will provide help in one form or another when they need it. A majority of those in a study I made argued they saw no reason for concern. As one woman put it, "Why worry that I'm losing social security benefits? Everybody says it's going broke anyway—and besides, when I can't work any more, I'll just go on welfare. The money's all the same and I'm not proud." Another, whose three out of four children were born with congenital heart deformities requiring repetitive surgery (one child had already had seven operations by the age of six), said she believed the health coverage she received as an unemployed single mother was far more generous than coverage received by her friends from their job-related health plans. These attitudes reflect a belief that, in a society with various kinds of safety nets, one may be a consumer of public resources without contributing to specific programs. There are enough funds to insure coverage and, further, others are willing to underwrite the costs.

Interestingly, not one of the several hundred people with whom I worked ever made the point that they, too, were paying taxes that contributed to the public purse from which they were or might eventually be drawing. They seem to ignore the fact that every consumer buys goods and services that are taxed. Prices for consumer items include charges paid for licenses and permits or import/export duties collected by the government. They purchase fishing and hunting licenses (in some rural areas a significant portion of the food consumed by the less affluent are wild resources) and permits to drive cars. Further, even the poorest pay taxes on gas and vehicle repair parts, telephone or cable TV services, alcohol and cigarettes, and purchase state-run lottery tickets (to which, according to 1996 U.S. figures, some 20 percent of the least affluent allot an average of 5 percent of their income). In short, they pay taxes on a wide range of purchases that range from over-the-counter medication to entertainment, clothes, and personal toiletries. Thus, because they are consumers, those frequently categorized as enjoying a "free lunch" still participate in the production of resources (taxes) that are transformed into goods and services. For example, medical research, the military and police, the highway system, and the agencies that monitor food and drugs for purity are provided by governments to even the most affluent citizen consumers.

It's not only the less affluent who work in the informal sector; physicians, lawyers, and other businesspeople may work off the books. Indeed, even the United States federal government has certain expenditures that escape on-line scrutiny. In most cases, the affluent cheat in order to reduce their tax liability, some concealing as much as one-third of a six-figure income through failing to record certain payments or arranging to barter services (e.g., dentists or plastic surgeons will exchange their services with a building contractor, a tutor for their children, or a caretaker for an elderly parent). Lately, money laundering of illegal gains adds to the distortion of economic data.

Aside from the problems that result when the citizens perceive the government has a surplus, surpluses present difficulties to producers (e.g., farmers with too much grain) and distributors in the business sector. Certainly, those who produce for exchange don't want to build up a surplus of unsold merchandise. Yet, many manufacturers have to prepare ahead for special selling seasons (such as Christmas or Easter). On the one hand, they must plan in advance in order to have adequate supplies to meet consumer demand and increasing sales, avoiding the risk of losing customers to competitors. On the other hand, they wish to avoid the risk of being left with an oversupply when the season is over. Just-in-time production tries to address that problem, but it works for only some items and can create problems of its own. So, again, we are left with the question relative to consumption of how much of a surplus is not enough or is too much.

All of which should indicate that having an abundance of resources—being affluent—doesn't solve all our problems. Being poor is no fun—but being rich isn't everything it's cracked up to be either.

It should be clear by now that one of the crucial questions that individuals and groups need to address is, "How do we know when we have more than we need—now or in the future?" First, there is a fine difference between "having too much" and "having more than we need." Even assuming that we are able to identify that we have more than we need, what do we do with that knowledge? At the aggregate level, cutting back on consumption may only increase a surplus—unless you also reduce production. That's difficult to do because, in many countries struggling with high levels of unemployed, cutting production means cutting jobs, and in some cases, it may require that workers be persuaded to retrain and take up alternative forms of employment. This reallocation of the workforce may not succeed because those out of work, despite their desire for employment, will, explicitly or out-of-awareness, resist doing certain jobs because the jobs are "not their kind of work" or are perceived as impossibly difficult to learn. Coal miners, steel workers, and fishermen don't want sedentary desk jobs, and for example, many males reject the idea of delivering services in hospitals or homes for the aged. Thus, despite that the highest rates of unemployment in North America are found on tribal reserves, many Amerindians reject the placement of turn-key operations on their lands; they don't want to work in factories. Many older workers, who spent years working at one particular type of work, become frustrated and feel an increase in their sense of worthlessness when they struggle—and fail—to acquire skills useful in the new HT and IT job sectors. Minorities often resent what they see as The Establishment's attempts to track them into menial and low-paying jobs. And not a few of the "surplus" unemployed find themselves being trained for work in which there are too few opportunities—leading them to complain, often justifiably, that the training programs were really dead-end jobs designed simply to "get them off the streets."

Aside from the rather implausible scenario of destroying much of our current productive technology and imposing a return to living as early humans did, our remaining options seem to be to (1) invent new ways to consume, (2) spread the wealth around, (3) preserve the resources for future use, (4) use less and invest those we do use (i.e., employ them in ways that produce future resources), or (5) waste it. Here is a short review of the trade-offs involved.

1. *Inventing new ways to consume.* We may assume, like the open-handed (spendthrift?) individual, that "There's plenty more where that came from," and raise our level of consumption by increasing the amount consumed, broadening the variety of goods and services consumed, or increasing the number of consumers. The ancient Athenians (as well as, among others, some Amerindian groups) held this attitude. The Greeks expressed the belief in the symbol of the cornucopia, the mythic "horn of plenty" that poured forth the earth's resources in a never-ending flow of riches. Similarly, until recently, many assumed that the oceans would never cease to supply an abundance of fish. And, currently, it's the position held by those celebrating the New Technology that they view as being capable of eliminating scarcity because it is now possible for humans to create a constant supply of new resources—

through, for example, genetic engineering. However, raising the level of consumption is a risky strategy. History shows it is rarely a sustainable policy because, for one thing, it rests on relying on the little we know while minimizing or ignoring the possible consequences of attempting to "manage" the vast and still largely unrealized complexity of the total world biosphere.

2. *Spreading the wealth around.* We may give the resources to those who lack them (e.g., food to the hungry, education for everyone) and identify an increasing number as entitlements. Indeed, there is a global phenomenon that a growing number of goods and services, once considered luxuries that only a few of the rich could enjoy, are now considered necessary components of life for all humans—e.g., telephones and, increasingly, e-mail addresses so that the unemployed and the elderly are able to maintain contact with those who can provide jobs or emergency medical services; specialized medical care (including extended physical therapy, access to costly "designer" drugs for rare illnesses, and psychiatric services); and access to higher education. The problem here is that, as populations expand, there are growing numbers of people who expect to receive their entitled allocation. Though expectations will grow that such entitlements will expand to include innovations initially available only to the affluent, continuing population growth may demand that we consider limiting the addition of new benefits or even require that we reduce existing quantities in the face of increasing scarcity of resources. Inevitably, it seems, we will face a situation in which "throwing more resources" at the problem will not be a viable solution; those who argue that societies can and must continue to meet the growing demand seem to assume the same kind of world as those discussed in option one—that, somehow, we will always be able to find sufficient the resources to meet increasing demands.

3. *Conserving resources for the future.* We may reduce present consumption (e.g., not cutting forests, limiting the use of water), or we may preserve and store present resources (e.g., information, semen or blood, historic buildings, or a portion of the fall harvest). This perspective is based on memories of past scarcities or on concerns that the current scarcities others are facing will soon also be a problem for us. In an extreme form, it is expressed in miserly behavior, that is, hoarding. There are two problems here. First, such conservation is not always acceptable—especially to those who are only now beginning to enjoy the benefits of the resources. Thus, many in developing nations resent attempts by affluent nations to conserve what they now consider world resources but which the former consider their own property to do with as they will. They ask why they cannot continue to use the labor of children as the poor of their locales have always done; or why they should not be able to benefit from the world demand for timber from their forests when, as their forests are exploited, they gain in employment, in cleared lands for agriculture, and in added resources for governments to increase or improve the level of goods and services they receive.

The second problem is that, despite the intention of protecting current resources from declining or disappearing, a natural deterioration or catastrophic destruction can still lead to their loss or diminishment. We may preserve a historic site only to have it destroyed in an earthquake; save an aged forest and then see it devastated by a major fire; preserve a "traditional" tribal way of life and then see the region ravaged by a flood that not only destroys thousands of lives but irrevocably alters the context in which such people have managed for centuries. In short, despite frugality, you may end up no more ahead than had the resources been consumed.

4. *Investing current resources.* The resources themselves are used to produce still more resources, that is, we are not depleting nonrenewable resources but "are putting them to work" in a productive process that, it's assumed or hoped, will allow a continued supply. The problem here is that we currently lack an adequate amount of information concerning the extent to which we may draw down resources or replace them with something "just as good." The results can be that: (a) we err in determining what constitutes a renewable base and, as in the case of fish stocks, deplete the resource below its capacity to reproduce itself; (b) in focusing on the key resource we overlook the extent to which that resource has a synergistic relation with other components (some of which have no value as resources) and thus unwittingly affect the whole interdependent chain; (c) we discover that our substitution is not "just as good" as the original.

Forests are a good example of these three results. Trees are a renewable resource but, between the time we cut them and the time the forest is restored, insects or birds responsible for various forms of life that assist the reproductive capacity of the forest can be eliminated. Further, slow-growing trees are often replaced with fast-growing species that do not have the same interface with the other species of plant and animal life that depended on the particular type of trees that are now gone. Similarly, we may err in not understanding the reproductive prerequisites of a species (e.g., schools of herring have been eliminated from certain areas because, having been fished below their sociological floor of reproducibility, the remaining herring left traditional grounds to join larger schools elsewhere). Further, some resources, (e.g., "normal" rainfall levels) may not return until the time frame has exceeded the human capability to survive.

5. *Wasting resources.* Despite good intentions we may utilize resources in ways that leave large segments of the resource's usability untouched. Though many idealize the Amerindians as "guardians of the environment," we have archeological evidence that, in some areas of

North America, massive buffalo kills took place because various groups used the technique of stampeding the herd over the edge of cliffs—resulting in only the top buffalo being butchered (and even then, often only the tongues were cut out) while those further down were left untouched.

But there are other ways we may waste resources: we may, for example, refuse to use humans to their maximum utility on grounds of age, sex, physical disabilities, sexual preference, "race," and so on. University students are among the major wasters of resources, many preferring to use their time that should be allocated to attending classes and studying for a variety of alternative activities, ultimately wasting valuable resources for learning—their professors, the libraries, or the classroom. A relatively rare form of waste is the destruction of resources for sacrificial or ceremonial purposes—for example the (now-banned) destruction of "surplus wealth" through barn burnings by the Canadian Doukabour communities. Relatively common, however, is the deliberate and selective destruction of segments of the population in war. In World War I, much of an entire generation of Europe's young men were killed or maimed during the senseless see-sawing of trench warfare; in World War II, the number of Soviet citizens who lost their lives or were left disabled was equally staggering; and, in the process once called "genocide" but now labeled "ethnic cleansing," a majority of Europe's Jews and Gypsies were selected for elimination. The waste of human resources, through one technique or another, matches in its damaging potential for the future, the destruction of natural resources. Yet it appears that this last option is the most commonly employed of the five suggested. Why should this be?

To address this question we come to the final issue that must be addressed in this discussion of consumption. In today's world, it's not easy to mark the point at which something has been "consumed"—if that word is meant to identify when a good is ended, finished, and gone forever. We may drain all the utility we need or desire from an object, but that rarely causes its disappearance; as already noted, even the actual act of consumption, the intake of food and drink, is followed by the elimination of certain products called "human waste."

It's interesting that, in the face of all our concern about managing the growing mountain of the global population's garbage, economists (and many other social scientists) continue to claim that there are only three possible paths that resources may follow: they may be invested, saved, or consumed. There's one more logical possibility: Resources that are no longer viewed as resources (they no longer have any utility) simply may be thrown away, i.e., wasted. It may be last year's fashion, an old piece of furniture, food that has been too long in the refrigerator—or it may be a building, a moral precept, or even another human—children, adults of either sex, the elderly, fetuses, or cadavers. The last sounds shocking but, in the real world, quite often that's what happens when we have a surplus. In a society where we have a lot of things, stuff, goods, anything for which we have no use—we have a problem, a big problem, a growing problem. We may call it garbage, trash, junk, debris, waste, (rather elegantly) refuse or, if we're archeologists, "material residue of the past." We may discard it or even just abandon it—as when on moving we just leave unwanted stuff behind.

However, it's important to realize that goods and services classed by some as waste may continue to have utility. This is not a new idea; after all, archeologists would be unable to construct the past if all the debris of the past totally degraded every ten years. Indeed, at the rate we're destroying and recycling waste, we may be leaving very little of the present for future generations to discover! Instead of throwing an object away we may invent new uses, as when an old-fashioned butter churn is made into a table lamp. Parents may be recycled into babysitters. Other elderly are being hired as "mall sitters." Equipped with beeper phones and on the alert to call security, they are keeping an eye out for disruptive teenagers, lost children, and bewildered customers.

Or we may discover that there is a use for the waste and debris itself: Early humans ultimately discovered that, with certain kinds of rock, the "waste" flakes they chipped away to fashion a projectile point (a spear point and, later, also an arrowhead) could themselves be used as scrapers or other kinds of points. The urban poor in emerging economies cut up old tires and make sandals from them. We may use old clothes to make quilts or rugs, and plastic bottles are now being processed and are reentering the marketplace as a new product, for example, CDs. We may invent a new product that utilizes waste or leftovers (think, for example, of casseroles). Crude oil, which only a few hundred years ago was viewed as nothing more than "ugly black goo" that made land worthless for farming or stock raising, became liquid gold when we found a use for it.

Not every item for which we no longer have a use is discarded, however. We may save something because our human sense of past and future tells us it may come in handy someday. This is why many of us have a certain drawer in our homes where we put a strange collection of things for which we have various rationales for not simply discarding—a broken pair of glasses; a key whose use is unknown; one earring, cufflink, or glove; loose change; a couple of paper clips; discount coupons (some long expired); an old receipt or invoice that we think we may someday need (e.g., for proof of purchase); some rubber bands; and so forth. The time when you finally clean out the drawer usually offers an excellent lesson on saving; for some mysterious reason, shortly after you dispose of something, you discover a need for it. To come full circle back to archeology, as anyone knows who has ever cleaned out the attic or the basement, we may use trash to retrieve knowledge about our past and the lives of the people who made it. Sometimes, however, it's knowledge and memories we want to get rid of.

The current concern with how to deal with waste exists because, as the world's population increases, and as we produce more and more things (as well as ways to package them), garbage keeps piling up and, as well, we have a growing awareness of how waste contaminates. No matter how creative we become in our use of garbage, the modern world is excreting a growing mountain of trash. And it makes no difference where in the world—as witness those emerging third world countries where, as in Cairo, thousands of people live on and make a living by scavenging in dumps.

Where does it all come from? Well, for one thing, in the process of accumulating pleasurable wealth, we also accumulate a lot of no longer pleasurable "stuff." These are goods that cease to provide us with the utility they once did and that are now simply nuisances or burdens. It becomes an aggravation when we try to get rid of them and must decide how the recycling laws ordain what we must do with that old car battery, a few almost-empty cans of paint, and a broken-down sofa—I mean a Coke-stained, cat-clawed, cushion-sagging, really broken down piece of furniture that even the Salvation Army wouldn't want—that won't fit in a trash barrel or down the incinerator of an apartment building.

Trash is full of information about you, your neighborhood, your company, your society. What is trash in Vancouver isn't the same as trash in Moscow. The garbage of each locale is unique. Archeologist William Rathje has led the way in the sociocultural analysis of modern garbage. His research is unique because he is able to talk with the people who make the decisions about what to keep and what to throw away. He has discovered that how people think they live their daily lives is often quite different from what their trash tells.

To identify trash as stuff no longer wanted may not be accurate. It may never have been wanted. There was a church pastor whose name somehow ended up on lists for catalogs featuring seductive lingerie—and even more exotic commodities. It took her over seven months to get her name off such lists but, in the meantime, the catalogs ended up in her trash. She was late in discovering that was a mistake. It isn't just those who practice industrial espionage, seek news items, want legal evidence, or practice archeology who go through trash. She discovered there was a great deal of local interest in her trash.

I once lived in a small southwestern U.S. town with a large number of fundamentalist Christian churches whose preachers regularly gave "hellfire and brimstone" sermons on, among other things, the evils of drink. The sermons were so successful that five successive votes to legalize the sale of alcohol in the county failed to pass. Shortly after my arrival, I discovered that our trash bins, sitting in the alley behind our house, waiting for collection, regularly accumulated a collection of beer cans and wine and liquor bottles. And they weren't ours. Unaware of the intensity of the town's anti-alcohol segment, our first thought was that people ran out of space in their own trash bins so they sneaked over at night and filled ours. But a local informant soon gave the true explanation: "Lots of people in the town do drink, secretly, but if they throw the empty cans and bottles in their own trash bins, the garbage collectors might tell others whose trash contained what. They might even report the backsliders (or hypocrites) to the appropriate preacher, and not many Sundays would pass before the guilty parties would have their names called out in church and the congregation would be asked to pray to help save such sinners."

Of course, there is a popular saying that "one person's trash is another's treasure." That explains the popularity of thrift shops, flea markets and yard sales. Besides, there is always the possibility that one will discover an item whose true "market value" is not known to the seller. Recently, a cheap print was bought at a garage sale for ten dollars; the buyer was really only interested in the frame. When the frame was removed, it was discovered that behind the print was an original copy of the Declaration of Independence that would later sell at auction for $2.4 million dollars. Is it any wonder TV increasingly is filled with programs on antiques and collectibles?

It's a good thing that there is a market for trash, because it's really difficult to avoid its production. A variety of attitudes is to blame: our tastes or the fashions change (think of all the clothes we give away); we become bored with certain items or pastimes (collecting stamps isn't interesting anymore); we become satiated (surely there is a limit to how much Elvis or Princess Di memorabilia one can amass?); we receive items as gifts from relatives and friends who think they know what we like (Whatever made Courtney think I'd wear earrings like that? Did my husband's sister really imagine he'd wear that tie in public? And why did six different people, in one holiday season, give me six [different] electric cooking woks and how can I ask them where they were purchased because I'd like to return them?). We grow too fat, too thin, too old, too tired (there is an enormous secondhand market for home exercise equipment). We've extracted all the usefulness from the object (think textbooks from completed courses and paperback novels). The "thing" becomes stained, battered, broken, dented, or is missing an important part. Go to the city dump or a thrift shop and see the remnants of incomplete sets of things: a piece of costume jewelry missing three stones, one cufflink, dented and stained pots and pans, jackets with one or two buttons missing, and the list goes on and on.

An individual's reassessment and transformation of "pleasurable wealth" into "irritating stuff" is what supplies those flea markets, charitable thrift shops, garage and yard sales, and antique dealers. Pawn brokers usually have a large quantity of musical instruments and golf club sets—though such shops also carry items that still have value for the owner who, needing emergency funds, only planned to surrender the item temporarily. It's estimated by Egyptian social scientists that thousands of people live in and make their living from the trash heaps of Cairo. Such poignant examples of how valuable garbage can be exists in many large cities where the poor search daily for usable waste that they may sell, exchange, wear, or eat.

One of the things that limits the accumulation of wealth and adds to the amount of discards is the lack of some place to put material things. Many lack the space to store goods. People who live in apartments or who rent rather than own frequently complain of a lack of storage space. Their dwellings lack attics or basements, and, often, closets are small and limited in number. This is one reason that the poor and the young as well as geographically mobile professionals are usually modest accumulators of material things. They prefer to spend their resources on acquiring goods and services that are readily consumable, quickly used up or worn out. Their consumption patterns not only increasingly emphasize entertainment, leisure travel, eating and drinking, but involve the type of goods we label "use-once-and-discard."

Though research indicates that residents of "poor neighborhoods" discard as much, and even more, trash than residents in more affluent locales, this may be because, in addition to lack of accumulation space, repairing a good, assuming you can find a repairer and the job can be done in less than, say, ten weeks, may be just as, if not more, costly than replacing it. The replacement item has the added virtue of being new—thus less likely to have something else break down after being repaired. And as well, it's capable of being purchased on extended, "easy" credit, not always available from those who repair goods. Another reason there may be more curb discards in poor neighborhoods is that the poor are discarding stuff that has already gone through multiple use cycles and there is no next "taker."

The urban homeless represent the extreme case of people who lack storage space. Like mobile populations everywhere—to name a few, sailors, hunters and gatherers, Gypsies, migrant farm workers, hobos and tramps, refugees and displaced persons (especially the many who refuse to give up the expectation that one day they'll be able to return home)—the need to travel light in order to avoid the energy costs of carrying a burden keeps such people relatively free of material goods. They may collect and acquire, but their "goods" are more often nonmaterial wealth, such as tattoos, games, riddles, stories, songs, dances, rituals and magical spells, and knowledge about the world they move through. But, even here, there are some possessions, as witness what is carried about by "the bag lady"; the hobo; the traveling preacher; or that temporary wanderer, the college student on a summer trip through Europe. Each carries the necessities for their current lifestyle in a bag, backpack, or small case of some sort—and, minimal as it might seem, they, too, can be tracked by the trash they leave behind.

Aside from the costs of acquiring goods, there are costs of packing and transporting them when one shifts residence (a housing pattern marked by high mobility and shared by both the poor and affluent single professionals—though for different reasons); costs of storage or display space; costs of protecting goods from theft or vandalism, catastrophes (such as floods or fires), and natural deterioration.

Trash seems an inevitable part of modern life. To some extent this is inevitable, because we are part of a global process marked by a constant search for new goods and services. For example, a great deal of waste results from failed or only partially successful experiments. This raises an important question: How can we calculate the real costs (and benefits) of so-called wasted time, energy, resources, and effort when such experimentation is both necessary and capable of providing useful information?

The tough view says such waste is inevitable if we want to explore all options (so-called "crackpot ideas" sometimes produce major changes in scientific thinking) or test results (think of wasted laboratory animals in medical experiments). When people wanted to eliminate malaria, they had to drain mosquito-infested swamps—even though it required destroying breeding habitats for a vast number of plants, animals, fish, and fowl. Was this ecological waste an adequate trade-off for saving humans from the ravages of malaria?

If each "failure" results in eliminating one dead end, has it been a waste? If a physician tries various medical routes to find a cure for an illness, are the negative results of a series of tests "just a waste of time"? If I enroll in college but drop out at the end of my sophomore year, am I a failure with two years wasted—or have I added two more years of new learning and acquired that much new knowledge?

The most popular view argues that we must continue attempts to "fine tune" for an ever smaller margin of error. First, mistakes waste scarce natural resources. In the early twentieth century, ripping up the tough-rooted wild prairie grasses on the North American Great Plains of the Midwest in order to plant corn and wheat led to the Dust Bowl of the 1930s—and to a continuing loss of thousands of acres of productive soil even today. Second, mistakes can cause human suffering and waste human potential. However, it's not easy to decide on the trade-off in waste when we decide to allow a logging company to cut the timber that, when exported, brings in money to upgrade rural services, schools, and hospitals—knowing that even when claims are made that logging is carefully monitored, it has resulted in thousands of people dying in mudslides from hillsides that, stripped of trees, became destabilized during the rainy seasons and also choked rivers and destroyed fish habitats.

A surprising amount of waste is "preventative necessity." There is the plastic "popcorn" used for protective packaging, not quite a waste since it can be used in future packages and, as well, is now being used to prevent dirt from falling through the drainage holes of pots for house plants. There is, today, a great deal of excessive packaging of small items in order to prevent shoplifting (the sharp increase of which is seen by some as a growing enslavement to the desire to acquire at any cost—or at no cost, unless one counts the potential price of a criminal record or a felony conviction). There is the "excessive" amount of packaging to prevent theft or tampering and the increasing amount of time we must "waste" standing around in airports because of the need for heightened security checks.

Most people, if asked if they opt for a short-term gain that would benefit living populations but deliver worrying costs to future generations (as in the current concern for preserving the environment for our descendants), would answer no. Yet, our ethical and moral commitments to saving lives and lessening human suffering says that we should offer, say, kidney transplants to those in need. Certain kidney diseases are genetic and, in one recent case, one family's five of six children had the defective gene, requiring kidney transplants and dialysis. Until the recent advances in medical science, most serious congenital mutations didn't allow affected individuals to have many surviving offspring. Now, medical advances are allowing individuals with "bad genes" to live to reproductive adulthood. It's been suggested that "bad mutations" are like a tax on the human species: one solution is to pay the tax promptly (that is, we can let those people with serious genetic defects die while continuing to do medical research on the problem and how to address it). Another alternative is to save them so that they make it to reproductive age and begin producing children who have a high statistical probability of inheriting the disease, who then produce more children, and so forth. This will not only increase the "genetic tax," it will also add to the costs of the health care program. And it will mean that future generations may have to bear the social cost of making cruel and personally devastating decisions about who will and won't get a kidney transplant (do we stop at a certain age—if so when? Do we bar prison inmates—if so, what types of crimes will render some inmates eligible and others not?). Do we manage to help only those who must depend on the public purse, recognizing that the rich can always afford to buy what they want? Do we waste individuals now or risk the future of the species later? Or do we use genetic modification either to modify the lethal gene or, as is now possible, to create a new kidney for a transplant? All are costly options; all have valuable benefits. Do we have the resources to do all three? Do we want to do all three? If not, which do we favor?

Some of the questions just asked may soon be out of date. The current urgency that surrounds the issue of the future path of and limits on genetic engineering is at least partly based on the awareness of geneticists, medical scientists, and public policy managers that human society is approaching a crisis of "genetic overload," a situation where the costs of addressing the health problems of genetically impaired individuals will exceed our ability to meet them. Those urging caution are concerned that science often pushes the limits without an adequate knowledge of the possible consequences. Others argue that we face a crisis in which the only path is pushing ahead on the scientific road.

As I said at the beginning, surpluses—of people, maladaptive genes, grain with no place left to store it, water when it reaches flood proportions, waste, or even, as many would charge today, scientific debris—can cause problems just as much as scarcity. In any case, it's very clear that, in dealing with human behavior, there is a surplus of issues, a great scarcity of ways to address them and, in the meantime, a growing waste of resources.

Chapter Ten

Comes the Revolution—Again

We are currently living through a period of transition (most would say a revolution) that has at least three important aspects. I'll briefly review the first two and then look at the third in some depth. The first change taking place is the extent to which human labor is moving from an emphasis on the production of goods to the production of *services*. True, the goods are still there—indeed, in ever increasing number. But the number of people engaged in producing hard goods is shifting just as dramatically as the number of people once engaged in agriculture was altered due to the Industrial Revolution. The service economy is replacing the industrial economy.

The second aspect is derived from the growing interdependence of people and societies around the globe. As that interdependence grows, more and more people are informed about events around the world, and their voices are increasingly heard. The result is a recognition and growing acceptance that their input cannot be ignored. This demand to be heard and the recognition that those with authority and power must take heed are producing a significant social change in government, corporate management, and, in general, the ways in which decisions are being made. Public choice theory is an important analytical model: *consensus* and *empowerment* are the key terms.

The third aspect is at once the most dominant and the most speculative. It derives from the view that we humans are not just rewriting the rules of the economic game, nor just building a whole new playing field. We are inventing a whole new game—*a new economy.*

Let's examine each of the following aspects of the current "revolution."

The Shift to a Service Economy

Though, along with artifacts, technology has always included mentifacts—that is, ideas of how to organize production, distribution/exchange, and consumption—it has only been in the last few years that people everywhere are beginning to recognize that "software" plays as important a role in technology as "hardware." True, even now, the material stuff in our lives still has the power to skew our view of reality. Certain "tools of the trade" are so linked to certain kinds of production that people assign a job to individuals merely on the basis of their association with the tool. As an example, a friend who is the vice president of a large company called me recently, torn between anger and high humor, to tell me how (on a dress-down Friday morning) she had dropped a cup of coffee just outside her office door. Expecting an out-of-town visitor, she rushed a few doors down the hall to get a mop from the janitor's closet. As she was cleaning up the spill, someone came down the hall and, looking at the mop, said, "Hey, hon, you better get a move on, the boss [my friend] is due to meet me here in a couple of minutes."

But the new emphasis on ideas, organizational structure, the flow of information, and the whole multitude of nonmaterial stuff is changing our emphasis on hardware. Nineteenth-century economists agreed that the increasing use of machinery would require ever higher spending as more productive but increasingly costly machines were invented to advance the industrial revolution. Although some optimists predicted a future in which machines would free humans from the drudgery of labor, the general public, government and church people, workers and capitalists alike assumed that, as human labor was displaced by machinery, jobs would be lost and massive numbers of unemployed people would become dangerously adrift, homeless vagrants. Some were concerned for humanitarian and moral reasons, but others had more secular worries. Those in government were apprehensive that this turmoil of change would end in a collapse of the social order as the unemployed and working poor rioted in the streets and turned to rural and urban banditry. But businesspeople (especially the new entrepreneurs) also began to be vexed by concerns as to how people who lacked the means to buy what was produced would be able to fuel the growth of commerce. There was, of course, the possibility of establishing markets in colonialized countries. However, most of these places were not populated with people who could afford these goods and thus were not capable of providing commodity markets on the scale of which the industrialists dreamed.

The Industrial/Fossil Fuel Revolution had made it possible to turn out relatively cheap, mass-produced commodities. Industrialists wanted to expand their markets, but, cheap as goods were becoming, there were growing numbers of people who were paid little (if they could find work at all) and who felt lucky when they could afford the basic necessities.

Manufacturers had the resources, and the machines and the energy to run them were there; the new steam-powered railroads and ocean vessels, along with the frenetic building of canals, bridges, and highways, promised more extended and faster distributional capabilities. But this potential would be stifled if there was an insufficient supply of that most fundamental component, consumers.

The Industrial Revolution didn't fail, and except for a few scattered outbreaks of violence (directed toward smashing the machines) and a brief outbreak of civil unrest that flared throughout Europe in 1848, the social wars didn't materialize—and for a number of reasons. First, the Industrial Revolution opened up other employment opportunities. Second, labor unions emerged to fight for laborers' rights. Finally, though it took several generations, those relatively small and localized disturbances that did occur led governments as well as business leaders to begin to weigh the trade-off between, on the one hand, the costs of providing social nets such as unemployment protection, pensions, and welfare programs (which provided goods and services as well as money with which to buy others) and, on the other hand, the costs of widespread civil unrest, even bloody revolution and the possible overthrow of the government itself. Not surprisingly, enlightened self-interest led the political establishment to conclude that not only did the benefits of providing some kinds of protection for the workers exceed the costs, the costs of doing nothing exceeded the costs of doing something.

Other trade-offs took place as well. Labor was not so easily displaced by machinery. Someone had to make the machinery. And it was true then as it is still true that some tasks need to be or are best done by hand. For one thing, machinery lacks the ability to discriminate certain product qualities—which accounts for the still intensive use of migrant farm labor, especially at harvest time. Further, once the decision is made to purchase a machine, it has to be paid for whether used or not but, when business is slack, companies can engage in cost cutting by dismissing human labor. Finally, and perhaps most critically, as just noted, machines don't buy things.

The problems are still with us, but they occur on a global scale and involve the decisions of many governments with many different policies. Various approaches have been suggested and used to solve the problem of how to increase production but also lower costs while, at the same time, maintaining both a flexible labor pool and increasing demand for goods and services. The "solutions" fall into two main categories. The first looks to providing adequate wages so that everyone can afford to satisfy all of their basic needs and even have some discretionary income (i.e., resources available after basic needs are met) to buy some of the things they want. The second solution relies on the community, through shared contributions of its members, to enable the government to provide minimum incomes, safety nets, the necessities as well as facilities for, say, education and recreation, that make for a healthier and better informed citizenry. These are issues that have emerged only recently (in the last one hundred years or so), and none of the solutions really have worked satisfactorily.

The new market in services seems to be able to leap over a great many of our long-standing problems with labor. While the emphasis in the service economy is on IT and Knowledge Workers (KW—the HT-end of the industry), there also has been an explosion in the Low Tech (LT) sector, in the jobs that must still, for a variety of reasons, be performed by people. Though, for the moment, the pay scale for most of what we often (and sometimes wrongly) label as "unskilled" service occupations has lagged far behind the increases for HT labor, the value and thus the price of LT labor is advancing as well. Partly this is because even work labeled LT often requires a level of technical expertise. Further, there are many tasks people can't or won't do, for example, car or TV repair, washing the windows in your apartment, sewing a torn seam. Do you plan to do any of these things yourself? Thus, in addition to HT service workers, we are developing an enormous dependency on LT service workers—and there is a growing interdependency among the two segments. The HT segment must hire people to do jobs that full-time housewives used to do or that the HT segment used to do themselves after work or on the weekend. HT people make more money, but expenses rise as they hire others to mow the lawn, clean house, run errands (such as picking up clothes at the cleaners or even shopping for wedding and birthday gifts), and as they squeeze in time at the health club or on the squash court. Gone are the babysitters one or two nights a month; now it's live-in nannies (with all the worries they bring to parents these days); eating out or stopping at the deli section replaces cooking dinner—and the house cleaner takes care of whatever dirty dishes there are. But the LT workers need HT (and other LT) workers, too. They need childcare providers, maintenance workers in their buildings, trash collectors, and medical aides; they need teachers and social workers, scientific researchers, computer programmers, and statisticians. In short, just as the manufacturer needs to hire more workers to increase production, workers need to hire more workers to increase their own production. So there's a trade-off between laboring for others (no matter how highly paid the job) and the need to rely on others to work for you.

For the affluent, the stresses of their own HT jobs combine with the difficulties of finding trustworthy and reliable people in the LT sector. It's no surprise, then, that some people are opting to adopt the lifestyle depicted by adherents of the Voluntary Simplicity Movement (VSM). True, those celebrating the VSM seem not to make the shift until they've achieved a reasonable amount of financial security and a reasonably healthy risk fund. Still, what is interesting is that the growth in the HT service sector is giving rise to the desire to return to more artisanal roots.

People may not encourage or look forward to their children being house cleaners, auto mechanics, carpenters, plumbers, or weavers—and especially not in textile mills—but they want to establish a lifestyle in which they are able to perform some of these tasks around the house themselves.

The Empowerment Process

There is growing recognition that, in an increasingly interdependent world, it is important to listen to the voices of those whose lives are affected by the changes occurring around them. As the world grows ever more interconnected, we are all coming to realize that decisions about production, distribution, and consumption are not simply issues to be addressed by the government, by union leaders and management and, in some cases, by those corporate coadventurers we call shareholders. We are hearing calls to include, at a minimum, the members of the communities in which production, distribution/exchange, and consumption occur as well as those whose environments, social and natural, will be affected by the decisions made and the actions taken. The perception of who has a stake in the outcomes is broadening—along with the realization that, while stakeholders may reap some benefits, they surely will be forced to eat the bitter harvest of any negative consequences.

There is also a growing awareness that productivity should not be considered only by counting work output; looking at how many widgets a worker has produced. For one thing, this is difficult if not impossible to do in the service segment of the economy. However, we are also more aware that decisions that affect those in the faceless segment of the economy called production do have an impact on the real people, even those who are not directly engaged in production. Belatedly, we are discovering that producers relate productive activities to the sum total of their lives. They want the opportunity to have an increased voice in and responsibility for the productive process. As noted earlier, studies have shown that people who say they like their jobs are much more forthcoming with suggestions as to how to improve the productivity of those jobs.

There is now recognition of the need to include this broader range of involved stakeholders in decision making. This, as well as the expanding role of the service sector and the growing interreliance between HT and LT workers in that sector, gives evidence of a future that will be marked by significant changes in the social relations of production. But the third aspect of the revolution we are undergoing also involves changes in the relation between humans and the natural world.

The New Economy

The recent rise of the IT/HT revolution is following a trajectory begun in the nineteenth century; it's reducing the ratio of capital to output by lowering the cost of capital. For example, in just a few decades the same information that in the mid-1970s required equipment that cost one million (U.S.) dollars to generate has fallen to about U.S.$25.00.

Let's return to the Law of Diminishing Returns, the economic law predicting that, over time, returns on incremental growth will decline. Recall (in chapter 3) how adding more workers may, at a certain point, actually lead to a decline in productivity. One worker produced ten widgets; two workers produced twenty-five; but three produced only thirty-three. Add a fourth worker and we may find that the number of widgets produced is forty-one. Add a fifth worker and the number of widgets turned out is forty-six, four below the expected minimum fifty! What happened?

Possible explanations: The company couldn't avoid increases in variable costs for, among other things, producing more widgets requires more raw materials and hiring more workers. So, trying to increase profits "on the cheap," the company tried to avoid increasing fixed costs (the costs that remain the same whether one hundred or ten thousand widgets are produced). The company didn't want to borrow money to buy more land and expand the plant; that would have increased fixed costs for, whether business continued to boom or suddenly dropped, interest on the loan would have to be paid each month. Moreover, the decision makers ignored the fact that putting five people into a space where the maximum production efficiency would allow for only three would result in crowding—which led to flow-pattern confusion, which led to inefficient work patterns, which led to a drop in production per worker—and in addition made for unhappy workers.

The same rule seems to apply to distribution: Add one new road, traffic moves more easily; add two, then three additional roads and traffic flow continues to move with increasing efficiency—though, again, each additional road doesn't increase efficiency as much as the first. But adding a fourth road gains us little, and when we add a fifth, we may encounter a peculiarity; the traffic flow declines in efficiency; drivers find themselves returning to the traffic jams, bumper-to-bumper traffic, crawling along at five or ten miles an hour. There is a rise in the number of accidents and, of late, a growing number of instances of road rage. Just adding more highways not only may not help, but it can hamper traffic flow; for one thing, those new facilities attract a growing number of drivers from older, "less efficient" roads.

The Law of Diminishing Returns may be applied to consumption. As anyone hankering after "The Body Beautiful" knows, increasing the amount one exercises ultimately begins to bring diminishing returns; despite added effort, one's body weight begins to stabilize. Similarly, decreasing one's daily caloric intake can go only so far; soon, we begin to feel the diminished utility of losing that extra half-pound over a period of three weeks relative to the value of the extra calories of a single meal with a good-sized steak.

Return for a moment to the VSM. Whole communities are now appearing whose membership is dedicated to trying to "cure the disease of affluenza"—that is, that seemingly insatiable desire to increase the number of things one has, the things one does—activities usually accompanied by an increasing concentration on getting the money to achieve these goals. However, those signing on to the VSM are opting to live slower, quieter lives in which family, neighborliness, and simple activities, such as gardening, talking around the dinner table, playing family games together, walking in the woods, and so forth, replace the compulsive drive to work harder and longer, so as to earn more income, so as to consume more and live faster. Of course, it's difficult not to note that both the VSM people and the poor or downwardly mobile are dealing with the issue of living at less than average levels of consumption. However, as noted earlier, paradoxically, the lives of VSM people are just as dominated by issues of consumption as are those of people still caught up in the rat race. Further, for VSM supporters, downsizing and increased frugality is voluntary; for the working poor, the chronically under- or unemployed, or those for whom downward mobility was from a low rung on the ladder to begin with, there may never have been any real chance of becoming a real competitor in that race. In any case, a major premise of the VSM supporters is that, in the drive to consume, we are pillaging nature and destroying resources. They combine with others who cry out that, unless we humans begin to consume less, we will leave an impoverished world for all future generations.

Now, however, there are economists and others who are rejecting most if not all of these old economic truths. These contrary voices maintain that, while these rules might still apply when you talk about farmers trying to grow more wheat or manufacturers trying to produce more widgets, they're increasingly irrelevant and even absolutely untrue when applied to the domain dominated by HT, IT, and KWs. There is, they maintain, a whole new world that began to take shape in the last decades of the twentieth century. In the debate, questions about productivity are key.

It's always been difficult to measure the productivity of those in the service sector. And, despite new and sophisticated models, it really doesn't seem to be getting easier. We may be getting more graphs, pies, charts, tables, and the like, but most are descriptive not explanatory. They show what is happening, but rarely do they address why—so that doesn't really help much. A simple example will show one aspect of the problem. An acquaintance, a computer programmer, tells me that when he reaches a certain point, he goes "brain dead"; he has to "turn off" and surf the Web or play a game. This, he says, allows his brain to work on the problem subliminally. "You have to back off so that you can get away from the details that stop you from thinking about the problem in new ways." Is a break to play a computer game productive or wasted time? A difficult question, and yet there's a growing attempt to constrain the amount of time that employees take on the job to use the computer for "personal" rather than "work-related" activities—though, as just indicated, it is sometimes tricky to define these terms. Employers say that research shows that as much as two hours of an employee's typical working day may be employed in what company heads consider non-work-related activities. Increasing numbers of employers are viewing this as a type of employee theft, and attempts are being made to control it. In the early summer of 1999, there was a widely noted case of an employee who was dismissed for "excessive personal use of his employer's computer facilities." Thanks to the Web, workers from all over the world have heard about the case and have used all forms of the media to express their outrage. A common response has been that such punitive efforts would be met by employees devising "ways of getting even."

So the question becomes whether four hours of "heroic effort" and, say, two hours "wasted," are more productive than eight hours of effort that is just enough above whatever is deemed average to win a raise or a bonus—or to avoid losing one's job. Further, how much attention do you pay to variable output per hour if you're concerned with measuring daily or weekly output? And how, especially relative to services, do you measure quality?

The questions being raised by these concerns are adding to a general (though sometimes concealed) feeling of uncertainty. As we lose old methods of and standards for evaluating and measuring, there's a growing sense that the future (any time from next month onward) is unpredictable and volatile. Adding to the confusion is the clamor of voices that claim that the economic rules that made sense of yesterday's world won't help to make sense of what's going on today—nor, more importantly, what may be going on tomorrow.

Let's return yet again to the Law of Diminishing Returns. That law is based on the premise that the basis of production includes not just labor and capital but raw materials as well—especially land resources and the water, timber, minerals, and fossil fuels the land offered. Since these resources are finite and most are nonrenewable, sooner or later, goes the argument, we'll run out of them. But, worse, even before that happens, these resources will become so expensive to locate and, if found, so difficult to retrieve, that costs will exceed benefits. Indeed, ultimately they will have to be priced at a level that will exceed the ability of most people to purchase them.

Link up the Law of Diminishing Returns with one of the more curious findings of biologists and botanists who have addressed the interesting question of why, given that growth is an integral part of living things, people and plants (e.g., trees) at some point stop growing. Why don't they just keep getting taller, and taller, and taller? You've now arrived at the more general argument that there are natural limits to growth.

Economist Paul M. Romer, for one, rejects all this, and his ideas have already gained sufficient interest that he's been suggested for the Nobel prize in economics for his insights. He has a favorite way to dramatize his vision of the World of Tomorrow. He asks that we take note that modern chemistry now provides us with the tools to reorder the basic building blocks of life. This being so, he argues, there are no longer limits to growth. Because the life sciences (e.g., chemistry) now have the potential to create anything, we now have the promise of an infinite supply of resources. We are, for example, now capable of redesigning the natural protein structures made up of carbon and hydrogen, thereby producing new resources created from the limitless supplies of these components. As a case in point, he asks us to consider a world made up of hundreds of thousands of small chemical refineries, each capable of directing itself to a new locale, as well as searching for its own input. It maintains itself and, if damaged, can in many cases, repair itself. It can produce copies of itself and, best of all, none of this requires human intervention.

Some find this vision exciting but distanced too far in the future; just as many others find it frightening and far too immediate for comfort. Romer tells both (but especially the latter) to relax; we already have such a chemical refinery. It's called a cow.

Say what? The point Romer is making is that the cow (as well as most other living things) took millions of years to evolve. But despite this long period of experimentation—species emerging, evolving into still more new species, some becoming extinct—there still remains a mind-boggling number of combinations of chemicals and atoms that do not exist and, to our knowledge, never have. But they could. There's no "law of nature" that would be violated if they did. And humans are now capable of exploring these possible combinations, of coming up with new forms of life, new chemical compounds, new substances.

Think, for a moment about a kaleidoscope. In its traditional form, it's simply a tube containing two mirrors forming a V and, at the bottom, usually a dozen or so bits of broken glass. As one looks through a small opening at the top of the tube and slowly turns the bottom portion, the different pieces of glass (only some reflected in the space formed by the two pieces of mirror) keep failing into an almost endless array of new arrangements. While a kaleidoscope consists of just a few simple components, the design recombinational possibilities are almost endless. So it is with the basic building blocks of the universe. Paul Romer and others are exploring what new kinds of materials their recombinations are capable of producing—and, as well, what uses we may find for them.

As I've noted in the previous chapter, very little matter actually vanishes, and we are often surprised to see how long material—and non-material—"stuff" can persist. The worlds envisaged by Romer and others offer numerous possibilities, and only one of them is a never-ending recycling of materials that will provide us with an equally endless supply of resources. Resources can be utilized yet ever continue to hold the potential for further reutilization. This means, says Romer and others, that we are on the threshold of discovering how to create new combinations of the inorganic and organic stuff of life and to deal with the age-old problems of human existence. Are certain species in danger of becoming extinct? Clone them. Are certain resources running dangerously low? Replenish them by creating or even replacing them with new supplies out of materials that are plentiful. Do we encounter new problems? Address them by utilizing the never-depleted resources of human creativity and imagination. Use the capacity of our species to weave past, present, and future together so that we may see (and foresee) such problems and work out new ways to address them.

A concrete example of life in this Utopian world: Statistics show that the first year of life is the most vulnerable. This is especially true in emerging economies. Infectious diseases (particularly from polluted water and inadequate or nonexistent sewage systems) are the major culprits. But current research shows that we soon will be able to alter the DNA of cows so that their milk will contain a protein to protect babies from these diseases. In many emerging economies, a common rationale for large families is the need to overproduce in order to insure some will survive to adulthood. Since many die in their first year, a decline in deaths might well lead to a decline in births, and fewer would then suffer the various problems caused by malnutrition; fewer would grow into adults suffering regimes of poverty. One major objection: Mother's milk also produces such protective inhibitors and, in addition, provides certain psychological benefits due to the loving, tactile interplay between mother and infant. However, mothers (who in some sociocultures may nurse children until the latter are age six or seven) may not have enough milk to provide for all their nursing children; their milk may dry up due to their own health problems; or the mother may die in childbirth. Another objection: What do we do about those populations where there is a widespread lactose intolerance that restrains the use of bovine milk? "Not to worry," say the New Scientists, "we'll be able to invent other ways to address that problem."

By now, I assume you're waiting to hear the trade-offs, the Bad News after the Good, the costs that go along with the benefits. And, sure enough, they're there. For, of course, when laying out the future, we can never be sure we've covered all our bases: What might be the unanticipated or unintended consequences of such human meddling? More importantly, are the problems capable of emerging and multiplying so rapidly that we're incapable of addressing them before we are overwhelmed by them? We already have come face to face with the problem that not only does the human body build up a resistance to antibiotics, there is growing evidence that over time the organisms these drugs were designed to attack have, through natural selection or mutation, begun to create new forms that are immune to the drugs. Those who oppose or wish to constrain our headlong rush to create new solutions urge that we move more slowly and cautiously, pointing to the new "superviruses" that have already emerged and are currently beyond the reach of our existing medical and pharmaceutical capabilities. We could be vulnerable to a pandemic for which we couldn't prepare a timely response. In the world-wide influenza epidemic that occurred in the fall of 1918, it's estimated that at least 20 million died in a few months.

There is growing worldwide concern about the increasing manipulation of nature when there is so much we do not yet understand about the possible consequences. A number of European countries have barred genetically altered foods from the United States from entering their markets. Dolly, the famous sheep who was cloned to produce an exact replica of herself, caused great concern in many sectors—the general public, scientists, and government personnel alike. It was recently announced that Dolly's clone has demonstrated aging effects indicative not of her own date of creation but representative of the age of the animal from which she was cloned. Again, part of the dilemma is we're not sure that Dolly's clone's "premature aging" is a trivial matter (just keep cloning; what difference does the life span of the clone make?) or a significant problem. Meanwhile, as the debate intensifies, we continue to destroy lands where existing plants provide valuable remedies already tested over time by native inhabitants but that both we and the current users are now at risk of losing forever.

In the growing and increasingly heated dispute about biotechnology, proponents and opponents are divided by various concerns. They range from issues as to the kinds of risk, the degrees of uncertainty as to the magnitude of various risks; long-term versus short-term costs/benefits of biotechnology; the urgency of addressing needs according to a triage model; and, most fundamentally, whether it is better to err on the side of caution or go for broke and trust that humans will be able to solve any problems as they arise. Many fear that, in the desire to focus on present needs and future benefits—the capability to end famine, alleviate the effects of drought, wipe out illnesses at a cost of a penny or two per capita, eliminate genetic defects in fetuses, the list grows daily—we will create . . . what? Think back to the debate over the NewLeaf potato and other GM products. Note, too, that farmers in India are claiming that GM cotton is violating their human rights. They're concerned that such crops will inevitably produce a boll weevil that is resistant to the toxin that now destroys it. Then, they say, their crops and their livelihood will be wiped out by what may be a super boll weevil, one so powerful that it will wipe out cotton worldwide before we are able (if we are able) to come up with a way to fight it. And it's possible. In any case, say those who urge caution, inserting new genes into an organism leads to the creation of new proteins, and no one can predict the effect of such proteins on human health.

It was not too long ago that DDT was hailed as a major breakthrough in ending worldwide famine. Insecticides would be a universal panacea to protect plants from the ravages of disease and insects. But, as years passed and generations of plants, animals, birds, and humans came into existence showing the deleterious effects of exposure to DDT, we began to discover the trade-off. Now DDT is banned, although in some cases it didn't happen soon enough. Again, we were told that various other insecticides held no risk for humans; we sprayed corn to prevent corn weevils from boring through the husks to the juicy kernels and cores. Now, however, some research is suggesting that the two-decade leap in allergies among North Americans may, at least in part, be the result of ingesting insecticide-laden corn foods. Question: What option do you select? Is your choice going to be GM Sweet Corn (free from insecticides); insecticide-laden but GM-free corn; organically grown but, for the poor, prohibitively expensive corn; or adding all corn to the list of "foods we shouldn't eat"?

Remember, however, according to Romer and others, reinventing nature isn't new. All forms of life have been doing just that since the beginning of life. Humans have been doing it since the beginnings of agriculture and stock raising. The major difference is that, prior to the biotech revolution, cross-breeding techniques to select for specific genetic characteristics were crude, haphazard, and time-consuming; now they are faster, the results are more predictable, and we now are capable of cross-breeding species that, formerly, we could not.

In the latter half of the nineteenth century, the entire wine-growing area of Burgundy was devastated by the joint attack of cryptogamic diseases and, more significantly, by the insect phylloxera, which attacked and killed the roots of the vine stock. Both the new disease and phylloxera accompanied North American vine stocks, brought to France by growers attempting to introduce new grape varieties. In the nick of time, it was discovered that grafting the few remaining old vine stocks onto the phylloxera-resistant American stocks would save French vineyards. True, critics warned that the quality of the Burgundy wines would diminish, and growers would end up with the distinctively "foxy" tasting wine produced by North American grapes. The unique wines of France, going back thousands of years, would, they warned, disappear forever. Fortunately, the grafting not only allowed the native Burgundian vine stocks to survive, but the crisis created the need to look at the vines as well as wine production in new ways. This led to new technologies that, in turn, led to improved varieties that—surprise!—French consumers found more to their liking than the original wines. So we have another Bad News/Good News example.

We were lucky in the case of attempts to manipulate vine stocks, and other experiments have also worked well. Suppose, however, that the catastrophes predicted for GM plant and animal foods do become real;

will science *always* be competent (or lucky) enough to be able to deal with the consequences—and in timely fashion? Further, are agribusinesses, chemical concerns, and farmers, as well as the general public, risking upsetting the long-term equilibrium in nature in order to cash in on short-term gain? Will future generations have to pay compound interest on the resources we are purchasing for consumption now? Or are proponents of biotechnology correct in asserting that there is nothing to fear, since such GM is only the latest development in a long history of hybridization?

So far, Europeans are much more concerned about the GM issue than are North Americans: In England, for example, the debate is so open, widespread, and heated that public icons such as former Beatle Paul McCartney and Prince Charles have weighed in, announcing that they will spurn such foods. In a recent debate in the British House of Commons, one member of Parliament labeled Monsanto "Public Enemy No. 1" (ignoring the fact that other firms, e.g., both the Swiss company Novartis AG and the British company Zeneca Group PLC also produce similar products). In response to the public outcry against GM foods, the major supermarkets in the United Kingdom have withdrawn them (or, at least, those currently under siege in the media and by environmental activists). In France, farmers are burning fields and shops they suspect are related to the production or distribution of such foods. It may be that since the powerful Rockefeller Foundation has weighed in on the debate we will see a major shift in efforts to restrain if not prohibit GM production. It seems likely, however, that this is only a temporary setback for the supporters of GM agriculture, and the issue will not soon be laid to rest.

What might have been the choice of the potato farmers in Europe at the time of the Great Blights of 1845 and 1846, blights that destroyed potato harvests from Ireland to Russia? Ireland, whose farmers were the first to adopt the potato after its introduction from the New World, became particularly dependent on the potato; it was especially hard hit when disease destroyed harvests two years in a row. The loss resulted not just in famine and starvation but in scurvy, dysentery, and other health problems. The Great Famine had enormous social consequences as well; over 12 percent of the Irish population died, and almost 20 percent of the population was forced to emigrate. Rural villages were left in internal disarray as social networks collapsed when the healthiest young adults were forced to leave the oldest, the youngest, and the sickly behind to deal as best they could. Faced with the alternatives of, on the one hand, starvation (even death) or forced immigration to England, North America, or Australia versus the possible long-term risks of the blight-resistant potato on the other hand, which would they have chosen? For those who chose immigration, the massive number of arrivals so overwhelmed the foreign cities into which they poured that they became increasingly unwanted; until well into the 1880s, public places in North America often had signs reading "No dogs or Irish allowed."

There is one more, very recent example of the dilemmas being posed by the question of how to proceed with ongoing experimentation on genetic modification of plants. A report in the prestigious weekly scientific journal *Science* (A. S. Moffat, Geminiviruses emerge as serious crop threat, December 3, 1999, p. 1835) notes that recently the global transport system has expanded the range of the white flies that carry what has been labeled the geminivirus from remote corners of the world where the virus received little attention to regions important to world food production. In just the 1991–92 growing season, Florida farmers saw $140 million in tomato crop damage; in the Dominican Republic, up to 95 percent of the tomato crop, primarily planned for export, was infected.

Various control techniques (e.g., plowing under the infected plants and the use of pesticides), have proved ineffectual. In the meantime, the unique characteristics of the virus allow it to swap DNA with other species of viruses that are distantly as well as closely related. Thus, maize (corn), cotton, pepper, beans, and cassava are also threatened. In other words, the geminivirus is itself engaging in the production of GM organisms.

Several potentially helpful strategies are being pursued in laboratories but all involve adding a protein to the plants' DNA. Despite the increasing furor about such GM activity, Claude Fauquet, director of the International Laboratory for Tropical Agricultural Biotechnology, believes growers will accept plants modified to resist the geminivirus threat: "When you have plenty of food on your plate, you may choose against transgenic techniques. But when you lose 35 percent of your income to crop losses, you don't care. . . ."

Despite all the talk about broadening stakeholder empowerment, are we actually *implementing* the choices of those to whom we say we are listening? Equally important, does everyone really have a choice? Suppose, for example, that farmer Brown chooses GM seeds while farmer Jones in an adjoining field chooses traditional potatoes and either grows potatoes organically or employs traditional herbicides to protect them from the blight. When natural selection produces a superfungus, the result of farmer Brown's choice, the potatoes of both farmers will be equally vulnerable. Did Farmer Jones really have a choice—or did Farmer Brown make it for him? Did Farmer Brown really have a choice, or did market forces select his "choice" for him? Who is better suited to make the choice: scientists, government officials, informed members of public advocacy groups such as Greenpeace, the farmers, members of the amorphous entity we call "the public" (which includes any and all of the above)? And if we try to adhere to Coase's formula, can we achieve a timely decision—indeed, can we reach a decision at all?

In sum, should we try to deal with pressing current problems and assume that if or when unanticipated consequences emerge as a result of our "solutions," we'll be able to deal with them? Or should we be cautious, though it may mean a continuation of human misery and suffering, for untold generations to come? Do we go for short- or long-term solutions? Do we do what we can with the scientific capabilities we have to address current problems—or, to avoid (or at least minimize) future risk, should we let the misery continue? (Remember, the crucial decisions are often in the hands of affluent members of affluent societies.) Will the consequences of these revolutions be as massive as the emergence of the Industrial Revolution and the capitalist global market system? What other revolutions lie just around the corner, currently as unimaginable to us as those in which we're participating were to our parents and grandparents?

In any cost/benefit analysis, we have to make decisions about the future on the basis of limited (in some instances woefully inadequate) information, trying to measure current costs, benefits, and risks against some nebulous, flexible "future" costs, benefits, and risks. If you or a loved one had a need now, were at risk now, would you know *all* your options? Assuming you did, how would you go about weighing them and choosing between them? What choice would you make? Would you plunge ahead and try the chancy drug or operation; would you experiment with the new seed, the new crop; would you raise taxes to help fund another new highway? Or would you opt to delay until more studies were done to determine possible consequences? Do you vote for employment now and "worry about the environment later," or do you choose to "protect the environment now" despite concerns that you may spend months, perhaps even the rest of your life, unemployed?

It's an odd thing about the concerns to which humans address their attention. For example, most studies show that a majority of Euroamericans express fears about the "hazards" of nuclear-powered generating plants. Yet hundreds of coal miners every year die in mine accidents and from work-related diseases, and no one expresses a desire to eliminate the use of this fossil fuel because of those proven occupational hazards. Our attention relative to coal focuses, instead, on the environmentally polluting effects of this energy source. Why?

A number of people ranging from anthropologists to zoologists, money managers to management gurus, philosophers to politicians, are studying the risks and the promises of these various "revolutions." The only consensus so far is that no one, anywhere, can remain aloof from them. A reasonable question, however, is which of the revolutions will simply fizzle out, which will be only partially successful, and which may prove to be only a prelude to some real revolution, a truly dramatic change just around the corner? Think small for a moment and consider the example of teenagers—or the growing number of seniors more than seventy years old—who have forsaken TV and malls to hang out in chat rooms and surf the Web. Consider the exchange we are making; chat rooms and the Internet in return for the loss of actual neighborhoods with real faces at the windows we pass (faces of people who may be spying in order to spread gossip but also may be there to lend a hand or a shoulder when we need it). Think more expansively and consider farm wives in rural Kansas or Saskatchewan charting on household computers the world commodity markets for wheat or pork belly futures in order to make production decisions about the family farm—but whose "decisions," in point of fact, may be little more than responses to the actual decisions that have been made by global agribusinesses and the forces at work in the worldwide commodities market. Think globally and consider, on the one hand, recent International Labor Office studies that show that an estimated 60 million children between the ages of five and eleven labor as much as eighteen hours a day—but also stop and consider how, in isolated villages all over the developing world, incalculable numbers of children are learning with the aid of satellites and computers.

Information and the speed with which we may acquire it are growing, but perhaps the trade-off here is a decrease in that information-synthesizing ability we label "knowledge." Common sense may be becoming increasingly uncommon. On the one hand, businesses appear overnight and in a matter of days become multibillion-dollar players in the global markets. On the other hand, businesses disappear overnight as major mergers occur and companies, in an orgy of corporate consumption, fight to consume for fear they'll be consumed. People have a mobility of which no nomad ever dreamed: they move around the globe casually, travel thousands of miles for a few days of vacation or for some special event (in the course of 1999, some fifteen hundred couples flew from Japan to Disney World in Orlando, Florida, to get married); work for two or three different companies at a time as consultants; take it for granted that they and most of their friends will not work longer than a year or so in any one position.

When our species first emerged, we lived as mobile hunters and gatherers, starting each day with a rough sense of what we were after but always on the lookout for some special prize—or, when unable to get what we really wanted, ready to settle for whatever we could find, even scavenging the carcasses that other animals left behind after they'd eaten their fill. When you're an opportunistic forager or scavenger, you hope for the best but are ready to accept that something is better than nothing.

Since our beginnings, we humans have gone through a series of changes and transformations. Now, some four million years later, we are entering a new era—call it the New Millennium, or the HT Revolution, whatever—an era marked by a growing number of people (and things) on the move. The human tide consists of immigrants, part-time workers following the job markets, and members of the growing army of consultants, advisors, and so forth. They may be refugees forced from their homes by war and hunger, or they may be one of the legions of jet-setting, globally focused governmental personnel, military, business professionals, and entrepreneurs. Their territory is a landscape filled with risks and rewards because of the continual streams of innovations and other unfamiliar "stuff" that may make life better—or worse. Just as early humans did, we have had to invent new concepts and terms (some would even claim a whole new language) in order to have ways to think about this new, unfolding world.

And the human historical process has taken an ironic twist: Today, as we deconstruct the Agricultural and Industrial Revolutions, we are once again adopting the mobile and unpredictable lifestyle of our ancestral hunters and gatherers. The resources may seem different. Early humans were after meat, edible roots, fruit and nuts, perhaps the unanticipated honeycomb find, the right material for a necessary tool, safe shelter for the night; we modern folk seek jobs, the right connections, information, an unexploited commodity niche, the right software for a necessary task. But, at base, the needs and wants are the same. Like earlier humans, we still seek to satisfy our need for food and shelter; we fear illness, old age, and death; we enjoy sexual partnering; we celebrate birth; and we find pleasure sharing "the good things of life" with friends and family.

Never in our history have we humans had so much information and knowledge about the world available to us. Yet, despite this increase (perhaps because of it), we are really no more capable of predicting the future than were our ancestors. They had far less information, but they also lived in a far more finite and immeasurably slower world. Indeed, given the growing velocity of change and innovation, moderns may be even more in the dark than our ancestors. But, through it all, we humans have, perforce, continued to try to make sense of the world, employing give and take—trade and trade-offs—both in everyday life and in the context of major world events. No matter how revolutionary the current (and future) revolution(s), it's not likely that this will change.

Glossary

Terms frequently have multiple usages; a glossary helps a reader to see which usage is central in the specific context of the work. However, any definition is risky and bound to be controversial. Specialists disagree with each other but become vitriolic when a generalist invades their turf. A commonly used strategy to avoid attack is to note that what is presented is an "operational definition," that is, the term is built on the researcher's basic premises and is specific to the context in which the concept is employed. It is considered to offer insight into the perspectives, biases, and foci of the definer. All of the following terms are to be considered operational definitions.

Affluence (cf. *Poverty*) Both affluence and poverty are relative terms. We cannot define one without having the dimensions of the other. Whatever the words mean, they should not be measured in terms of access to material goods only; services and such Goods as respect or power also matter. Further, since the identity of valued resources varies from group to group (even individual to individual) and shift as our information about uses for and access to such resources change, neither is an absolute. Whichever we address, few if any affluent persons or groups do not find themselves poor in some thing(s)—and those who live in poverty may have access to some resources that even the most affluent might lack.

Alienation (of property) The loss of control over the utilization of a good or service through its surrender to another, for example, through sale, as a gift, or forced seizure. The latter situation, however, does not carry the same bundle of alienation characteristics since the individual or group that loses control did not agree to the alienation.

Allocate To partition or set shares apart for a particular purpose according to a purposeful plan.

Altruism Altruists are those who perform acts in which their own benefits are not only disregarded, they are not even considered. Altruistic acts are selfless, that is, they are performed solely because actors are concerned with the welfare of others, without thought for one's self. In philosophy, it is a doctrine that argues that the proper concern of all individuals should be the common good, not personal rewards or satisfaction.

Those who believe that there are genuinely altruistic acts are deeply uncomfortable with a cost/benefit model. For example, R. W. K. Paterson in *The New Patricians* (1999) has identified "Patricians" as those individuals for whom a life based on achieving optimum benefits at the least cost would be a life not worth living. The actions of Patricians, Paterson argues, are based on beliefs and values, and guideposts for action that embody idealism, heroism, generosity, disinterestedness. True Patricians (and class, wealth, or station of life has no relevance) possess the ability to make such fine and reckless gestures as giving up their own lives to save that of strangers. They live lives based on a rejection of whatever is calculating, self-serving, and materialistically reductive, all qualities that Paterson argues mark the lives of "Plebians."

However, the cost/benefit model presented here argues that, while decisions are calculating and self-serving, they need not be base or materialistically reductive, and they may, at the same time, serve the larger good as well (cf. enlightened self-interest, in which selecting from the broader populace improves ones' own life as well). At different times and in different contexts, all of us are capable of choosing to be either Plebians or Patricians, to use Paterson's terms.

Arbitrage In economics, a term that refers to the purchase of a good in one market and its quick (often instantaneous) sale in another locale where the price is higher than in the first. Actual delivery may be delayed for months. The objective is to profit from the price difference in the two markets. But, from an anthropological perspective, if one combines this concept with the role of the entrepreneur, the term may be broadened usefully by identifying entrepreneurs as arbitragers who profit by exploiting the difference between labor costs, consumer preference, and so forth in different locales. Globalization and the Internet have brought new importance to this strategy in the world trade system.

The economic anthropologist Harold Schneider (see Bibliography) offers a classic example of arbitrage drawn from the Turu of East Africa. Among the Turu, cows are valued more highly than steers because, while a steer is a steer, a cow has the potential to reproduce herself. At one time, the central government to which the Turu were subject set up a government market program. It valued steers more highly than cows. Turu arbitragers were able to buy steers relatively cheaply in local markets and sell them in the government market at a higher price, thereby reaping a handsome profit.

Artifact (cf. *Mentifact*) Any material thing whose use has been determined by its physical or cognitive shaping by humans. A rock, unaltered except as it's repetitively held and used to hammer something—nuts, for example—becomes an artifact because a human has identified it as a useful tool. Over time, usage alters the shape of the rock. But all material goods that are the product of human imagination and utilization are artifacts (the preferred British spelling is "artefact"). Mentifacts, on the other hand, are nonmaterial; they are the ideas, the rules, the procedures—the "software," if you like—of human existence. Cars are artifacts; the idea of the assembly line to produce them is a mentifact. A material religious object is an artifact, but the ideas that shape what the object means relative to its religious identity—whether as an object to revere or to be destroyed—are mentifacts. A mountain or rock may be designated as "sacred" even though its identity relating to other mountains or rocks is invisible to, say, a geologist or nonbeliever. A house is an artifact, as are all the planks, nails, plumbing, wiring, and so forth, that go into it and, as well, all its furnishings. But the word "home" is more of a mentifact, bringing to mind all sorts of life experiences.

Authority (cf. *Power*) This is the legitimate exercise of the capacity to manage the lives of others according to the authority holder's decisions. "Legitimate" usually means such actions are accepted by those being managed as appropriate and proper.

There is a distinction between authority and power: Power is the ability to persuade/compel others to do as the power holder wishes. This may be accomplished by sheer force of personality (e.g., the charismatic leader), persuasive speech, the threat/use of negative consequences (e.g., rewards withheld), or the promise of benefits (e.g., bribery).

Power without authority is common. However, though it is more unusual, authority may exist without power (the United Nations is often used as an example of the latter). As President Andrew Jackson said, during a dispute with the newly established U.S. Supreme Court, "They [the Court] made the law; now let them enforce it." Similarly, Hitler is said to have responded to those who expressed concern about papal disapproval of his actions, "How many [military] divisions does the Pope have?"

Barter In premonetary sociocultures, barter is the exchange of goods and services, the identities and quantities given one for the other being determined by those exchanging. In modern societies, money is used as a measure of value for each commodity exchanged (as when Nigeria gives oil to Russia in exchange for wheat but uses the monetary price of these commodities on the world market to determine the ratios of each to the other).

Budget A system of allocation that distributes specified quantities of a resource for particular uses.

Capital (cf. *Social capital*) Capital is resource-producing resources. I've defined it this way in order to make the term cross-culturally and cross-temporally applicable. Capital is any resource that is neither simply saved (with no intent of using it for future investment) nor preserved until some future time when it will be consumed. The definition used here allows anthropologists to see "capital" in a wide range of contexts, including: hunters and gatherers imposing rules against killing females during breeding season; farmers saving seeds from one harvest in order to plant them for the next season's crop; a female's capacity to produce a live, healthy baby; information and knowledge acquired and being put to use in a work environment. *Capital*, as the *Oxford English Dictionary* puts it, is "wealth in any form used to help in producing more wealth."

Though economists make a sharp distinction between savings and investment (it is not until resources are invested that, for economists, these resources [wealth] become capital), this is a fuzzy area. Distinguishing between "working capital" and "potential capital" resolves some of the difficulties. If the owner of a resource identifies a resource as something intended, at the appropriate time, to be put to work, it is potential capital. For example, it's not uncommon in some rural areas of emerging economies for parents to be torn between preserving seed for next year's crop (potential capital) and the need to provide immediate food for their children. The children, if of an age to be providing useful labor, would be maintained (i.e., "paid") with the food provided by the seed (as flour); the seed would be turned into working capital rather than preserved for the next harvest (potential capital). On the other hand, since parents often see the production of children as a type of investment for the parents' future well-being, the children themselves constitute capital as defined here. In short, there is a transitional period in which it is difficult to differentiate between resources that should be designated "savings" and "investment" unless we know the intention of the resource owner. It may be, for example, that some buried treasure (normally labeled "hoards" and viewed as "savings") was actually potential or even working capital.

There are, of course, many definitions of *capital*. Among the more popular is that of anthropologist Scott Cook (see Bibliography), who has defined capital as "the stock of resources (i.e., existing assets) at a particular time available to increase the volume of consumption in future periods, either directly or indirectly, through production."

Another view of capital currently influential among many anthropologists is found in French sociologist Pierre Bourdieu's definition of capital as "resources that give those with more such resources advantages—power—over those with less." Bourdieu argues that capital is a social relation; one type of capital is effective in one context but may not function to the capitalist's advantage in another. For Bourdieu, there are many types of capital, for example, educational, economic, intellectual, biological (as with sports figures), and, particularly, symbolic and social capital. Symbolic capital consists of such things as knowledge, experience, wit, charm—intangibles that one accumulates during one's lifetime and, depending on the context, give individuals power in their everyday interactions with others. On the other hand, the positions, connections, and family that one possesses as a result of birth, marriage(s), offices held, associational membership, and the like are all social capital.

One final point: Today the word *capital* automatically leads many to assume we are speaking of money. However, in the traditional view, money is sterile; unlike land, animals, or seeds, money cannot reproduce itself. If you bury money in the ground, you shouldn't expect a money tree to appear. It is only when money purchases some factor of production that money is transformed into capital. Thus, the economists maintain that, of all things that may constitute capital, money is not one of them. Money is a commodity, useful for its exchange value in the acquisition of those resources (e.g., land, labor, seeds, information) that are necessary in production.

Capitalism A term surrounded by controversy and obscured by the smoke of ideological fires. Many economists avoid the term because it includes social relations and thus, it is claimed, is too broad for their analytical use. In essence, however, capitalism (though not capital or markets) is a system in which those who control capital use it to increase their wealth by organizing production, distribution/exchange, and consumption so as to balance supply against demand in ways expected to optimize prices and thus produce optimum profits. The owners of capital use profits to increase their store of wealth, which they may then consume, save, or invest. Capitalism is dependent on entrepreneurs (as well as those such as governments or venture capitalists who are willing to risk funding their endeavors) to create new markets and enhance the potential for profit.

It's often argued that a critical component of capitalism is the availability of "free labor" (labor free from preexisting social constraints that would prohibit workers from selling their labor to the owners of capital i.e., not slaves or serfs). However, the State itself may be the owner of capital; as in Soviet Russia or present-day China—and not only may it direct workers to perform certain tasks, prohibit them from leaving such employment, and set the terms of their wages, but may employ prisoners of the State as slave labor in production. This indicates that "free labor"—the freedom of workers to sell their labor on the market to whomever they wish—is not a necessary condition for capitalism.

There is confusion—as well as irony—because of the multiple meanings of the word "free." Not uncommonly, workers have little choice as to whom, how, or when they will sell their labor. They must sell to whomever will buy—or accept deprivation as their option. It seems reasonable to suspect that, when Marx in *Capital* talked of "free labor" as required for industrial capitalism (though he never used the term *capitalism*), he was employing a bit of sardonic wit.

Many types of capitalism have been suggested by various scholars, the three main types being: (1) laissez-faire capitalism—a competitive system of production in which the government plays little role except to maintain order, prevent marketplace abuses of the citizens, and carry on certain activities that encourage the production of goods, the search for profit, and the protection of property, including profits, gained through activities in a market; (2) mixed capitalism—some important aspects of production, distribution, and consumption are controlled by the State and other aspects are privately controlled; (3) State capitalism—the State controls and directs the flow of capital and sets the terms of production, distribution/exchange, and consumption. An array of subtypes has been suggested, for example, booty capitalism, managerial capitalism, welfare capitalism, and a variety of other terms that follow below.

The origin of capitalism is also debated and has been variously argued to originate in very early times to recent times. Five suggested points of origin are (1) in early Near Eastern states (e.g., Egypt, Mesopotamia) or in the Far East (e.g., China); (2) in the Roman Empire or Aztec Empire (commercial capitalism), independent of each other; (3) during the European Renaissance (mercantile capitalism); (4) during the Age of Discovery when, beginning around the fifteenth century, Europeans began their exploration and eventual colonization of much of the world (colonial capitalism); and (5) in eighteenth-century Europe as a result of the Industrial or Fossil Fuel Revolution (industrial capitalism).

Whenever it began to take shape, capitalism today exists as a self-organizing system, a structure of interdependent markets, supply and demand, prices, profits, capital, entrepreneurs, and labor (free or otherwise) that affects and is affected by production, distribution, and consumption.

Cartel An association of individuals, firms, or corporations established in order to limit access to a particular resource (e.g., a diamond cartel) and to establish the price at which all participants buy/sell as well as settle on the quantity of resources to be released to consumers. Governments often attempt to restrict cartels as "illegal restraints on free trade" because such cartels are seen as ways to manipulate market supply and prices to the disadvantage of the consumer.

Chattel A movable item of personal property, for example, jewelry, furniture, an automobile, livestock. At one time, it included humans—slaves, and even wives and children. Such property can be sold, used as a gift, or be offered as security for a loan. In the latter case, the tender holds a chattel mortgage that entitles the lender to take possession of the chattel if the debt is not repaid.

Circulatory exchange That portion of a economic system of production, distribution/exchange, and consumption that involves the movement of goods beyond the local point of primary production.

Class A layer in a hierarchically structured socioculture, often defined by birth into one of the segments or by economic standards. Class is different from other stratification systems, for example, castes, because economic changes, marriage, or personal behavior may bring a change in one's class, moving up or becoming déclassé (moving down), while caste membership is unalterable. One's class may be ascribed (established by birth) or achieved (established as the result of an individual's activities).

Commoditization (also identified as **commodification**) The process of transforming goods and services once produced for self-use into products for exchange in markets. Any product produced and distributed via the market has a price (determined by supply and demand), and this is the major, sometimes even the sole, consideration for the characteristics of the product in production, exchange, and consumption.

Commodity Any good or service that can be exchanged in an institutionalized marketplace or via a system of trade. Though many use the term, few define it since, especially among Marxians, any definition (as opposed to a description) is problematic. For example, one common definition (see above) is "a good or service produced for the market and priced according to supply and demand." This, however, makes it difficult to deal with things not originally intended for exchange but, ultimately, entering the market (e.g., an infant whose parent(s), unable or unwilling to care for it, offer it for exchange in "the baby market"; or, again, the medieval market in religious relics). The two examples given suggest that however we identify a commodity, one useful criterion is the characteristic that it has an exchange value that can be priced in money.

While consumption has increased due to the commoditization process (i.e., the standardization of production so that price is the chief factor differentiating, say, one car or watch or professional service provider from another), it is also the case that the increase in consumption has led to a growth in competition—and the growth in competition has led to the need for rivals to compete with each other on the basis of value added. But, in today's world, that often requires tailoring a product to the specific demands of particular consumers. If it were not for the new technological abilities created by the computer, meeting specific demands would be so cost-inefficient that it would be rejected as a viable strategy for producers. Thus, ironically, whereas it once was the case that the mass production and cheaper prices achieved by homogenizing commoditization was the incentive for increased consumption, competition for the customer is now reversing the commoditization process as producers are forced to customize products to individual demands.

Complex system (cf. *Synergy*) Since all systems are aggregates of functionally interdependent parts, it may seem strange to speak of "complex" systems because, from one perspective, a system is by definition complex. Some systems, however, are closed and stable; others are open and are constantly in a feedback relation with forces external to themselves. In such open systems, some new input can alter the system and thus alter the entire functioning of the system. This may not be due to the input in and of itself but because the new input combines with some existing part of the system to create something that was not part of the input, the system, or any of its components. Thus, for example, when two parts of hydrogen are combined with one part of oxygen, the combination results in something totally new, not predictable from any characteristic of the components in their precombinational state (i.e., H_20 = water).

Consensus A general agreement among an aggregate of participants as to the ground rules, dimensions, or other aspects of an issue that must be addressed—and, as well, the decision(s) that must be made.

Corporate group An aggregate of individuals who, as one of their defining characteristics, have access or use rights to and control over the allocation of resources within the group or the alienation of specific resources to those outside the group.

Corvée Enforced and unpaid labor for the secular and/or religious governing authorities. It is a type of tax paid in the form of labor for those who exercise control over a community.

Costs (fixed and variable) Fixed costs are the expenses that must be met regardless of whether the level of production stays the same, goes up, or declines. Thus, an individual may be earning an income or be unemployed (unproductive) but still must face such expenses as food, housing, utilities, clothing, and health care. Though shifts in productivity do not alter such costs to any significant degree, and they remain relatively constant even when productivity increases or declines, these usually will vary over the long run.

Variable costs are those that increase/decrease as production increases/decreases. In business, if sales are growing and you increase your advertising, add sales staff, spend more on research and development, and so forth, your variable costs increase. In personal life, a growing list of clients might require that you spend more time away from home, hire a house cleaner, buy a more impressive automobile (that uses more gas than your former vehicle), or spend more time and money attending specialized seminars.

Covenant A mutual but conditional agreement between two or more persons to do or refrain from doing certain acts relative to each other. As long as both adhere to the stipulated conditions, the agreement stands (e.g., the covenant between the early Hebrews and God, or the Mayflower Compact made by the Pilgrims).

Culture (cf. *Society* and *Socioculture*) A learned, shared system of arbitrary beliefs, values, and norms whose patterns emerge in the process of humans living within the context of group life. It emerges over time as a group's members attempt to retain connections with the past while adapting to current necessities and long-term aims. Cultural components are considered arbitrary because each human aggregate creates the system and its parts, that is, they are not preordained by "nature," biology, or some supernatural agent. Culture is dynamic; it is responsive to and capable of generating change. Without culture, societies (specifically, nonhuman aggregates) are able to change only through such biological processes as natural selection, mutation, or the accidents of nature. Culture may be viewed holistically (as when we speak of the human capacity for culture) or segmentally (as when we speak of "cultures"). In this latter case, we focus on the patterns of specific sociocultural aggregates that select certain patterns to point up their distinctiveness relative to other aggregates (e.g., ethnic or religious groups).

Distribution The movement of resources according to sociocultural guidelines, rules, laws, or values that indicate the who, what, where, when, and how of such circulation. When Captain John Smith said, "Those who don't work, don't eat," those to whom it was said assumed that the edict applied only to able-bodied adults and not infants, infirm elderly, or those who were ill. The deprivation of food from those in these categories would have violated both common sense and the settlers' moral values.

Double-entry bookkeeping Every transaction, whether a sale or a purchase, is entered into a record as both a debit and a credit. The underlying premise or accounting principle is that a firm's assets equal liabilities plus net worth. If a firm buys something for $10, it lists a $10 asset (since it has the merchandise), but it must also record a $10 liability (since the firm must pay for the merchandise). The important point is that the accounts are kept on a daily basis and, at any given time, the managers of the firm, investors (or potential investor), or current/future debtors know the value of the ownership equity (assets minus liabilities).

This was not the case prior to the invention of this bookkeeping technique and is assumed to have occurred prior to A.D. 1340, the dating of the earliest accounts discovered. These are already in so sophisticated a form that it's assumed the technique was invented much earlier.

In "social accounting," individuals and groups are concerned with particular transactions that show cost and gain/loss. The "books" need not "balance" at the end of the day; there is no attempt to analyze every transaction in terms of the profitability of "the firm" (an individual or a group). Records are often kept in one's head.

Duties Individuals or groups are required to accept that there are legitimate and inescapable expectations that they will provide certain Goods, goods, and services to specified other(s).

Economic anthropology Anthropologist Richard Wilk (see Bibliography) has defined the field as "the study of the social and cultural bases of rationality and choice" and makes the important point that rationality should be the subject, not an assumption, of economic anthropology.

Economic system (cf. *Economies*) A model constructed in order to select, observe, measure, and analyze particular phenomena that researchers identify as relevant to whatever aspect of production, distribution/exchange, or consumption on which they focus. In this sense, there is no specific entity (e.g., "the economy") that we can observe. Rather, there are aggregated activities and products that are labeled by actors or analysts as "economic."

Economies of scale There is a decline in unit production costs as the quantity produced increases. The first widget produced may cost millions because of research and development and setting up the machinery (or producing a prototype model by hand). Even the first thousand may cost four or five times as much as the next nine thousand. The general public is aware of this; one often hears (relative to a new product), "I'll wait to buy till they come down in price." The assumption is clear that once the innovation becomes popular and the scale of production increases, prices will decline.

Economizing Selecting the combination of costs and benefits that allows decision makers to achieve their own optimum utility—the optimum benefits at the least cost.

Elasticity The relation between the price of a good or service and demand for each as the price goes up or down. The relation is expressed in percentages. If the demand percentage declines less than the price percentage increases (e.g., the price goes up 10 percent and demand drops by 1 percent), demand is said to be elastic. If, however, a 10 percent price increase produces a 15 percent decline in demand, demand is said to be inelastic. A rise in the price of milk barely affects demand; the demand for milk relative to price is elastic. A rise in the price of beef leads to a decline in the demand (people seek cheaper substitutes); the demand for beef relative to price is inelastic.

Entitlement programs Tax-supported aid that channels assistance to various groups composed of individuals whose needs are seen as less than that to which they have a human right. All people should expect, it is argued, that they will receive at least the necessary minimum access to food, housing, protection from natural disaster or human predators, education, and, in general, caretaking and the provision of life's necessities when unable to provide these adequately for themselves and their dependents.

Entrepreneurs Individuals who innovate and introduce change, by finding ways to (1) enhance existing markets or (2) discover/invent new opportunities for consumer goods and services. Entrepreneurs are opportunistic niche-seekers who, in seizing opportunities for profit, not only risk their own resources but persuade others to risk theirs on the hope that by using such resources as capital, that is, by investing rather than saving or hoarding them, such investors will increase their rewards (profits). The British anthropologist I. M. Lewis (see Bibliography) has defined an entrepreneur as "an innovator who can turn a situation of unfulfilled potential demand to profit."

Equilibrium In economics, a concept concerned with the balance between supply and demand. For example, in a competitive market, when a widget is priced so that all demand is satisfied and all suppliers have cleared out their stock of widgets, the widget has achieved its equilibrium price.

Ethnocentrism (cf. *Value judgment*) The transference and imposition of the concepts, rules, norms, and values developed by one socioculture onto the guidelines for living of another socioculture. It leads to, at the least, a misreading and distortion of the patterns of another group and, at the worst, to disaster and even death (of persons or whole sociocultural groups) when one socioculture has the power to force its ways on another.

Ethnography Individual studies of particular societies, usually pictured at some relatively fixed or stable point in time. Many ethnographies tend to be as all-inclusive as possible. Other ethnographers choose a particular aspect on which to focus, such as the subsistence system of a specific village or the governing system of a specific nation-state.

Ethnology The study of the same or similar socioculture theme(s) in order to compare and contrast specific ethnographic data. It is the cross-cultural and, often, cross-temporal study of various general sociocultural phenomena (e.g., religion, kinship, gender, child rearing), utilizing ethnographic data to explore broad theoretical or methodological issues.

Evolution I've found no more useful definition than that supplied by the anthropologist Robert Carneiro (in a paper entitled "Successive Reequilibrations as the Mechanism of Cultural Evolution," 1982): "Evolution . . . is recurring changes of structure accommodating to function, accumulated and projected over an extended period of time."

Exchange Individually grounded decisions to use what has been received through the distribution system or from previous exchanges in order to obtain what is personally needed or desired. At the least, the process operates according to some minimal sociocultural rules but may also be subject to complex rules and factors of exchange.

Externalities The costs or benefits derived by or imposed upon those in one group/aggregate as the result of events that occur outside the boundaries of the affected group. Public goods (see *Public goods*) are one such externality. One of the difficulties in using the term is identifying the boundaries of where my "group" or backyard ends and yours begins.

Factionalism Disputes that divide the members of a group into opposing aggregates that we label factions. Factions are made up of subsegments of the group. The entity divided by factionalism may be as small as a household or as large as an empire. The point is that people "take sides" on some contentious issue. The dispute may become so bitter and intense that members of the opposing factions employ physical violence against each other (e.g., pro- and anti-slavery factions that ultimately resulted in the U.S. Civil War [or, as they say, in the American South, "The War between the States"]). The Amerindian town of Isleta in the American Southwest split over whether to allow the Roman Catholic priest to pave over an area used for public dances linked to the pre-Christian religion and the result was several years of intense violence. Members of factions may differ on a number of issues, but they unite to oppose those who do not support their stand on one particular issue.

Factors of production Often identified as "land, labor, and capital" (though various anthropologists [e.g., Harold Schneider and Fredrik Barth] rightly include entrepreneurs). Given, however, the broadness with which I define capital, they are any resources that are used to produce Good, goods, or services. Thus, they may be mentifacts; artifacts; natural resources such as land, water, minerals, living creatures (e.g., fish, bees, fur-bearing and food-providing animals); a sociocultural bundle of property rights; duties, privileges, and responsibilities; or even a scenic view, religious celebration, or historic site that attracts tourists.

Gift Any good or service that is transferred to another and is, at least in theory, "free." In reality, however, it may entail a rule of reciprocity, or it may be something that seeks to establish or recognize a social relation.

Good (cf. *Goods*) Humans do not merely hanker after material goods. They are emotionally rewarded by intangible rewards that I label "Good." All sociocultures place a positive value on certain nonmaterial qualities of life—that is, respect, freedom from fear, caretaking when incapacitated, leisure time to relax with family and friends, prestige, children, honor. The list varies from one socioculture to another and even within a given socioculture, depending on age, sex, condition of life, and so on. But in all places, all individuals are able to identify certain components of what they, and the aggregates to which they belong, identify as "the good life."

Gross income Total income before costs of production, taxes, transportation, and other charges are subtracted. The amount left is the net income.

Hominids Modern humans (*Homo sapiens sapiens*) and all of their ancestral forms. Hominid ancestors are distinguished from those of other primates by certain physical characteristics such as the habitual use of upright posture for standing, walking and running (i.e., bipedal locomotion) and, as well, by evidence of certain cultural abilities, as in the use of controlled fire and the manufacture and sustained use of tools (i.e., tools that are used repetitively and carried from place to place rather than discarded after a single usage). All ancestral forms of modern *Homo sapiens sapiens* are extinct (unless, as with Neanderthals, they simply were genetically absorbed in *Homo sapiens sapiens* through interbreeding).

Hypothesis A testable statement, generated by a theory, and usually stated, "If A . . . then B. . . ." Data collected do or do not support the statement and lead either to its modification and retesting or to its rejection. An important part of sciencing is that the falsifiability of a hypothesis (i.e., the data do not support the statement) rests on whether multiple investigators, testing the same hypothesis, under the same conditions, will obtain the same results (supporting or refuting the initial hypothesis). When such results do concur, the hypothesis is said to be intersubjectively supported, that is, the results correspond regardless of who tests the hypothesis. It's important to note that even a falsified hypothesis can advance knowledge and provide valuable new data.

Income The return received as a result of resources (e.g., human labor) invested.

Inelastic (see **Elasticity**)

Inflation An increase in the money supply, wages, and/or prices. We are said to be experiencing inflation when the demand for goods and services increases faster than the supply, leading to increases in prices. The reasons for demand increases may be a fear by consumers that goods will be in short supply (due, say, to a war) or (a chicken/egg problem) of higher prices/wages leading to claims that prices/wages need to be raised, which in turn leads to the claim that prices/wages need to be increased yet again, and so on and so on. Inflation may also be due to an increase in government spending, which increases the supply of money and leads to a decline in its value in the marketplace, that is, one dollar will buy only ninety cents worth of groceries this week, only eighty-five cents next week, and so forth. Sometimes the public's fear of inflation itself leads to inflation, as people begin to rush to exchange their money for goods in order to escape a feared loss of purchasing power. The rush to buy may create shortages, which leads to higher prices at the same time that the money is declining in value. Some countries have undergone hyperinflation: The historian H. Thomas (*History of the World*, 1979, p. 299) has noted that in Germany, in the one year between Fall 1922 and Fall 1923, prices increased 1,422,900,000,000 percent over those at the beginning of the World War in 1914! In essence, of course, the money became worthless (though people were photographed carrying baskets half as tall as themselves to the markets to buy a one-day supply of bread and milk). People resorted to barter or sold goods abroad to obtain foreign currency.

Informal economy Any form of production, distribution/exchange, or consumption that is untracked and thus unrecorded in public statistics, that is, it takes place off the books and can only be "guess-timated" in the national economic statistics. Other terms for the phenomenon include "black," "underground," "unregulated," "parallel," "unregistered," "second," and "private." In some countries, it is estimated that some 40 percent of economic activity takes place off the books; estimates for the size of the informal economy in the United States and Canada range from 5 to 15 percent.

Information (cf. *Knowledge*) A precise bit of datum that, alone or, especially, when combined with other such bits, can be very useful, signify nothing much that is useful, or even be erroneous (though, in this latter case the discovery that the datum is incorrect will lead to the bit being reclassified as "noise"). The greater one's ability to discern a larger schema—being able to discern which bits properly fit with others—the greater one's knowledge. Think, for example, of the letters of the alphabet: Possessing such bits does little good unless one grasps how they can be utilized to read and write. Thus, the alphabet provides bits of information; understanding the principles of how to fit the letters together, then, more importantly, recombining the letters, and—most important—grasping the utility of the literacy system, is an example of knowledge.

Institutions A conceptual tool of social scientists that identifies and models the various organizational contexts that, among other things, enable groups to structure, interrelate, and manage the production, distribution/exchange, and consumption of socially essential goods and services. It is the organization of various structures and processes so as to sustain those activities considered vital to the well-being of the group (e.g., religion, health care, households/families, defense, education, governing). Institutions consist of (a) structured networks of social positions and their attached roles, as well as (b) a bundle of techniques and rules that are designed or emerge in practice to implement the aims of the institution.

Interest Payment for the use of loaned resources. Lenders require the return of what was originally borrowed (or its equivalent) plus additional compensation (i.e., interest) for the loss to the lender of the ability to use the resource for alternate purposes.

Loans do not always have interest (indeed, Muslims specifically prohibit it). Further, interest is not always calculated in monetary terms; since what is loaned can vary widely, so too can the form of interest. For example, it may be a number of lambs added to those required to replace the original sheep loaned. The concept of rental is related. I may appear to pay no interest on the use of someone else's property if I pay a rental fee but, in point of fact, since the rental costs always exceed the purchase price, the return to the owner of the rental is similar to that of a loan with interest.

Knowledge (c.f. *Information*) A set of principles that allows bits of information (i.e., data) to be assembled in ways that provide a greater understanding of, say, the dynamics of a phenomenon than the data in and of themselves can provide. Knowledge provides a sense of coherency. Knowledge enables one to take a given assortment of data and not only assemble them appropriately but even import or imagine pieces of information not in the original collection.

Language A learned, shared cognitive system expressed through arbitrary vocal symbols (and, very recently, symbols of these symbols, i.e., writing). Language serves to organize sensory phenomena and facilitates the storage, retrieval, and transmission of information about such phenomena.

Language consists of units of sounds (phones/phonemes) and shapes (morphemes) that, together with organizational rules (syntax), can be endlessly recombined to create *new* utterances. Thus, for example, I'd be willing to wager that no one has ever before in the history of human life said, "I have a *fnerfl* that's red with yellow polka dots." Again, the English sounds written as "p," "t," and "æ" (the so-called "short a"), may be recombined to produce "tap," "rap," or "apt." And while "Jack climbed the tree" may be of little interest to most people, telling them "The tree climbed Jack" would probably produce a shudder of horror.

Language may be the major way that humans communicate with each other and other animals but it's also part of a larger communication system. Humans use various communication systems, some of which have much in common with those of other species, such as the use of space (e.g., being "too close for comfort" or "standoffish"); voice (e.g., shouting, screaming, growling—i.e., a low, harsh, raspy voice; a soft, drawling voice that seems to soothe; plus whimpers); or body motions (e.g., smiles, winces, frowns, hand and arm gestures, or a raised eyebrow). There is even message sending based on involuntary, physiological responses to events —e.g., "breaking out in a cold sweat" when nervous and fearful, dilating pupil size or increasing eyelid movement when excited, or the involuntary start when one is frightened by a loud noise or sudden movement.

Nonhuman animals are unable to transfer the information using a system of symbols, that is, for example, a chimp can't tell another chimp how to use a rock to break open a hard-shelled substance containing food in the absence of the rock and the hard-shelled substance. Further, while most if not all species have *communication* systems that allow them to signal information among their own and to other species, no nonhuman species has invented a language. Nonhuman species can acquire (and even invent variations) on language-like skills only in a process initiated by language-using humans.

A human child has an innate cognitive capacity for language. Even a deaf and dumb child can be taught how to think with language, despite being unable to articulate sounds (i.e., use speech to communicate). Yet no child deprived of true language during its critical learning period—say, birth through the age of five years or so—is capable of inventing language independently. Not only is such a system too complex for a single individual to create out of nothing but it is the essence of language that it is an aggregate activity, something done by sociocultural groups.

Law of Diminishing Returns Each added unit of input leads to a smaller increment in output.

Law of Diminishing Utility It's best to begin a definition of this law with an example. For most people, most of the time, the distance between cost and benefit is narrowed or broadened depending on availability. If, as farmers, we have been suffering through a drought, we place great value on the first inch of rain. Each additional inch of rain will, for a while, bring us an increase in pleasure—though not as much as the first inch brought. Indeed, each inch of rain brings less.

Lifeboat ethics A phrase suggested by biologist G. Hardin (see Bibliography) to make a case against altruism. Suppose, he said, you were in an already overloaded lifeboat and people in the water were crying to be saved. If you behaved altruistically and surrendered your place in the boat, you would drown and the person to whom you gave your seat would survive. But, argues Hardin, that would result in the elimination of the noble and self-sacrificing individual and the preservation of the reproductive potential of the self-interested, nonaltruistic individual. If enough such situations occur over time—the altruistic surrendering his or her future to protect or save the future of those selfish enough to value their own survival over that of the altruist—we would ultimately have a society of those whose survival "proved" that greed and selfishness were, if not good, at least the realistic path to follow. All the altruistically minded would have disappeared—and, along with them, their moral and ethical concerns. Thus, Hardin claimed, it's wrong to send food to the hungry; this will only keep them alive, allowing them to continue to reproduce, pursuing their selfish goals of having children. Though some will die of hunger, disease, and natural catastrophe, the more children they have (or as Harden and others argue people in certain sociocultures believe), the higher the chance that some will survive both to care for the parents and perpetuate the family line. In the long run, however, argues Hardin, what is more likely is that those unable to care for themselves will become so numerous that they will be too great a burden for even the most altruistic (if any still survive). At that point, a real worldwide catastrophe will occur. Thus, by being kind and altruistic now, Good People are only increasing the number of people who will suffer in the future. It would be better, says Hardin, to let a few die now rather than encourage the population of future sufferers to grow.

Lifeboat ethics is a variant of Hardin's widely cited article (1968) on the tragedy of the commons. Looking at the growing degradation of the environment, he held that any resources belonging to everyone (e.g., public lands, fish in the ocean's international waters, the air), are owned by no one. Therefore, those with access to the resources will seek to maximize their returns, regardless of what damage is done to the resources and their use by others. The premise of the maximizers is, "It's not mine, so why should I care? What I don't take or despoil somebody else will." This leads Hardin to the conclusion that only private property insures that resources will be used wisely. The self-interest of owners leads them to protect their resources in order to maintain sustainable returns. Private property, concludes Hardin, is the only way to avoid the general ecological disaster that he labels the "rape of the commons."

One of the most fundamental flaws in Hardin's argument is that he misunderstood the institution of "the commons" (communally held and managed resource areas), confusing it with open-access systems. The latter is what he was talking about. Historically, "the commons" is, paradoxically, public resources—usually land—that are held privately by a specific aggregate, for example, residents of a neighborhood, village, or several such cooperating aggregates banded together. The commons consists of resources held in trust for community members by community members. Contrary to Hardin, this "common wealth" is far from unregulated; there are always rules regulating its usage, such usage is carefully monitored, and, as well, rules are strictly enforced by fellow shareholders. Despite this and other weaknesses, Hardin's arguments are still popular and frequently turn up in debates on such issues as how to manage resources or what to do about aid to the needy.

Macroeconomics (cf. *Microeconomics*) That segment of economic analysis that focuses on statistical aggregates rather than specific variables. For example, macroeconomists are concerned with the aggregate cost of labor rather than the specific labor costs in the production of say, widgets.

Marketplace (cf. *Market system*) Unlike the market system, which is an abstraction, marketplaces are specific and real locales. Marketplaces and the market system have in common the feature that both buyers and sellers engage in exchange transactions. Both parties must reach agreements that bring at least that minimal degree of benefits for each that allows the exchange to take place. Societies in which marketplaces are the only medium through which people can transfer goods and services outside the contexts of household, kin, and other obligatory channels of distribution are often labeled marketplace (or bazaar) societies.

Marketplaces may be very local and operate on a cycle (e.g., the first Thursday of every month), or they may be regional and operate with some frequency, even daily. They may be large fairs (generalized in what they sell or very specific—as, for example, the annual book fair in Frankfurt, Germany, which draws in buyers and sellers from around the world). Marketplaces may conform to the ancient mode whereby merchants and buyers meet and negotiate prices according to the concerns of each at the moment, or, as the example of the Frankfurt Book Fair illustrates, prices may be subject to the market system.

Market system (cf. *Marketplace*) Ideally, a market system is an institution with self-regulating prices that vary according to supply and demand on the part of both producers and consumers. Demand is determined by scarcity/abundance, price, and preferences; supply is determined by scarcity/abundance, price, and sensitivity to demand.

Although governments and individuals attempt to manage the market, its complexity and volatility—plus that (a) it is sensitive to externalities and (b) it appears to be a self-organizing system—make the market difficult to predict (let alone "manage"). All components of the market system are focused on and coordinate the production of commodities, as these produce the profits that stimulate production, exchange, and consumption.

Mentifact (see **Artifact**)

Microeconomics That segment of economic analysis that focuses on the mathematical (rather than statistical) analysis of activities in the competitive market. It deals with the movement of single goods or pairs of goods as they move in small segments of the market. It concentrates on a static analysis of partial and general equilibrium.

Minimax rule This "rule" involves taking the worst case scenario and selecting the option that will bring the least ill effects if the worst outcome of that option occurs.

Model This is a generalized abstraction constructed by scholars to represent some sorts of data or real phenomena. The construction may vary widely, depending on what it is that the modeler wishes to test or represent to others. It may, for example, be a book of etiquette (a model for appropriate behavior); a particular verb paradigm that represents how all regular verbs in a language operate; a statement that lists a set of relationships among a specific set of variables (as in a kinship chart setting out the positions, roles, and networks among members of a particular socioculture who see themselves related biologically, through marriage, or via some legal fiction [e.g., adoption]); or a flow chart illustrating the standard ways of management decision making.

Money Anything that has general acceptance as (a) a medium of exchange, (b) a store of value, and (c) a measure of value. It's common to distinguish between general and special-purpose money. The latter is limited in its range of circulation or applicability. For example: In some societies different domains of goods and services require specific forms of money that cannot be used in other domains (e.g., there is a specific form of money that may be used only to pay bridewealth but not to pay for any other goods and services). Thus, poker chips are a kind of special-purpose money since they may be used in the issuing casino but not in a competitor's casino. Some special-purchase money may, under certain circumstances, expand its domain, for example, during wartime, ration coupons and in peacetime, food stamps may serve as money—i.e., used as a medium of exchange—in the informal economy. In North American socioculture—even today—a few companies issue—and even pay—employees in "company specie," redeemable only at company-owned stores or as rent on company-owned houses. The current popular tactic of new cyberbusinesses paying employees at least in part with stock options is another example of special-purpose money. The option represents money to the employee but, until the employee exercises the option to buy the stock at some predetermined and presumably lower price than the stock's current market value, the option has no exchange value outside the company.

Net income (see **Gross income**)

Norm "The norm" may refer to whatever most people, most of the time, do (or are said to be expected to do). In this case, "norm" is defined as whatever is the most prevalent behavior. People may vary in what they say is the norm and what they do in practice (e.g., "a red traffic light means automobiles stop"—well, yes, sometimes). French anthropologist Claude Lévi-Strauss differentiated these as the mechanical (ideal) norm versus the statistical (a count of actual behavioral events).

Norms, along with values and laws, guide or regulate behavior in specific groups. Norms and values are highly variable, one aggregate to another, and it's not uncommon for individuals and groups to employ different, even conflicting, norms as they move from one aggregate, place, and time to another.

Opportunity costs Positively weighted options and choices that one rejects in order to produce or consume a selected alternative. For example, if I decide to cut short my education in order to obtain current income, the lost potential for a higher income later in life as a result of foregoing further education is an opportunity cost. Similarly, if I extend my education on the assumption that, over my lifetime, this will allow me to earn a higher income, potential current income not earned (as well as the costs of the education while I attend school) represents opportunity costs. Thus, we give up one or more benefits elsewhere when we choose which opportunity to seek. It's a trade-off.

Out-of-awareness Thinking is a complex process, and much of it goes on at a deep level, beyond our explicit awareness that we are engaged in considering certain, often quite specific, information. These "deep thoughts" often given rise to responses that we can't dissect and instead characterize as "intuition," a "hunch," "guess," or even "a feeling." For example, people often announce that they want to "sleep on the problem" and wake up with some sort of solution.

However, we actually are utilizing a great deal of information that we may not even be aware we know. It is not deleted or lost but is stored and retrieved as "deep thought." For example, in evaluating another individual we may not know that, say, we're picking up on certain clues of speech (e.g., social dialects, vocabulary, tone of voice). We may be unaware that we have taken note of facial and body movements (some very minimal and fleeting—as when another gives a quick tap of the fingers that perhaps will register with me out-of-awareness as, say, a sign of the other's impatience or annoyance). Or an increase in the number of eye blinks per second leads me to have a "hunch" that the other is excited or nervous. The range of things we notice but don't always consciously note include: clothes worn, body posture while sitting or standing, makeup shades or type of scent worn, the way another uses personal space—especially relative to one's own personal space.

When we enter a new social context, we note certain bits of information that are bundled together to create "a sense of scene" (or "seen"). It may be the seemingly imperceptible tempo at which people move during a party ("hectic" or "relaxed"), the extent to which members in a group smile at each other as they pass or keep their eyes down and their expressions remote, the way the office furniture is arranged, whether there's a hum of activity or a restrained silence, and so forth. Again, though we are often unaware that we have noted such information, we still use it to assess a person or a situation. In one classic study (Pittinger et al., *The First Five Minutes*), it was determined that those psychiatrists studied made critical evaluations of their patients in the first five minutes of the initial physician–patient meeting and rarely altered their "out-of-awareness" judgment call, even after intensive and extended interaction with the patient.

Peasant This is another of those highly contentious terms. Indeed, noted anthropologist Eric Wolf (in a 1955 paper that he labeled "a preliminary discussion" of "Types of Latin American peasantry") began addressing the issue of defining "the peasant" by preempting attacks. He noted that ". . . definitions are tools of thought and not eternal verities." He limited his focus to those who met three criteria. First, peasants are agricultural producers, and he eliminated, for example, "fishermen, strip miners, rubber gatherers, and livestock keepers" as well as "rural craftsmen." Second, the peasant is one who controls the land the family works. In contrast to tenant farmers, the peasant pays no dues to an outside landowner—save, I would add, taxes to local/regional/national government(s). Third, the peasant aims at subsistence, and while he may sell some of his crops, the money, says Wolf, "is used . . . to buy goods and services which he requires to subsist and to *maintain* his scale of operations, his social status, rather than to *enlarge* his scale of operations" (my emphasis). Wolf contrasts peasants with farmers and sees the most notable distinction as being that "the farmer views agriculture as a business enterprise" while "the aim of the peasant is subsistence."

These remarks of Wolf generated much discussion and provided a talking point that saw major rethinking on the subject—including much by Wolf himself.

Persona The public or social identity of individuals (a) as they wish to portray themselves to others and (b) as others create or impose such individual identities on others as a result of specific characteristics and behavior. An individual usually has multiple personas.

Poverty (see **Affluence**)
Power (see **Authority**)
Preferences (see also **Utility**) Questions of what, where, how, when and who that are used to help us focus on, prioritize, and select for our needs and wants. Preferences shift depending on time, place, practical implementation possibilities, and so forth.
Price (cf. *Value*) The payment that an individual or group is willing to give and the recompense someone is willing to accept for a good or service.
Prisoner's Dilemma Two prisoners are given a choice: (a) deny everything—and possibly both go free; or (b) betray their partner—and receive a reduced sentence. Most who play the game in a test situation elect to betray their coprisoner on the ground that, while they are sensible enough to see that the best strategy is to keep silent, their fellow-prisoner is not that sensible and will admit to the crime, thus reducing the confessor's sentence while maximizing the sentence of the one who remained silent.
Privileges Individuals or groups are conditionally granted access to specified Good, goods, or services. The original grantor(s) may later withdraw or limit such access and, unless the conditions that satisfied the original granting remain unaltered, the grantee has little, if any, legitimate recourse to prevent the loss or alteration.
Production Any process by which humans transform resources into goods and services for their own use or for transfer to others in order to satisfy needs and wants. Human productivity requires natural resources and labor (human energy, skills, and knowledge). Even more broadly, production may be defined as the expenditure of energy (generated by humans and other animals, as well as natural or mechanical means) in order to generate more energy, for example, working to produce food (or whatever is necessary to obtain food), which, when consumed, produces the energy necessary to produce more food. It is any activity that creates goods or services utilized for self-use or exchange.
Profit The sum remaining (net income) after direct and indirect costs. Expenses (labor, physical plant, research and development, purchase of materials, etc.) are deducted from gross income (total sales). Profit is what is left after costs are deducted.
Property Any resource to which is attached a bundle of rights, duties, privileges and responsibilities held by certain individuals or groups.
Public choice theory Bruno Frey (in "Keeper and Keeper's," *The Social Science Encyclopedia*, 1985) emphasizes that "the traditional idea of government maximizing the welfare of society has to be replaced by an emphasis on the consensual choice of the appropriate rules and institutions." Essentially, public choice theory is concerned with the way the aggregated results of individual political and economic choices are utilized by political parties, government agencies, and public interest groups (e.g., The League of Women Voters) to make choices as to how to deal with matters of concern to the general public.

Public good(s) A particular type of externality (sometimes, rather cutely, contrasted with "Public bads") that is shared by or imposed on everyone. Public goods may be negative (pollution) or positive (medical research). The market system tends to undersupply beneficial public goods because freeloaders will benefit without anyone in the market profiting, thus reducing the incentive to supply such goods and services. On the other hand, the market system tends to oversupply negative public goods because, given that the costs are diffused, any group (or individual) generating the externality is able to reduce the costs relative to its own benefits.

Rationality The term is used differently in different contexts. Logicians, for example, define it as a cognitive process that shows a logical relation between, on the one hand, inferences and, on the other, conclusions; mathematicians use it to designate a function that can be expressed as the quotient of two polynomials; economists maintain that individuals are behaving rationally when they maximize their utility, that is, aim for the greatest benefit at the least cost. In everyday life, we tend to equate it with "being reasonable," displaying "common sense," or viewing things the way we do. In general, it is a process in which a particular form of behavior results in reaching the goal the behavior is undertaken to attain.

Here, the term is used to describe the taking of actions that, given the actor(s), the context, and the goals, have a greater probability of success than other alternatives. In rational planning, each action should be judged as reasonably expected to result from the previous action and have a reasonable expectation of laying the groundwork for the next action in the sequence. The whole sequence should show a coherency relative to the end purpose.

H. A. Simon (see *Satisficing*), in discussing ways to evaluate the consequences of administrative (or managerial) behavior, suggests there are three kinds of rationality: First, an activity may be deemed "objectively rational" if the behavior results in maximizing the benefits sought; second, an activity is "subjectively rational" if, relative to the information of the actor(s), it attains the maximum benefit; and third, an activity is "consciously rational" if, during the decision-making process, there is an explicit process of readjusting the means being utilized to attain the desired end.

Simon suggests that rationality is always limited (no one can ever have total information or full knowledge as to the consequences of a decision). Further, studies of executive decision making show that many of their decisions are made on the basis of what might best be called "fuzzy logic." This is a kind of decision making where the cognitive process follows no neat formula and where bits of information and different kinds of knowledge are not bundled into neat, distinctive categories but, rather, overlap and merge into each other. Thus, executive decisions are often made on the basis of what we call "hunches," "in-formed guesses," and the like. This leads me to suggest there is a fourth kind of rationality—"holistic rationality"—one that occurs out-of-awareness and follows seemingly random pathways and links widely separate and even what may appear to be disparate information and knowledge. However, it is frequently used by political leaders, entrepreneurs, executives, and other types of decision makers to make what are, in fact, highly informed—though difficult to explain—decisions.

Reciprocity This is another term that is complex and tendentious. It has been studied and analyzed by a wide range of social scientists, most of whom have suggested various refinements. Anthropologist M. Sahlins identified three types: Generalized, balanced, and negative reciprocity. Others have added a temporal dimension (immediate versus delayed return). Still others have focused not on the items exchanged but on the social relations created or ended through reciprocity. There is also a vast amount of literature that relates the role of the gift to issues of reciprocity. Finally, anthropologist A. Weiner has argued that the central point of reciprocity involves determining what is held back rather than what is given. Rather than enter this quagmire, let this simple definition serve for our purposes. It is the act of receiving something the giver and taker expect will result in something being given in return.

Resources Resources are defined by economists as factors of production, for example, land, labor, capital, minerals, water. For anthropologists, it is any material or nonmaterial entity that is socioculturally identified as having a use value, that is, that may be drawn on to satisfy a need or a want. Anything defined as "useless" is not a resource because it has no use value. Thus, for example, what for centuries has been defined as "wasteland" or "swamps" were labeled undesirable because such areas were unusable for agriculture and often were the source of disease (such as malaria). We humans derive ways to get rid of or eliminate such nuisances. In the case of swamps, we now label them "wetlands." We have come to recognize how valuable such areas are (e.g., as breeding areas for fish and fowl) and now see them as a valuable resource. Another example: A little more than 150 years ago, areas with surface evidence of oil or natural gas were shunned; they were deemed useless and dangerous to one's health. Then, the Industrial Revolution found a use for such materials; land rich in oil and gas reserves became coveted, even fought over. The current state of Oklahoma, prior to the discovery of the usefulness of oil, was considered a region of little value, assigned as a relocation area for the forced migration of assorted Amerindian groups (the U.S. version of ethnic cleansing) and designated "Indian Territory."

Responsibilities Individuals or groups accept or agree to become accountable for (a) providing for specified others' specific goods or services; (b) maintaining or sustaining the current condition of resources;

and (c) dealing with the consequences of certain actions. Such acceptance or agreement may be abrogated or changes in the designated responsibilities may be negotiated.

Rights Individuals or groups have a legitimate, inalienable claim to or expectation of access to certain specified resources (i.e., Good, goods, or services).

Risk (cf. *Uncertainty*) An actor knows the rough probability of different outcomes. For example, if you know that a professor marks on the curve, you can predict that only 10 percent of the class will receive As, 10 percent will fail, 15 percent will receive either Bs or Ds, and 50 percent will receive Cs. Calculating various factors, you should be able to estimate what grade you'll receive. It should be noted, however, studies show that over 50 percent of students believe their work is better than average; the same is true of automobile drivers who evaluate their driving skills relative to the general public.

Risk assessment is the attempt to quantify the hazard of failure—an impossible task since there are always unknown and/or chance variables that can't be assessed. However, in general, the exercise is an attempt to prevent the recurrence of past or new mistakes in future situations through the application of current information or knowledge.

Risk fund A store of resources that acts as a kind of safety net to protect individuals when trying new ventures or engaging in activities that, if unsuccessful, will result in a loss. The possible loss is assumed adequately "insured" by the risk fund.

Rites of passage Ceremonies that mark transitions from one life phase to another (e.g., from childhood to adulthood, from civilian to military life and back, from single to married life). These rituals may be performed by a group that maintains a certain identity or cohesion through time (the class of the year 2000 will always be the class of 2000 and may hold periodic reunions) or it may be a temporary assemblage (the mass marriage ceremonies of several thousand couples performed for his followers by the Reverend Moon). Some have a permanency (that same class of the year 2000), and others end when the ritual is completed (the assembly of people who gather to become citizens of another country). Some changes are marked with great ceremony (the coronation of a new monarch), and other changes are ignored (marriage is often accompanied by a religious ceremony, but divorce is not).

Satisficing A term coined by H. A. Simon in a landmark article (see Bibliography) that played an important role in his being awarded the Nobel Prize in economics. He argued that, when faced with decisions and selecting choices, people don't always seek the maximum or even the optimal return, benefit, strategy, or solution. Rather, within a context of search costs, constraints on search time, practical considerations of access to an availability of various options, and so forth, it is not uncommon that the first option that is deemed "good enough" is selected. It is a satisfying choice given the circumstances. When making decisions or determining choices, people are aware they face limitations and, being practical, use "bounded rationality" to "settle for the best that, realistically, they can hope to achieve."

Scarcity (cf. *Surplus*) A vexing concept that many economists identify (in the words of S. L. Brue and D. R. Wentworth [see Bibliography]) as ". . . the central problem underlying all economic decisions" (p. 285). It has both objective and subjective dimensions. In either case, it addresses the issue of insufficiency. Objectively, scarcity refers to inadequate access to what is required to obtain an end; it has limits that, when exceeded (at the high or low end of supply), can lead to disaster, satiation, substitution, or innovation. Since scarcity is related to demand (what is unwanted or unusable is never viewed as scarce), it may change as variables (e.g., taste, price, and, above all, utility) affect demand. However, there are cases where an insufficiency is absolute, not subjective. Despite that many affluent women believe (as one such famously put it), "You can never be too rich or too thin," there is sure to be disagreement from those dying because they lack adequate access to food—or, perhaps from at least some of the affluent when, just before they are killed by those who seek to seize their resources, they realize the consequences of a large gap between scarcity for many and abundance for few.

Chapter 10 presents the claim by some that new scientific breakthroughs mean an end to material scarcity. Remember, however, that it is possible for other kinds of scarcities to exist in a world of material abundance. Further, since both "scarcity" and "abundance" have relative as well as absolute dimensions, it seems safe to assume the relative gap will persist.

Self-organizing system (cf. *System*) This is a complex but exciting concept that is difficult to compress in a brief definition but is basic to many of the arguments about change and innovation presented in this volume.

The systems with which we are concerned here are—as are all systems—entities that consist of interdependent components that collectively support the functioning of some bounded entity as a whole. More importantly, while systems may be closed or open to new external input, the systems with which we are concerned—human sociocultures—are open. Thus, while the system has identifiable boundaries that allow us to distinguish between the system and its environment, those boundaries are porous, allowing the system the capacity to send and receive information (matter and energy) between itself and its environment. This means the system is dynamic, that is, subject to change as a result of new input. Closed systems, on the other hand, may change over time as the result of negative or positive feedback, but this feedback is built into the original system. The thermostat of a furnace is one such closed system.

Some open systems, over time, begin to exhibit certain performance characteristics that did not previously exist. The components begin to interact in ways that do not relate to the specific characteristics of either inputs or the system's components. Change emerges spontaneously from within the system itself. Further, the changes are regular and demonstrate patterned behaviors; that is, they conform to certain rules, follow nonrandom routings, and show consistency at various levels of scale in the system (i.e., they repeat from the smallest to the largest segment).

A description rather than a definition might serve us best. The Web is a good example of a self-organizing system. No one manages the Web; its structure and functioning are the result of millions of individual decisions made daily. Yet, as Jocelyn Kaiser recently reported ("Netwatch" *Science,* September 17, 1999), research by the physicist Albert-Laszlo Barabasi and his colleagues has suggested that ". . . for the estimated 800 million pages on the entire Web . . . several dozen pages have 1,000 or more incoming links. If unmanaged, undirected users, following their own individual preferences as to the links they establish, should select for a more diffuse field of sites. A mere handful of sites attracting a high incidence of hits seems highly improbable if not downright impossible. The pattern of Web links, however, is conforming to a distributional law that is neither built into the Web nor to specific actions performed by the Web's components (i.e., those who initiate the links, be they human or software programs). Kaiser reports that Barabasi and others conclude that the average number of clicks it takes to get from any one page on the Web to any other page is only 18. . . ." This degree of interconnectivity gives evidence that the system itself is capable of self-organization.

Serf An individual who had an obligation to perform agricultural labor on the land for whatever person or institution (e.g., temple or church) owned the land. Theoretically, a serf received the right to be protected by the landlord, who had the duty to defend his property and those subject to him. Serfs and landlords had bundles of duties, obligations, rights, and privileges. For example, serfs had the obligation to perform so many days of nonagricultural labor per year, landlords had an obligation to protect the serfs, serfs had the privilege of access to certain resources (e.g., gathering fallen branches for firewood in the lord's forests), and the land-lord had a responsibility to allow the serfs to retain a sufficient portion of their production to meet family subsistence needs. Serfs were bound to the land and were not free to leave without permission. If the land was sold, the serf was part of the deal. Serfs, as chattels (i.e., movable property), could be used as security for a loan (chattel mortgages) and in some locales could be sold to other lords.

Slave Definitions of slavery vary considerably because the conditions of slavery vary widely from place to place. In general, slaves are human, not animals or machines; however, like animals and machines, they are the property of their owners. Slaves may be acquired through purchase, through reproduction by existing slaves, as gifts, or by defeat and capture in war. They usually perform tasks viewed as inferior in the socioculture in which they are enslaved—though in some societies it was possible for slaves to achieve high positions (e.g., a ministerial position in the government) and even be entitled to own a business and possess slaves of their own. They are held in their position by the use or threat of force, as well as what they perceive as "the inescapability" of their situation (i.e., where would they go? who would help them? how could they reach home?). Slaves technically have no kin since spouses or children have obligations to their owners that transcend any of the usual kin obligations to each other. In some sociocultures slaves could gain their freedom by purchasing it from their owner or by the owner giving it as a gift. In both cases, a formal act of manumission had to be made by the owner. They may also be freed through a general law abolishing slavery or, of course, by escaping from their owners. As United Nations studies show, slavery still exists in certain parts of the world.

Social capital (cf. *Capital*) This is a new term (though the concept has been around for many millennia). As is often the case with a new term, it's being variously defined by a variety of scholars and in line with their own research interests. For example, the historian F. Fukuyama has defined social capital as the values that underwrite human cooperation to serve the mutual benefit of all. I would define it as the investment we have in the goodwill of others as such goodwill serves as a resource for and has a bearing on our own well-being.

Society (cf. *Culture* and *Socioculture*) A structure of positions (i.e., group-identified statuses), the roles attached to such positions, and the institutions that create a network of relationships. Although society changes through time, descriptions of societies tend to be either synchronic (a view of the society as it is structured at a single or compressed "point in time") or pseudo-diachronic. In a pseudo-diachronic analysis, two or more synchronic statements are linked sequentially. This juxtaposition of a series of static states, however, is a false presentation of the actual ongoing, dynamic processes at work. A typical pseudo-diachronic analysis, for example, might begin with a chapter on prerevolutionary France, followed by a chapter on nineteenth-century France, followed by a chapter on twentieth-century France. This would not be a truly diachronic (multiple time frames) analysis. This latter type of analysis requires a concern with process; it focuses on what is going on in the interstices (that is, the spaces) between the synchronic nodes (think of a fishing net and think of how different is our description of the construction of a net versus the view we have if we concentrate on the net in use—the changes in the spaces between the knots as the net fills, empties, and fills again). A genuinely diachronic analysis looks at the processes of "becoming-ness," of the movement between

Times A, B, C . . . rather than Times A, B, C . . . in and of themselves. Clearly, I favor performing a diachronic analysis when attempting to understand human behavior.

It is important to note that it is not only humans who have social systems. Other species also live in aggregates whose members are differentiated by holding different positions. Studies of such groups (wolf packs, whale pods, coral colonies, etc.) tell us much about the group structure and interactional processes of social existence (not a few of which provide insights into the social behavior of humans). Further, the social structure of nonhuman aggregates can change through time as a result of learned behavior ("learning" is defined here as any newly acquired information that leads to a modification of previous behavior). However, only humans are capable of initiating preplanned alterations in social structure and organization (see *Language*). Human society, however, is unique because of our species-added cognitive capacity for culture. This blend of society and culture, with the latter's special capacity for introducing and responding to change, creates a unique synergy for adaptation strategies that transcends the much slower biological processes of adaptation imposed on nonhuman species.

Socioculture (cf. *Culture* and *Society*) This term is indicative of the synergistic relation between society and culture as the two interact and affect each other so as to generate changes (calculated or assumed to be adaptive) through time. The two aspects have a feedback effect on each other as well as with the larger context in which any given socioculture exists.

Subsistence economy A style of production and distribution that is carried on to provide for the consumption needs of the local household or community. Groups don't aim to produce surpluses though unplanned overabundances may occur from time to time.

Surplus (cf. *Scarcity*) A surplus is whatever quantity of a given resource an individual or group identifies as excessive to current or short-term future needs and wants. For economists whose focus is on an equilibrium market (demand matches supply and vice versa), the idea of a situation in which there is a surplus over and above the demand is in the long term impossible and undesirable; when supply outruns demand, production should decline until production and demand are equal to each other.

Synergy This is the collective, often emergent energy that results from the combination of two or more components. Each component has its own identity and qualities, and each is capable of autonomous existence, but the combined energy or identity of the collective is more than the sum of its parts. Synergy may be based on competitiveness (two teams playing a game) or complementarity (labor, management, and government negotiating a work contract). When two or more companies merge, when various States form an alliance, when individuals form a household, it is usually assumed (sometimes incorrectly) that positive synergistic results will occur.

System (cf. *Self-organizing system*) A system is an orderly, integrated entity of functionally interdependent parts. Systems may, among other things, be simple or complex, open or closed, in dynamic equilibrium or static.

Theft An act that deprives the legitimate holders of resources of their use rights over these resources.

Triage Originally, a system of assigning priorities of medical attention to the wounded on a battlefield. Using various criteria (e.g., urgency of care given the type of injury or wound, time, and staff available to treat certain medical needs relative to the number and types of injuries or chance for survival), patients were ranked as to when, how, or even whether, given the needs of others, they were to be treated. Making triage decisions involves myriad factors; even the identity of the wounded is relevant. For example, assume two patients arrive from a battlefield at the same time—with the same wounds requiring the same immediate attention. Available medical staff and facilities allow only one to be treated at the necessary level of caregiving. Does the next available surgeon work on the pilot of a rescue helicopter or on one of the camp cooks?

The medical usage of the concept has now been broadened and is being used to establish priorities for the distribution of various resources. The issues may involve: environmental cleanups, multiple regions simultaneously requiring economic aid, famine relief, disease control, and how to distribute scarce resources among such competing programs such as overcrowded prisons and entitlement programs. In short, triage involves building a model for establishing a hierarchy of priorities that allocate limited resources to a variety of needs. Triage recognizes that all issues cannot be handled simultaneously and in a totally equitable fashion.

Turn-key factories A complete factory (including office and production-line operations) is assembled in one locale, then disassembled and transported to another locale. Once reassembled, those employed literally need only turn a key, walk in, and begin to work. Such operations have long been part of development programs that industrialized countries have made available to emerging economies. The government of Norway, for example, has assembled a number of fish processing plants and then transported them for use in emerging economies. Private firms may also utilize the concept: Japanese companies have, over the past several years, set up turn-key computer chip factories in various part of Asia where labor costs are lower than in Japan.

Uncertainty (cf. *Risk*) The outcome of a specific event cannot be absolutely predicted. For example, though you may know that, according to the laws of chance, whether a coin is tossed ten times or a thousand times—and has come up heads each time—on the next toss, the odds still remain 50/50 on whether the coin comes up heads or tails. This is very counterintuitive for most people. Each successive "head" leads the average person to become increasingly convinced that the next time, odds are against another throw producing heads yet again. They will argue, "the coin has to come up tails." Yet the chance of it coming up heads is still 50/50.

Utility (cf. *Preferences*) This is the capacity of a resource's ability to be used in order to satisfy wants and needs. It is measured by the resource's use function and is the subjectively determined degree of satisfaction or pleasure derived from a good or service at a specific time. Not uncommonly, the utility of a good or service is subject to change over time; for example, the more we possess of a given resource, the less utility it will have relative to some other resource. Thus, money may come to have less utility than, say, good health or one's future salvation. Contrariwise, the less we have of a desired resource, the greater will be its utility. Polls show that, for many North Americans, time is the resource of greatest utility.

Economists tend to assume that (a) all individuals have a single, unified utility model in their heads; (b) preferences are ranked relative to each other; and (c) preferences are transitive (i.e., if you like A better than B and B better than C, you must, logically, like A better than C). However, most anthropologists and, increasingly, some economists question why we should expect people's preferences to be stable over time. For one thing, the notion that each person's utilities are independent of everyone else's assumes that individuals are, indeed, individual; that they are not embedded in a sociocultural matrix in ways that substantially contribute to an individual's needs and wants, preferences, and so on. Anthropologists and other social scientists are more likely than economists to take this matrix into account and explore the ways in which preferences are sensitive to the activities and relations that individuals share with others.

What economists seem to dismiss is the fluidity of preferences. The kinds of choices made often give little real evidence for preferences since any given choice may actually rank very low on a scale of preferences. Other factors, natural and sociocultural, often play a deciding role in determining choice. For example, I may choose to spend my summer vacation painting my house; this is not, however, evidence that I prefer using my time that way.

There is also the problem of circularity: As some economists would have it, people have preferences because they make choices and these specific choices are evidence of their preferences. But people often believe that what they prefer is not a realistic or practical choice—and, often, they're right.

"Utility" has also been defined as an individual's subjective sense of "well-being," the psychological "satisfaction" any individual feels at a given time.

Value (cf. *Price*) The desirability or undesirability of a good, service, or Good, as it is ranked relative to other goods, services, or Good. What holds great value for one individual or group may be of little or no value to another. Value is a far more subjective estimate of worth than is price.

Value judgment (cf. *Ethnocentrism*) An assessment that is colored by a perception of what is right or natural or of how people ought to behave or what ought to be the case.

Variable and fixed costs (see **Costs**, fixed and variable)

Veblen effect In certain situations we encounter cases that run counter to the usual arguments regarding elasticity. The Veblen effect is evident when, as the price of a good or service increases, demand also increases rather than dropping or remaining the same. There are various explanations: Higher prices make a good or service more attractive because of elitist or snob appeal; or, as in the current HT stock market or Beanie Baby craze, people believe that the increase in price is evidence that price will continue to increase and, no matter what price they pay now, it is less than they will pay in the future.

Venture capitalists Individuals who are willing to invest money to support new, usually highly speculative entrepreneurial ventures.

Widgets (and Widgeting) A blanket term invented to talk about any kind of good or service you want to think about, whether battleships or tubes of lipstick, brain surgery, or trash collection. Widgeting is the act of producing widgets. Economists seem to believe (and I agree) it is more "user friendly" than page after page discussing X-product. My personal preference, however, is "fnerfl."

Suggested Reading

A number of this book's readers may never have taken any anthropology courses. Both of the following are recommended for those who want a lively and readable overview of cultural anthropology:

Bodley, John H. (1994). *Cultural anthropology: Tribes, states and the global system*. Mountain View, CA: Mayfield Publishing Company.

Bohannan, Paul. (1994). *We, the alien: An introduction to cultural anthropology.* Prospect Heights, IL: Waveland Press.

For a broad introduction to anthropology—one that, in the American tradition of the field, incorporates biological anthropology, linguistics, archeology, and applied anthropology as necessary components in attempts to understand human behavior—the following is not only an exceptionally well-written introductory text but, as well, emphasizes current world issues:

Ferraro, Gary, Wenda Trevathan, and Janet Levy. (1994). *Anthropology: An applied perspective*. Minneapolis/St. Paul: West Publishing Company.

There are a number of excellent readers, but for an unusual and attention-grabbing collection that is sure to stimulate thinking in fresh ways about familiar human ways, this next resource is among the best:

Carlson, David L., and Vaughn M. Bryant, Jr. (1997). *Through the looking glass: Readings in anthropology.* New York: The McGraw-Hill Companies.

Annotated Bibliography

Acheson, James M. (Ed.). (1994). *Anthropology and institutional economics*. Society for economic anthropology. Monographs in economic anthropology, No. 12. Lanham, MD: University Press of America. A collection of 15 papers reviewing the field of institutional economics, especially as two concepts, property rights and transaction costs, relate to decisions and strategies of individuals and how these are guided by institutions. Recommended are Acheson's introductory review of the field (pp. 3–42); R. H. Bates's essay, "Social Dilemmas and Rational Individuals . . ." (pp. 43–68), which has a particularly good discussion on Coase's theorem; J. Marti's case study, "Vendors and the [Mexican] Government . . ." (pp. 195–212); J-P Colin and B. Losch's paper, ". . . French Africanist Rural Economics and Institutionalism (pp. 331–64); and R. Wilk's discussion, ". . . Modeling Household Budget Structures" (pp. 365–90).

Appadurai, Arjun (Ed.). (1986). *The social life of things: Commodities in cultural perspective*. New York: Cambridge University Press. This collection of papers by historians and anthropologists, and particularly Appadurai's "Introduction: Commodities and the Politics of Value" (pp. 3–63), had a major, immediate impact in ahthropological research. As has been the case with Appadurai's introduction, some articles in this collection are sure to become classics, such as I. Kopytoff's "The Cultural Biography of Things: Commoditization as Process" (pp. 64–94); C. Renfrew's "Varna and the Emergence of Wealth in Prehistoric Europe" (pp. 141–68); P. Geary's "Sacred Commodities: The Circulation of Medieval Relics" (pp. 169–94); and B. Spooner's ". . . The Authenticity of an Oriental Carpet" (pp. 195–235).

Arrow, Kenneth. (1951). *Social choice and individual values*. New York: John Wiley. A seminal work on the linkages as well s the similarities between economic and political behavior. If politics is essentially concerned with the allocation of economic resources, economic resources are fundamentally linked to the allocation of political resources.

Becker, Gary S., is an economist (another Nobel Prize winner), and long before the behavioral economists began to modify the narrow concept of rationality held by the classical economists, he was exploring the ways in which seemingly irrational behavior was really rational. His work is of special interest because, among other things, he is concerned with the role emotion plays in decision making. In 1960 (*Demographic and economic change in developed countries*, Princeton University Press, pp. 209–31), he argued that people's attitudes about the economy influence the number of children they decide to have—if any. In 1968, he addressed the "riskless choice" model to question the risky choices made by criminals (Crime and punishment: An economic approach. *Journal of Political Economy 76*, 169–217). He has studied a wide variety of decisions, including suicide, drug addiction, the formation of emotions and the way they relate to religious beliefs, and marriage (see, e.g., A theory of marriage. In T. W. Schultz [Ed.], *Economics of the family* [pp. 299–344]. Chicago: University of Chicago Press, 1974. Caution: Parts of his material are mathematically challenging, but his work has been and continues to be too important to be overlooked).

Binswanger, Hans Christoph. (1998, July 31). The challenge of Faust. *Science 281*, 640–41. A noted European economist contributes one in a series of essays, "Science and Society," solicited by the editors of *Science* to celebrate 150 years of the journal's existence. Faust is described as "a vigorous entrepreneur"—and that's the good news and the bad news for his employees. Binswanger has also written *Money and magic: A critique of the modern economy in light of Goethe's Faust* (University of Chicago Press, 1994).

Brue, Stanley L., and Donald R. Wentworth. (1988). *Economic scenes: Theory in today's world* (4th ed.). Englewood Cliffs, NJ: Prentice Hall. An introductory text by two economists, unusual in that it combines both macro- and microeconomic perspectives and concepts, blending the two to give holistic perspective of the discipline. The authors use a series of well-selected case studies (as well as a welcome touch of humor) to illustrate the points in the text. The material and its organization (including the study questions at the end of each chapter) make it possible for independent use by the self-directed who would like to review or gain some background in economics.

Carneiro, Robert L. (1961). Slash-and-burn cultivation among the Kuikuru and its implications for cultural development in the Amazon Basin. In Johannes Wilbert (Ed.), *The evolution of horticultural systems in native South America: Causes and consequences* (pp. 47–67). A supplement to *Antropologica 2*. Caracas, Venezuela. A readily available reprint of this article appears in Patricia J. Lyon (Ed.), *Native South Americans* (pp. 73–91). Prospect Heights, IL: Waveland Press, 1985. This is a tightly argued paper with an abundance of ethnographic data discussing, e.g., the relation between environmental factors and cultural change among various tropical forest settlements, and focusing on the way in which people who, despite their common practice of subsistence agriculture, arrive at different solutions via rational decision-making processes.

Carrier, James G. (Ed.). (1997). *Meanings of the market: The free market in Western culture*. New York: Berg. This is an outstanding set of eight papers (plus an afterword by W. Roseberry). Carrier's introductory remarks and the titles of a few of the papers should be enough to attract interested readers: "Demons, Commodities and the History of Anthropology" (Joel Kahn, pp. 69–98); "The Free Market as Salvation from Government: The Anarcho-Capitalist View" (S. L. Brown, pp. 99–128); "Oriental Despotism and Sugar-Coated Bullets . . . the Market in China" (A. Smart, pp. 159–94); and "Markets,

Transaction Costs, Economists and Social Anthropologists" (this last a somewhat dated critique of institutional economics by M. Chapman and P. J. Buckley, pp. 225–50).

Castells, Manuel. (1999). *The information age*. Cambridge, MA: Blackwell Publishers. This is a massive three-volume set that establishes Castells as among the leading figures in IT studies. His Marxian background leads him to emphasize the extent to which computers and the Internet are empowering "the people" (formerly "the masses"?), altering the ways people identify themselves as well as undermining the power of States and the elite. He's enthralled by and unabashedly enthusiastic about the whole affair.

Clammer, John (Ed.). (1978). *The new economic anthropology*. New York: St. Martin's Press. Although, as the publishing date indicates, no longer new and, indeed, given the neo-Marxian perspective of the contributors, apparently taken over by historical events, this publication still deserves attention. For one thing, the papers cover material that raises the kinds of issues that help explain the attraction of the Marxian approach. For another thing, despite claims that we now live in a post-Marxian era, there are many (not a few in key posts in government, in universities, and in nongovernmental organizations) for whom Marxism (as "socialism") still serves as a guide to thinking and action. Those who naively discard or ignore such thinking do so at their peril.

Coase, Ronald H. (1960). The problem of social costs. *Journal of Law and Economics 3*, 1–44. Since this has been discussed in the text, no further comment seems necessary. It deserves to be read firsthand.

Cook, Scott. (1973). Economic anthropology: Problems in theory, method, and analysis. In J. J. Honigmann (Ed.), *Handbook of social and cultural anthropology* (pp. 795–860). Chicago: Rand McNally & Co. Probably one of the most widely cited reviews of the state of the art of economic anthropology—and still relevant for today. These 55 pages (plus the rich bibliography) could stand alone as an introductory text.

Cronk, Lee. (1989). Strings attached. *The Sciences*, (May/June). Reprinted in D. L. Carlson and V. M. Bryant, Jr. (Eds.), *Through the looking glass* (pp. 117–22). New York: The McGraw-Hill Companies. Like all of the papers in this imaginative collection of readings, this is an unusual perspective on an everyday activity. Using modern North American society, Cronk explores the various (and often surprising) strings attached to gifts.

D'Amico, Masolino. (1989, December 18). Letter from Rome. *Times literary supplement*, p. 14. Despite all the face-lifting that is going on in Rome to prepare it for the millennium and a religious Jubilee year, life goes on much as usual as the entrepreneurial activities of chestnut vender, Donato Tredicine, illustrate.

Davis, John. (1992). *Exchange*. Minneapolis: University of Minnesota Press. A cross-cultural examination of exchange, what it is and what are its social, ethical, and political consequences. In this slim volume of only 100 pages, Davis gives one of the most wide-ranging and sophisticated presentations available. Although it emphasizes exchange, more is delivered than promised. If I had to limit my list of recommended readings to ten items, this modest but excellent review would be one of them.

de Certeau, M. (1984). *The practice of everyday life*. Berkeley: University of California Press. De Certeau explores consumption as a hidden type of production, arguing that the twists and turns that people put on the products they consume have an ability to transform commodities into something else, and this process is, in itself, a type of production.

Douglas, Mary, and Baron Isherwood. (1979). *The world of goods*. New York: Basic Books. A pioneering study on why people want goods, why they save, and the ways they use goods to communicate with those around them—and to themselves about themselves. Drawing data from sources as diverse as Trollope's novels on Victorian England, the lives of the wives of the professional military, and dock workers, Douglas and Isherwood (the former an anthropologist and the latter an English economist and specialist on consumer behavior) make us think about "things" and their consumption in ways we rarely consider. The book is divided into two major segments: "goods as an information system," and the implications for social policy of the authors' findings.

Falk, Pasi, and Colin Campbell (Eds.). (1997). *The shopping experience*. Thousand Oaks, CA: Sage Publications. A collection of eight papers on a central experience in today's world, one that, as the editors note, is (paradoxically) a private activity performed in a public context (even when done on the Web), one that hovers between privacy and sociability, and, as well, is neither simply work nor leisure, but both. Some topics explored in the papers are: supermarkets, department stores, and super-malls; male and female differences in shopping; cultural variability of shopping in different countries.

Fine, Ben, and Ellen Leopold. (1993). *The world of consumption*. New York: Routledge. Fine (an economist) and Leopold (a regional planner and economic advisor) argue that "individual commodities create their own distinct 'systems of provision,'" a process that results in different styles of vertical integration of production, distribution, marketing, and consumption for different commodities. Thus, marketing fashion is better explained by looking to other aspects of the fashion industry rather than by comparing the process with that of, say, the food industry. Using extended case studies, Fine and Leopold explore both industries to support their thesis.

Firth, Raymond (Ed.). (1967). *Themes in economic anthropology*. London: Tavistock Publications Ltd. An important collection of ten papers by leading British scholars. Of particular interest, given the themes in this book, are papers by: R. Frankenberg (a review of various sides in some of the most important debates in the field), M. Douglas's paper on primitive rationing and primitive coupon systems, and S. Epstein's discussion on customary systems of rewards in India. Firth's introduction is an overview that is still capable of provoking discussion.

Frank, Robert H., and Philip J. Cook. (1996). *The winner-take-all society: Why the few at the top get so much more than the rest of us*. Glencoe, IL: The Free Press (Penguin ed. 1996). In 1993, Disney chairman Michael Eisner earned US$203 million, approximately 10,000 times that of the lowest-paid employee at Disney. Frank and Cook argue that in today's economy, small differences can make for very large differences in rewards, and this is leading not only to a growing gap between the rich and poor but also to a relentless even ruthless emphasis on "being at the top." The authors explore both the causes and consequences of income inequality and the implications of such inequality for social policy, taxes, and so forth.

Friedland, Roger, and A. F. Robertson (Eds). (1990). *Beyond the marketplace: Rethinking economy and society*. New York: Aldine de Gruyter. This is a collection of twelve papers by a mixed bag of social scientists. The introduction by the editors (a sociologist and an anthropologist, respectively) gives a wide-ranging review of the various debates about what markets are and do. The paper by R. H. Frank (an economist), "Rethinking Rational Choice," addresses his concern that "much of the model's apparent difficulty is the result of [economists] simply having focused the model's lens too narrowly," that when the model fails to predict, it's because other factors that economists discount, come to the fore.

Friedman, Thomas. (1998). *The Lexus and the olive tree*. Friedman is a journalist who looks at the globalization process from a distinctly American point of view. The book has attracted much attention since its publication and provides some excellent talking points because of the author's rather parochial perspective on a worldwide phenomenon. It is included here because it is typical of much of the popular thinking on the globalization process.

Gottlieb, Manuel. (1984). *A theory of economic systems*. New York: Academic Press. Substantive and free of mathematical models, this text is user-friendly for the noneconomist but requires careful reading. Gottlieb takes us through various modes of production, functions of the State in the economy, the institution of money, the institution of property, and the economic system as a whole—how it evolves over time and the ways in which various systems, despite their uniqueness, are related to each other. The presentation, written when Gottlieb was Emeritus Professor of Economics, is a distillation of his years of thinking on the subject.

Gregory, C. A., and J. C. Altman. (1989). *Observing the economy*. New York: Routledge. As the authors note in the opening line of their introduction, "This book outlines some general techniques for the fieldworker's collection and analysis of primary data on the economy." In a lucid and lively way it guides the reader through the tasks of preliminary desk work and establishing hypotheses—watching, timing, classifying, counting, measuring, recording, accounting, and describing. It is extremely useful not just for anthropologists but for those whose research is done within a different framework (e.g., marketing or organizational analysts, regional planners, emerging markets consultants).

Gubernick, Lisa. (1999, May 7). Buying your way on to a board. *Wall Street Journal*, pp. W1, W4. A sardonic view of philanthropy, "philanthropic" individuals, and "the price of admission" to the boards of various arts institutions.

Halperin, Rhoda. (1994). *Cultural economies: Past and present*. Austin: University of Texas Press. The book jacket notes that, "Halperin offers an analytical tool kit to studying economic process in all societies and at all times," using various key concepts (e.g., equivalences, storage, time). She relies on Marx's institutional paradigm and what she labels as Karl Polanyi's "generic model" of the economy. She is especially indebted to the latter scholar—and, indeed, announces that she started out to write a book about Polanyi's very influential contribution to the development of economic anthropology. Her procedure rests on "emphasizing economic processes and patterns as they are culturally and institutionally constructed" (p. 1).

Hamada, Tomoko (Ed.). (1999). *Anthropologists and globalization of business organizations*, a special issue of the journal, *Practicing Anthropology*, consisting of six papers with an emphasis on organizational change. The paper by Hendrick Serrie, "Training Chinese Managers for Leadership: Six Cross-Cultural Principles" (pp. 35–41), is especially interesting because it raises thought-provoking questions: Could similar nationally grounded principles be devised for any country? If so, how might they compare with those for Chinese managers? Is the Chinese view of American business accurate? Do they view Canadians any differently? If so, how? Hamada has also edited a special issue of *The anthropology of business organization* in the journal *Anthropology of Work Review 18*(2 & 3), 1998. Both collections are useful for those in business, management, and marketing.

Hann, C. M. (Ed.). (1998). *Property relations: Renewing the anthropological tradition.* Cambridge, UK: Cambridge University Press. This collection of eleven papers, which address issues of ownership, control, and power, rests on two key assumptions: (1) property has been and should again be a key integrating concept in anthropology as well as in the whole of social sciences; (2) property relations are not relations between people and things but are about social relations among people. A key to the approach taken by Hann and the other contributors can be found in the heading quote for chapter one by George Homans: ". . . the control of wealth is more important than its mere possession." Hann's introduction (pp. 1–47) is particularly useful and the essays that follow draw on data from a wide range of settings.

Hardin, Garrett. (1968). The tragedy of the commons. *Science, 162* 1243–48. An essay that argues for private property on the grounds that what is owned by all will be managed wisely by few (if any) because *all* individual owners, faced with even a few maximizing co-owners and assorted free loaders, ultimately will be forced to maximize their takings as well, a situation that inevitably leads to depletion of the resource. Widely cited by nonscholars, it was equally widely attacked in the academic world, not the least because Hardin failed to understand the important distinction between an open resource area (his concept of the common) and the common as this institution actually has existed in history, i.e., as a carefully regulated area to which specified persons have specific rights. Ironically, Hardin forced attention on the rethinking about ways in which humans have tried to manage resources—not only as maximizers but as stewards of nature.

Hardin, Garrett. (1974, October). Living on a lifeboat. *BioScience, 24,* 10. Reprinted in G. Hardin and J. Baden (Eds.), *Managing the commons,* (pp. 261–79). San Francisco: W. H. Freeman and Company. This is a deeply uncomfortable paper because it raises a number of issues (e.g., should we feed the hungry given that every life saved this year in a poor country may lead to two lives being lost next year? Should immigration be restrained to protect the living standard of those already "here"—wherever "here" is?). Not all of the questions raised are easily resolved.

Hayden, Brian. (1995). Pathways to power: Principles for creating socioeconomic inequalities. In T. D. Price and G. M. Feinman (Eds.), *Foundations of social inequality* (pp. 15–86). New York: Plenum Press. Though focused on the critical role of the entrepreneur (identified in various sociocultural formations as, e.g., "Great Man," "Big Man," "aggrandizer") in the transition from egalitarian to hierarchical societies, this excellent article discusses various theoretical issues involving trade, the emergence of chiefdoms and states, mechanisms for creating inequality, innovation, investment and much more. Hayden, an archeologist, gives a wide-ranging number of ethnographic and archeological examples, models for analyzing the emerging situations just listed, and provides an extensive bibliography—especially for those especially interested in the archeological aspects of these issues. It's highly recommended.

Herskovits, Melville J. (1940). *The economic life of primitive peoples.* New York: Alfred A. Knopf. One of the pioneering attempts to establish a foundation for the building of a particularly anthropological perspective on economic behavior. Chapter 2 ("Anthropology and Economics") sums up what drove Herskovits's effort: "In no conventional treatise on economic theory is primitive man [sic] depicted in a manner even remotely either in harmony with the facts of primitive life [sic] as known to anthropologists" nor, he goes on, "is it in line with anthropological theory concerning the nature of the interaction among humans, their environment, and their traditions" (p. 33).

Hunt, Robert C., and Antonio Gilman (Eds.). (1998). *Property in economic context.* Society for economic anthropology. Monographs in economic anthropology, No. 14. Lanham, MD: University Press of America. A collection of 18 papers that draws on a varied range of sociocultural settings, e.g., private landownership and debt in the ancient Near East; property, state, and self-destruction in Medieval Iceland; Amerindians caught up in the fur trade; and land and property in West Java (as well as another on the topic from the Ivory Coast). The papers are grouped as follows: "Part I: Concepts of Property"; "Part II: Property in Precapitalist Societies"; and "Part III: Modern Colonial Encounters." Together they provide a valuable perspective on the variability of the uses of the concept of property.

Jackson, Tony. (1999, April 27). Reflections of a knowledge worker. *Financial Times*, London, p. 12. This is a lengthy interview with the man generally acknowledged to be the dean of management studies, 89-year-old Peter Drucker, on the occasion of his most recent publication, *Management challenges for the 21st century*. Drucker's books are numerous and are all of excellent quality. It would be impossible to single out one for attention. Two quotes will give you the flavor of Drucker's work: "Profit is . . . very much like oxygen to the human body . . . absolutely necessary, but you don't exist for its sake"; and "Around 70–80 percent of commodities no longer conform to the marginal utility curve. Economists have still not adjusted to that."

Jackson, Tony. (1999, February 4). Stumped? Just pinch an idea. *Financial Times,* London. p. 8. A reporter for the *Financial Times* interviews four company heads, including the American entrepreneur Michael Bloomberg, and reports on their discussion on innovation.

Jevons, Marshall. (1978). *Murder at the margin.* Sun Lakes, AZ: Thomas Horton and Daughters. Normally focusing on such subjects as antitrust penalties and the relation between economics and law, two professors of economics team up (under a pseudonym) to write a mystery in which the hero—a professor of economics, naturally—uses basic economic theories (e.g., cost/benefit analysis, supply and demand, marginal analysis) to solve a murder. Commenting on the book, noted economist Milton Friedman said: "It is hard to conceive of a more pleasant or painless way of imbibing sound economic principles . . ." We first meet our hero as he does a marginal analysis in order to determine how to respond to a flight attendant's question as to whether he would like a glass of iced tea ("one dollar, please"). A good mystery and lessons in basic economic theories brings you good value for time invested. A second book, *The fatal equilibrium* (MIT Press, 1985) was also well received.

Kamman, Daniel M., and David M. Hassenzahl. (1999). *Should we risk it?: Exploring environmental, health, and technological problem solving.* Princeton, NJ: Princeton University Press. This is a demanding but a well-written and clear presentation of, among other things, risk, uncertainty, the use of statistics to identify levels of risk, and decision making in the context of health and environmental concerns. It's clear enough for an introductory undergraduate textbook.

Kauffman, Stuart A. (1995). *At home in the universe.* New York: Oxford University Press. If you want to know more about the kind of thinking that's going on at the Santa Fe Institute (where they do cutting-edge research on such topics as the end of scarcity, chaos theory, and complex, self-organizing systems), read this. Though written for the general public, it's not for lightweights. For those who like to be challenged and occasionally prefer a book that can't be summarized in 6–8 pages of current buzz terms, this is highly recommended.

Kilman, Scott. (1998, February 11). Farm wives step into futures, as brokerage firms woo them. *Wall Street Journal*, pp. C1, C19. An example from today's headlines on how the telecommunications revolution is changing life for everyone—changing both family farms and the families that work them.

Komter, Aafke E. (Ed.). (1996). *The gift: An interdisciplinary perspective.* Amsterdam: Amsterdam University Press. A collection bringing together 16 important, previously published papers on reciprocity, exchange, self-interest, and altruism. The papers in Part III, especially, are useful for this book's readers: "The Work of Time," P. Bourdieu; "Rational Fools: A Critique of the Behavioral Foundations of Economic Theory," A. K. Sen; "Reasons for Altruism," D. Schmidtz; "The Social Basis of Unselfishness," C. Jencks; and two papers by S. P. and P. M. Oliner, "Why Risk One's Life?", and "Moral Heroism and Extensivity."

Levin, Simon. (1999). *Fragile dominion: Complexity and the commons.* Reading, MA: Helix (Perseus) Press. For those interested in ecological issues such as the "costing of the earth" (calculating, over various time frames and as inclusivly as possible, the human and environmental costs of resource exploitation) and environmental pollution, this is a must read. Levin organizes the book around six fundamental questions (e.g., how do ecosystems assemble themselves; how, if evolution acts on individuals, does it shape aggregates?). More to the point for readers of this text, the later chapters discuss how to utilize such concepts as scale, self-organized criticality, chaos, and power laws, and, for example, the ways in which complex systems organize themselves.

Lewis, I. M. (1991). *Social anthropology in perspective* (2nd ed.). New York: Cambridge University Press. A basic introduction to the specifically European (notably British) emphasis on the structure and functioning as well as functions of society. The book earns a place in this bibliography because of its especially stimulating chapter, "Exchange and Market" (pp. 197–233), where, unlike most, Lewis takes time to address the important role of entrepreneurs (pp. 230–33).

Lien, Marianne Elisabeth. (1997). *Marketing and modernity.* New York: Berg. Lien's theoretical concern is to address questions of "modernity" (one of many definitions is that it is a self-consciousness, i.e., reflexive, thinking about the ways in which we humans behave). However, believing that modernity may be examined only in an ethnographic context, she studied it among the employees of a marketing department of a major Norwegian food manufacturer whose chief concern is reducing uncertainty in marketing decisions. Her detailed ethnographic analysis of the staff's attempt to deal with such questions as: How do you recognize an effective advertisement?, How can creativity be measured?, What's the value of a brilliant idea?, and What should poultry really taste like? is fascinating. Anyone interested in how commodities are merchandised should read this book.

Marx, Karl. No bibliography dealing with economics can ignore the contributions of an individual who (along with Engels) influenced the global history of the twentieth century—and will continue to do so in the twenty-first. Yet in a selected list of "supplemental readings," it would be silly to list, say, *Capital*; Marx is not a "quick and easy read" nor does his work deserve to be. No one who is concerned with global economic dynamics, no matter if local, regional, or international, can neglect the pull that Marx's ideas continue to exert on people's behavior, nor can one slight the real insights that his work offers. It must suffice to say that those who are ignorant of Marx will be incapable of a robust response to the geopolitical events that are unfolding around us.

Morrison, Scott. (1999, April 29). Cows head for market in cyberspace. *Financial Times*, London, p. 16. A mini–case study in how the Internet is changing the face of stock raising and livestock sales through global auctions.

Newman, Peter C. (1998, March 30). A revolutionary young economist. *Maclean's*, p. 46. Newman writes a succinct article reviewing the contribution that Paul Romer is making to economics with his "vision of a boundless future with unlimited growth." Though Romer's work has attracted much attention, it's not immediately accessible to a neophyte. This is an excellent one-page introduction to his work by the business editor of the leading Canadian weekly news magazine. Those interested in exploring more of Romer's work should consult his Web page: stanford.edu/~promer.

Not quite a billion. (1999, January 2). *The Economist 56*. Whether adding an inch to a shirt-tail to increase textile sales to China, or merchandising (for example a home-karaoke machine), despite the current average income of just $360 per person annually, China's population (1.2 billion) is a magnet for traders.

Ohmae, Kenichi. (1990). *The borderless world: Power and strategy in the interlinked economy.* New York: Harper Perennial. Ohmae is managing director of McKinsey and Company, an international consulting firm. This is one of the better examples of how such gurus guide others in how to think about such issues as management, trade, leadership, and decision making in the global economy. It is a different perspective on these issues from the view usually presented by Euroamerican analysts, especially since Ohmae was trained as a nuclear engineer and transformed himself into a management consultant—and one who begins by announcing that, despite all the time he has spent helping devise and implement strategies, he has "never discovered any formulas or algorithms for getting things right" (p. 1).

Ophuls, William. (1977). *Ecology and the politics of scarcity.* San Francisco: W. H. Freeman and Company. Given the date of this publication, it's interesting to read this book on scarcity as a study in futurology. "Section Two: The Dilemmas of Scarcity" (pp. 142–220), has four chapters that will provide material for a debate on whether Ophuls was on the mark or whether the strides being made by bioengineering are proving him wrong.

Orbell, John. (1993). *Hamlet* and the psychology of rational choice under uncertainty. *Rationality and Society* 5(1), 127–40. A fascinating paper that draws out the distinction made in this text concerning risk versus uncertainty. It offers an interesting re-reading of Hamlet's actions.

Palumbo-Liu, David, and Hans Ulrich Gumbrecht (Eds.). (1997). *Streams of cultural capital: Transnational cultural studies*. Stanford, CA: Stanford University Press. A really cross-disciplinary group of papers—contributors come from the fields of anthropology, comparative literature, philosophy, drama, and education. They're brought together to consider Pierre Bourdieu's concept of "cultural capital." As Palumbo-Liu points out in his introduction, culture is "eminently commodified and conspicuously consumed," and can be productively viewed in terms of its exchange value. Despite a heavy burden of deconstructionist jargon, the papers are stimulating, especially those by A. Appadurai ("Consumption, Duration and History"), J-F Lyotard ("Marie in Japan"), I. Schneider (". . . American Movies on German Television"), X. Chen ("Shakespeare, Ibsen and Brecht in Post-Mao China"), and M. Richardson (". . . An Archeology of Disneyland").

Parry, Jonathan. (1989). On the moral perils of exchange. In J. Parry and M. Block (Eds.), *Money and the morality of exchange* (pp. 64–93). Cambridge: Cambridge University Press. Although all ten papers in the volume are of value, this paper stands out for its provocative reversal of the way in which people may view gifts versus commodities (especially money). It's standard for investigators to note evidence for the way in which gifts are safe, good, and morally right, and to stress how in most communities commodities are threatening, barren, and morally wrong (or, at best, amoral). Parry discusses a situation in which *some* gifts embody evil and danger while *some* "commercial profits and market transactions are generally seen in a much more benevolent light" (p. 65).

Paterson, R. W. K. (1998). *The new patricians: An essay on values and consciousness.* New York: Macmillan. A rather romantic view of the virtues of nonmaterial qualities such as generosity, heroism, sincerity, and kindness. The book is listed because, for some, it will provide a welcome antidote to my heavy emphasis on material resources and self-interest.

Plattner, Stuart (Ed.). (1985). *Markets and marketing.* Society for economic anthropology. Monographs in economic anthropology, No. 4. Lanham, MD: University Press of America. This volume contains a collection of papers spanning a time frame from pre-Columbian America (Aztec and Inca markets) to today's urban markets, both formal and informal, in locales as diverse as India, Mexico, China, Nigeria, and Peru. Several stress the role of women as vendors. Two papers, one, "How to Count Onions: Methods for a Regional Analysis of Marketing," and another studying the growth of consumption and its relationship to urbanization in Malaysia, are especially interesting.

Plattner, Stuart (Ed.). (1989). *Economic anthropology*. Stanford, CA: Stanford University Press. A collection of 15 original papers, and identified by Plattner as "the first comprehensive text in economic anthropology since the 1970s" (p. ix), was designed to present an up-to-date introduction to the topic for "high-level undergraduates . . . [or] introductory graduate courses." There are so many outstanding contributions that it's difficult to single out particular items but, certainly, Roseberry's paper, "Peasants in the World" (pp. 108–26); Cancian's, "Economic Behavior in Peasant Communities" (pp. 127–70); the two papers by Plattner, "Markets and Marketplaces" (pp. 171–208) and "Economic Behavior in Markets" (pp. 209–21); "Industrial Agriculture" by Barlett (pp. 253–91); and Bossen's "Women and Economic Institutions" (pp. 318–50) deserve special attention. A summary, "On the Division of Labor between Economics and Economic Anthropology" (pp. 397–425), is very useful as is the extensive bibliography.

Rathje, William, and Cullen Murphy. (1992). *Rubbish! The archeology of garbage.* New York: HarperCollins Publishers. The introductory chapter (pp. 3–29) is especially useful for initiating people into the way archeologists use garbage, ancient and modern, to study human behavior.

Romer, Paul M. See bibliographic references for Newman, Peter C. or check Romer's Web page: stanford.edu/~promer.

Rutz, Henry J., and B. S. Orlove (Eds.). (1989). *The social economy of consumption.* Society for economic anthropology. Monographs in economic anthropology, No. 6. Lanham, MD: University Press of America. In addition to Orlove's and Rutz's excellent introduction (pp. 1–58), there are very useful papers, including: "Schedule Constraints on Household Consumption in Modern Vienna" (pp. 149–176); "Consumerism without Capitalism: Consumption and Brand Names in Late Imperial China" (pp. 253–280); "Houses as Consumer Goods" (pp. 297–322); and "Gender and Low Income Household Expenditures in Jamaica" (pp. 379–98).

Sahlins, M. (1972). The original affluent society. In *Stone Age economics* (pp. 1–38). Chicago: Aldine. An influential essay that has become a classic. Sahlins establishes the controversial thesis that, "By the common understanding, an affluent society is one in which all the people's material wants are easily satisfied. To assert that [impoverished] hunters are affluent is to deny . . . that the human condition is an ordained tragedy, with [humans] the prisoner[s] of hard labor of a perpetual disparity between . . . unlimited wants and . . . insufficient means" (p. 1). He concludes that poverty isn't a lack of goods, nor is it the relation between means and ends. Rather, it's a relation between people. Thus, it's a social status, a position structured by the emergence of infinite wants. In clearly distinguishing between needs and wants, and in demonstrating the extent to which "poverty/wealth" are culturally measured, Sahlins challenges traditional economics as well the cultural attitudes that influence our thinking about "underdeveloped sociocultures."

Schmidt, Leigh Eric. (1995). *Consumer rites: The buying and selling of American holidays*. Princeton, NJ: Princeton University Press. Beginning with the way that the calendar of festivals (especially those based on religious events and national holidays), links up to "the peddling of festivity," Schmidt (a professor of religion at Princeton) takes us through the consumerism of St. Valentine's Day, Christmas, Easter, and Mother's (with a nod to Father's) Day. Lavishly illustrated, it's a fascinating excursion into the evolution of commodities, markets, and consumption.

Schneider, Harold K. (1974). *Economic man*. New York: The Free Press. As with the book by Herskovits listed earlier, this title is included on the premise that those who don't know history are doomed to repeat it. Thus, this work in economic anthropology is listed to facilitate the understanding of some of the issues that anthropologists needed to address in order to establish a foundation for their particular view of economics.

Sen, A. (1981). *Poverty and famine: An essay on entitlement and deprivation*. New York: Oxford University Press. This publication set the stage for what has become a major theme for Sen. It is a study of four occurrences of massive famine in Bangladesh, Bengal, the Sahel, and Ethiopia. Sen gives poignant evidence to support his thesis that people experience famine not because food is scarce but because systems of distributing food to the needy are flawed and inadequate.

Shennan, Stephen. (1999, June). Cost, benefit, and value in the organization of early European copper production. *Antiquity 73*(280), 352–63. An exciting and provocative use of Ricardo's Law of Comparative Advantage (it's not worth producing X if, by producing Y and exchanging it for X, one gets a better return for less effort). He looks at the production of copper ore in central Europe beginning about 4000 BP (Before Present) and explores several interesting questions, one of the most important being why, given the presence of copper deposits throughout the region, some communities chose to mine it while others didn't. For nonanthropologists, it offers a fascinating example of how research on remote times is relevant to modern issues.

Simon, Herbert A. (1979). A behavioral model of rational choice. In H. A. Simon (Ed.), *Models of thought* (pp. 7–19). New Haven, CT: Yale University Press. This is the 1955 paper that made such a revolutionary contribution to decision-making theory, rational choice modeling, etc., that it ultimately led to Simon being awarded the 1978 Nobel Prize in Economics. Simon describes his task as the need to present a model of rational behavior "compatible with the access to information and the computational capacities . . . actually possessed by organisms . . . in the kinds of environments in which such organisms exist" (p. 7). Given the need to make decisions in a real world in which no one (a) has perfect information and (b) rarely has time even to attempt to gather as much information as might be considered necessary to make maximizing or even optimizing decisions, most people—recognizing such constraints—will adjust their goals to make "good enough" (i.e., satisficing) decisions.

Smith, M. Estellie. (1989). The informal economy. In Stuart Plattner (Ed.), *Economic anthropology* (pp. 292–317). Stanford, CA: Stanford University Press. A review of the various approaches to studying what is often difficult (even impossible) to study, i.e., economic activities (sometimes performed quite openly) that are not recorded in official statistics and are often criminalized by the authorities for various reasons. A key concern is that, since the size of this particular sector of a national economy may constitute a significant proportion of the GNP, the activities may result in seriously flawed decisions by economists, politicians, and bureaucrats as to what needs (or doesn't need) to be done when determining budgets and national entitlement policies.

Smith, M. Estellie (Ed.). (1990). *Perspectives on the informal economy*. Society for economic anthropology. Monographs in economic anthropology, No. 8. Lanham, MD: University Press of America. A collection of 15 papers on what is variously known as, for example, the "underground," "black," or "informal" economy. The papers look at the informal economy in such diverse settings as Brazil, Tanzania, Miami, India, Scandinavia, Burma, and Hong Kong. A wide range of people, from street vendors to bureaucrats, is examined.

Strasser, Susan. (1999). *Waste and want: A social history of trash*. New York: Metropolitan Books. Strasser presents a popularly written review of trash that forms an interesting contrast with the perspective of the archeologist (see bibliographic reference to William Rathje).

Terkel, Studs. (1975). *Working*. New York: Avon Books. In a few pages each, 130 people with a diverse range of occupations—e.g., farmers, cabbies, jazz musicians, hockey players, hookers, priests, executives, poets, housewives, and grave diggers—talk about working, about being productive (and, when retired or unemployed, what the difference means to them). Terkel, a self-described sometime writer, actor, mostly radio broadcaster, lets the people speak for themselves and, for many of us, this is a view of a world as unknown and as exotic as any studied by anthropologists in the most remote parts of the world. It's no wonder this book has never gone out of print. A must read.

Tett, Gillian. (1998, July 6). Files from Tokyo: Bridges over troubled waters. *Financial Times*, London, p. 11. The article describes the various make-work projects (especially in construction—even if it's only digging holes) that the Japanese government is utilizing to address its financial crisis and the specter of rising unemployment.

Thomas, Paulette. (1999, February 2). A tavern's fame spreads hand to hand. *Wall Street Journal*, p. B1. Entrepreneurs aren't always starting up new businesses. This is a mini–case study in which a waitress in a bar learns sign language and thereby expands her boss's client base. Was her decision to learn sign language based on altruism or enlightened self-interest?

Truex, Gregory F. (1988). Crime in the development process. In J. W. Bennett and John R. Bowen (Eds.), *Production and autonomy: Anthropological studies and critiques of development* (pp. 185–98). Society for economic anthropology. Monographs in economic anthropology, No. 5. Lanham, MD: University Press of America. Anything illegal is difficult to measure; much of it is hidden but if you can't see it how do you count it? We can only make guesstimates about a great deal of economic activity—e.g., political corruption, the sale of drugs, sweat shops, smuggling. And the problem is not only underestimation: Shoplifting may be overestimated as store employees filch from the company or embezzlement goes unreported because firms don't want publicity that might undermine public confidence in the firm. Further, what is defined as "crime" is heavily laden with cultural values and norms. This paper gives an overview of some of the problems.

Weatherford, Jack. (1997). *The history of money*. New York: Crown Publishers. Weatherford is an anthropologist who writes with wit and verve. After a brief look at the global society, we begin with "Classic Cash" (pp. 15–110), with segments that move us from "cannibals, chocolate, and cash," through the rise of Italian banking families to the price revolution. In the following two sections he covers first, the twists and turns of paper money (pp. 111–92) and (the final segment), electronic money (pp. 193–268). This highly recommended book is about more than money.

Weise, Elizabeth. (1999). Companies learn value of grass root anthropologist help adapt products to world's cultures. *Society for Applied Anthropology Newsletter 10*(4), 11–12. Despite the clumsy (to me unreadable!) title, this neat little two-page article encapsulates a wide range of ways in which anthropologists utilize their skills to assist industry in understanding things about people (whether their own workers, customers, or potential clientele). This run-through of what is called applied anthropology will be especially helpful for those who wonder what anthropology has to do with "the real world" as well as for potential anthropologists who have no plans to storm the citadel of academe for their employment.

Wilk, Richard R. (1996). *Economies and cultures: Foundations of economic anthropology.* Boulder, CO: Westview Press. This is a well-rounded overview of economic anthropology. When examining the divisive debates in the field, it's temperate in tone and moves easily between anthropology and economics. Though designed as a textbook, it avoids the dull, pedantic tone that is able to put so many students (and others!) in a stupor. It's less than 200 pages long but still manages to squeeze in an excellent bibliography and a very useful appendix: "Where to Look for More—Finding Literature in Economic Anthropology" (pp. 157–63). This is an extremely useful handbook for those who have had little or no anthropology or economics background (e.g., those who come from business, computer science, and management disciplines). I'm particularly indebted to Wilk for his comments on risk and uncertainty.

Index